Margaret Mehringer

276

GROUP COUNSELING

Concepts and Procedures

Second Edition

Robert C. Berg, Ed.D.
Associate Professor of Counselor Education
University of North Texas
Denton, Texas

Garry L. Landreth, Ed.D.
Professor of Counseling
University of North Texas
Denton, Texas

 ACCELERATED DEVELOPMENT INC.
Publishers
Muncie   Indiana

GROUP COUNSELING
Concepts and Procedures
Second Edition

Technical Development: Tanya Dalton
Delores Kellogg
Marguerite Mader
Sheila Sheward

Library of Congress Cataloging-in-Publication Data

Berg, Robert C.
    Group counseling : concepts and procedures / Robert C. Berg, Garry
L. Landreth. -- 2nd ed.
        p.   cm.
    Includes bibliographical references (p.   ).
    ISBN 1-55959-008-4
    1. Personnel service in education. 2. Group counseling. 3. Group
guidance in education. I. Landreth, Garry L. II. Title.
    LB1027.5.B44   1990
371.4'044--dc20   89-81013
                                                            CIP

LCN: 89-81013

ACCELERATED DEVELOPMENT INC.
Publishers
3400 Kilgore Avenue
Muncie, Indiana 47304-4896
Toll Free Order Number 1-800-222-1166

ACKNOWLEDGEGMENTS

We would like to acknowledge with our thanks the following editors, authors, and publishers for permitting us to quote from their materials in this book: the American Association for Counseling and Development, Association for Specialists in Group Work, the Council for Accreditation of Counseling and Related Educational Programs (CACREP); "Group Counseling" and "Interpersonal Skills Development" in *Encyclopedia of Psychology*, (1984), Raymond J. Corsini, (Ed.), John Wiley and Sons; Brooks/Cole Publishing Company and Basic Books, Inc.

Additionally, we extend our thanks to the editors of the following journals for their permission to reproduce sections of articles which we have personally authored and which initially appeared under the titles and journals listed: "Dynamics of Group Discussion," (1973) *The Clearing House, 48* (2), 127-128, a publication of the Helen Dwight Reid Educational Foundation; "Getting a Counseling Group Started," "Facilitating Responsibility in Group Counseling," "Maintaining a Group: Process and Problems," "Varied Time as a Factor in the Preventive Role of Group Counseling," "Structuring Group Guidance Activities in the Schools," and "Terminating a Group" all in the *Texas Personnel and Guidance Journal;* "Overcoming Initial Group Leader Anxiety: Skills Plus Experience," *The Personnel and Guidance Journal;* Encountering Carl Rogers: His Views on Facilitating Groups," *Journal of Counseling and Development;* "Group Counseling: To Structure or not to Structure," *The School Counselor;* "Group Silence in Counseling Groups Has Meaning," *Journal for Specialists in Group Work;* "The Experiential Component in the Training of Group Counselors," *Michigan Personnel and Guidance Journal;* and "Using Behavioral Change Contracts in Group Counseling," *The Wisconsin Counselor.*

PREFACE

In the preface to the first edition of this book we pointed out the marked interest in group work that crested during the early to mid 1970s. After a period of leveling off, we noted once again an increase in attention to group interventions in the helping professions. We believe that this is related to more than just efficiency of helper time—but rather to the recognition that group counseling is and should be the treatment of choice in many cases. As colleagues and teachers of group counseling at the graduate level since the mid-1960s, we have had an opportunity to observe and participate in many of the developmental shifts that have occurred during that period of time.

We continue to believe that groups offer a unique format for interpersonal exploration and growth and that the "success" of the group is most likely related to the skill and competency level of the group leader. Through our years of teaching, practice, supervision, joint lectures, and group demonstrations we have attempted to discuss and evaluate group methods, theories and procedures—always with a profound respect and fascination with the powerful intervention that we call group. We hope that our own development as group facilitators is reflected in this present volume as we attempt to address and share some of the topics that continue to grow out of our personal observations and research.

The purpose of this book is to provide encouragement to the beginning group counselor, to furnish support for the efforts of the practicing group facilitator, and hopefully, to contribute to the stimulation of both through the presentation of ideas and practices that we have found helpful in our work with groups in a number of different settings. The potential group leader should find this book especially helpful when initiating a counseling group as well as anticipating some of the practical group problems that can be anticipated throughout the working life and ending stages of the group.

The intention of the authors is for this text to serve as a primary resource in traditional courses in group counseling.

In addition, we feel that this book can be used as a method of acquainting the reader with group counseilng concepts and procedures in survey courses for human service providers in the fields of counseling, psychology, social work, rehabilitation, and sociology. The social impact of group work has become increasingly apparent as we move toward the twenty-first century. Professional practitioners in educational settings and the many community social agencies will need to extend and validate their knowledge, skills, and competencies as experts in the application of group dynamics in their work.

In many ways this is a very personal book in that the authors have insisted upon maintaining contact with the direct clinical aspects of group work rather than simply treating it as a theoretical intervention system. We continue to do groups as well as to teach and speculate about them. As such, our intent has been to present more than a cookbook or how to manual but rather a sharing of some of our deeply held convictions and personal experiences that have helped shape us not only as group leaders but as persons. It is our firmly held belief that those two things are virtually inseparable.

Remarks James Muro made about group counseling in our first group counseling text are still pertinent. Since questions he raised about the field of group counseling have been an impetus for exploration in this current text, we have chosen to include his original remarks at this time.

> While numerous authors have attempted to define group counseling in contrast to the more clearly established procedures labeled group guidance and group therapy, these attempts, though well meaning, generally have neither provided the clarity nor delineated the comptencies that are required of a professional group counselor. Certainly this gap is not because of lack of interest. Interest alone however does not provide the counselor/educator or practicing counselor with answers to the basic questions that are essential for complete professionalization.

> Why for example, should a process so personal and intimate as counseling be conducted in a group meeting? How does one delineate the thin line between group counseling and group therapy? How can the consumers of this process, the children and

adults, of our nation, have faith in what counselors profess when the counselors themselves are ill-prepared to provide evidence that the graduates of training programs are comptetent to deal with the sensitive issues that arise in the world of small group life? What must group counselors do? What must they know? Who should they be?

This book by Robert C. Berg and Garry L. Landreth attempts to address some of the areas that are neglected or ignored in many of the widely utilized books on group counseling. Berg and Landreth have elected to provide the reader with essential topics that are of concern to all group counselors regardless of philosophical orientation. This book is a needed and valuable resource in professional counseling literature.

Readers of this book are provided with responses to the basic concerns of the group counseling process. The "why" of group counseling is explored and defended in understandable, humanistic terms. One can initiate a personal philosophy of group counseling from this overview. Philosophical considerations however, represent only the tip of the group counseling iceberg. Readers, once oriented, can follow a developmental program of skills necessary to become active group leaders. The dynamics of groups are outlined clearly and the mechanics of organizing and maintaining a group are presented. Berg and Landreth also share with the leader the potential trauma and rewards of an initial group meeting.

James J. Muro

Following, listed in concise, summary form are what we consider to be some of the singular attributes of this book in that it presents:

- a thorough discussion of the rationale for using group counseling with emphasis on the group providing a preventive environment, a setting for self discovery, an opportunity to redefine self, and the development of interpersonal awareness.

- an insightful look into the personalities of the authors as manifested in their differing approaches to the development of a theoretical approach to working with groups.

- practical suggestions on the skills needed for effective facilitation of groups.

- an examination of the group facilitator's internal frame of reference and the overcoming of initial group leader anxiety.

- a rare look at Carl Rogers' personal feelings about group members as shared by Rogers.

- detailed guidelines for forming a counseling group and accomplishing the difficult task of facilitating the early stages of development with emphasis on encouraging interaction and member responsibility.

- an exploration of typical problems in the developing group process with suggested solutions that facilitate group cohesivenss.

- a description of frequently encountered issues in group counseling related to structuring and an analysis of the practical application of structuring.

- a thorough exploration of potential problems related to termination of a counseling group with recommended procedures for termination, evaluation, and follow-up.

- an insightful and practical examination of the application of group counseling procedures with children, adolescents, adults, and the elderly.

- topical presentation of group counseling with abused children, juvenile offenders, and individuals with chronic diseases, emotional difficulties, and addictive behaviors.

In conclusion, we would like to thank our friend and publisher, Dr. Joe Hollis, and his able editing staff at Accelerated Development. Their appropriate insights and suggestions have aided us greatly in the completion of this text. At the same time, we assume full responsibility for the final product, including errors of omission.

Robert C. Berg

January 1990

Garry L. Landreth

CONTENTS

6   GETTING A COUNSELING GROUP STARTED 135

7   PROBLEMS AND INTERVENTION TECHNIQUES 163

10 TERMINATION, EVALUATON, AND FOLLOW-UP 241

11 CHILDREN AND ADOLESCENTS 257

LIST OF FIGURES

CHAPTER **1**

RATIONALE FOR GROUP COUNSELING

Although counseling programs have become an integral part of most educational settings and social agencies, both public and private, group counseling has only slowly gained recognition as an approach having therapeutic applicability. Group counseling's effectiveness often has been limited by those who consider it only as a method for giving information, for planning, and for saving counselor time. Group procedures in counseling and guidance have long been considered and used by counselors as an expedient method for meeting the needs of increasing counselee loads (Pepinsky, 1953; Super, 1949). Although efficiency in terms of saving counselor time often has been considered a major attraction of group counseling, research has shown that the use of groups for various guidance and counseling functions provides advantages other than expediency. Group counseling programs can provide individuals with the kinds of group experiences that help them learn to function effectively, to develop tolerance to stress and anxiety, and to find satisfaction in working and living with others (Corey & Corey, 1987; Ohlsen, Horne, & Lawe, 1988).

What advantages within the group experience are possible for members? What are the unique features and values of the experience? Logically, the rationale for group counseling should be understood clearly before counselors attempt this approach. Counselors are unlikely to be very effective if they do not understand the process they are attempting to facilitate. Group counseling *is* a unique and valuable experience for group members.

PREVENTIVE ENVIRONMENT

Taxed by large counselee loads and faced with escalating demands upon their time and talents, counselors must continually evaluate their present methods of meeting these increasing demands and must launch out to investigate and appraise new approaches. As counseling programs expand, counselors will have to become innovators in order to cope with these increasing demands. Adoption or incorporation of a new approach however is never justified simply on the basis of expediency.

Most counselors in an educational setting usually concentrate on those students who seek assistance *after* they have developed emotional or academic difficulties. For many students, emotional or adjustment problems predispose them to develop maladaptive study habits and poor attitudes toward academic work which, in turn, lead to lack of achievement, to rejection of a teacher's authority, and often to rejection of authority in society. Such students often leave school (drop out) with a psychological predisposition to be hyperresistant; that is, they tend to react to the offerings of society with a mental set characterized by rejection.

Counseling should be preventive and developmental with an emphasis on therapeutic prevention of emotional or adjustment problems in students. The prevention of maladaptive academic habits and attitudes which may stem from such problems would enable more students to attain the educational experiences necessary in order for them to make the positive contributions to self and society of which they are capable.

The trend toward the application of group counseling procedures in meeting the needs of individuals is likely to grow, stimulated by greater acceptance of this preventive approach to problems encountered and by increased recognition of the effectiveness of group counseling. Sufficient research and experience with group counseling procedures has accumulated to suggest the worth of this approach as a part of the process of helping individuals to grow. As a result of extensive research and experience in group counseling, Rogers (1969) and Ellis (1969) have suggested that group counseling is more helpful to most people than is individual counseling. Krumboltz (1968) agreed with this position in part, and Gazda (1978) proposed that group counseling is the preferred mode of treatment for many individuals.

SETTING FOR SELF DISCOVERY

When Man is placed within the context of a group, he cannot continue to rely only upon himself for a view of himself. Through the process of group interaction he comes in contact with the group's perception of what he is or what he purports to be. Thus, it is within the context of the group that Man gains a greater self awareness. He is confronted with the perceptions of others rather than relying solely upon a subjective perception of himself. The catalytic nature of the group's reaction brings Man to consider other perceptions of himself as well.

It is only in light of this more refined awareness of self, provided by group interaction, that Man is able to gain a more complete awareness of his substance; and it is this more enriched concept of himself that enables Man to release his full positive potential to society. (Cohn, 1967, p. 1)

Inherent in the preceding statement is the theory of an adequate self concept and the significance of the group to individuals and their self awareness. Utilizing the advantages provided by the group, group counseling provides an accepting climate in which members can test new and improved ways of behaving. The process facilitates each member in discovering a new self and in revealing it to others.

The implications of this discussion for the educational situation, as well as others, can be seen when one recognizes that individuals behave in terms of the self concepts they possess. Even an individual's levels of aspiration are a function of the kinds of self concepts he/she holds.

Lecky (1945) pointed out that children who are not considered bright by their parents and who have therefore come to see themselves as stupid or incapable of learning, hold to this concept when they go to school. A given phenomenal self perpetuates itself by permitting only such perceptions as are consistent with its already existing structure. Rogers (1970) said in effect that the fundamental urge underlying all behavior was the need to preserve and enhance the phenomenal self. A tendency exists for individuals to regard themselves in certain fairly consistent ways and to behave in such ways as will maintain their view of themselves.

Group counseling provides the individual with an opportunity to explore behavior patterns that may be the result of a limiting self concept. We are faced with a situation in which few counseling programs have the development of positive self concepts as one of their major functions. Since every individual experiences personal problems, group counseling can be utilized as a developmental approach for all students, not just the problem cases.

DISCOVERING OTHERS

For those individuals who are threatened by a one-to-one counseling relationship, the group provides a degree of anonymity and the individual within the group feels less conspicuous and "on the spot." When group members feel threatened, they may withdraw verbally from the interaction and still be very much involved in the group through the experience of other members. Thus, their withdrawal is not complete.

Whether verbally active or inactive, group members discover that their problems are not unique to them and begin to feel less different, unwanted, and alone. They begin to relax and to be less defensive as they perceive themselves to be less isolated. Blocher (1966) and Gazda (1978) contended that the most terrifying part of working through developmental problems is the feeling of isolation and loneliness that comes from the delusion that no one else has ever experienced the same difficulties. "Even if all members of a group do not have the same problems, the awareness that others do have problems and the sharing of feelings about them tend to develop a degree of empathy and help in the understanding of self and others" (Warters, 1960, p. 191).

Realizing that personal problems are common is a process that helps group members to admit their own problems to full awareness and to deal with them in the context of a caring relationship. Thus members' problems are no longer unique to them, and they discover that others have problems too.

REDEFINING SELF

Individuals function most of their lives within groups. Against this background of interaction with others, one's self-concept is formed and many times distorted. This distorted perception of self and self in relation to others often occurs in the dynamics of the family group relationship. Seemingly then, the most effective place for dealing with adjustment difficulties is within a relationship that incorporates the basic structure which originally created the difficulty (Warters, 1960).

Through the process of the group counseling relationship, the group member discovers the meaning of giving and receiving emotional support and understanding in a different and more positive sort of way. Perception of self then is redefined in a context similar to that which initially resulted in the distortion (Lifton, 1972).

This process and the importance of the family relationship is viewed somewhat differently by Durkin (1964). She stated that "The idea of a group activates in the adult individual traces of the preoedipal mother image and the fears connected with it, causing him to become relatively submissive to the group and usually suggestible" (p. 79). Slavson (1955) described the counseling group as significant for individuals in that they receive from the group the satisfaction they originally desired from their parents (family group). The group's ego-strengthening acceptance aids attempts to find out about and redefine self. Feedback, which is a prerequisite for validating or developing one's self-concept and self-image is assimilated because the individual feels safe.

DEVELOPING INTERPERSONAL AWARENESS

Most problems are basically social and interpersonal in nature. Within the group counseling relationship, members can identify with others and develop understanding into their own difficulties by observing the behavior of others. The group provides immediate opportunity for discovering new and more satisfying ways of relating to people. When individuals begin to feel safe, understood, and accepted, they will attempt social contact at greater feeling-oriented levels and in effect will try out new behaviors. Group members then are confronted with interpersonal relationships which provide feedback. Through this experience, individuals recognize and experience the possibility of change.

Immediate opportunity is thus afforded group members to test the effectiveness of their ability to relate to people and to improve their skills in interpersonal relationships. For some individuals, having peer group members present has a facilitating effect on their social behavior. To see and hear another person extending himself or herself openly in an attempt to better understand self may encourage the cautious member to attempt similar behavior. When one person talks openly and honestly about feelings and attitudes denied in other social situations, the effect upon others may be contagious (Ohlscn, Horne, & Lawe, 1988). In a group counseling relationship, feelings and attitudes about self and others are examined in an immediate situation as the group brings into focus the individual's adequacy or inadequacy for social and interpersonal skills.

REALITY TESTING LABORATORY

The group itself provides an immediate, first-hand opportunity for the group members to change their perceptions and to practice more mature social living (Lifton, 1972). Since emotional difficulties and maladaptive behaviors that are not physiologically based often result from disturbances in interpersonal relationships, the group offers the most appropriate situation for their correction by providing an opportunity for reality testing (Slavson, 1955).

Each member in a group counseling relationship is provided with multiple stimuli to work through problems or difficulties in a situation which more closely approximates the real-life situation (Lifton, 1972). Yalom (1985) referred to the group as a matrix for reality. The group represents immediate social reality and enables members to test their behavior. In effect the group serves as a practice field in which members may become aware of their own feelings, how they feel and act toward others, and how others perceive and act toward them.

Group structure within a group counseling relationship becomes an extremely flexible reality-testing base. In the larger society, individuals encounter rather rigid and fixed structural demands which are inhibiting factors in their striving for self discovery and change. The flexibility experienced in the counseling group, which can be viewed as an immediate mini-society, is a freeing agent to individuals, providing an opportunity to experiment in their own way with reality as perceived by them. This exploring behavior is fostered by the absence of anxiety resulting from fear of punishment.

SIGNIFICANT RELATIONSHIPS
LEARNING TO HELP

In our society children learn at an early age that to withhold, repress, and deny awareness of feelings and emotions are considered appropriate behaviors. Consequently children do not know "how" to deal with their own feelings, to express themselves in a feeling/caring sort of way, or to respond to others out of the depth of their emotions. Within the safety of the group the individual, in the process of becoming less defensive, begins to experience fully, at an emotional level, another person, initially the counselor, who exhibits a kind of helping behavior unlike that which the individual has encountered previously.

Muro and Freeman (1968) asserted that "one of the key elements of group counseling is the opportunity for members to observe a model of helping displayed by the counselor and to acquire some of the helping behaviors themselves. Thus each member of the group is engaging both directly and empathically in the search for meaning" (p. 10).

Behavioral group counselors contend that the group process intensifies the principles of learning by providing a greater variety of models within the group and increased opportunities for reinforcement. Membership in the group is viewed as a powerful reinforcing agency (Vander Kolk, 1985). "The simulation of social reality and social environment created by a group can be systematically controlled and manipulated to bring about . . . learning or change in behavior . . ." (Varenhorst, 1969, p. 131).

For Slavson (1955), a key factor in group therapy was the opportunity for sublimation. ". . . the difficulty the neurotic experiences is due to the presence of unsuccessful repressions on the one hand and an underdeveloped superego on the other, a situation in which he can neither express nor sublimate these instinctual drives" (p. 142). Sublimation activities are viewed as freeing the individual to enhance interpersonal relationships.

Blakeman and Day (1969) described the significant relationships that develop within the group as the basic contributors to behavioral change. Group members come to function not just as counselees but as a combination of counselees at times in the sessions and at other times as helpers or therapists. Through the process of this experience, group members seem to learn to be better helpers or member-therapists. Although Lifton (1972) stated that possibly members may absorb some of the leader's attitudes and thus learn from the leader, he hypothesized that helping behavior can emerge only after group members have made progress themselves in counseling. He contended therefore that giving help is basically within the person and not external to the individual.

A general agreement is that in a group counseling relationship, group members learn to give as well as receive help. Experiencing the reality of being helpful to another person is especially growth promoting to an individual who has felt worthless and rejected.

DYNAMIC PRESSURE FOR GROWTH

According to Bach (1954), in the group counseling relationship a compulsion to improve is present. This drive toward sanity and health is so strong that groups "push" members toward normalcy. Group pressure to change or improve was viewed by Warters (1960) as originating in the verbal interaction with other members which helps to reveal to members the inadequacies in their self-image and the distortions in their views of others. "Group members observe the defensive distortions of reality expressed by other members, challenge these distortions, and accept the challenging by others of their own distortions. The tension and anxiety created by the others' impatience and criticism are dynamic forces that impel a member toward growth and good mental health" (Warters, 1960, p. 187). A similar view was expressed by Ackerman (1955, p. 257) when he stated "gradually the members of the group become conditioned to a code which promotes frank self-revelation, minus rationalization, alibis, and other self-protective dressing."

SUPPORTIVE ENVIRONMENT

As group members assist in the helping relationship, they realize the worth of human relations and feel less helpless and defensive. Experiencing the reality of being understood by others reduces barriers, and defense mechanisms become less acute. Group members then are encouraged to deal with their problems because they feel accepted and supported by the group (Rogers, 1970). This process of being understood and accepted by others as a worthy person results in the group member beginning to view himself or herself in a more positive way, to perceive self as being worthwhile and acceptable. This change in self-image results in more positive kinds of behavior (Slavson, 1955; Hansen, Warner, & Smith, 1976).

Experiences of trusting and being trusted can be extremely effective in meeting the needs of alienated individuals whose fears of our manipulative society have forced them to withdraw or to adopt maladaptive behavior patterns. "In group therapy a person may achieve a mature balance between giving and receiving, between independence of self and a realistic and self-sustaining dependence on others" (Hobbs, 1951, p. 293). The group provides an anchor to reality, and group members learn to understand that different people will react to them in different ways (Wolf & Schwartz, 1962).

Ohlsen, Horne, and Lawe (1988) supported the view that the giving and receiving of acceptance, assurance, and support from others within the group are quite therapeutic. Bonds of common concern are developed and members begin to develop a positive interest in the growth and well-being of others. This can be a very powerful and significant force in the life of individuals who have been able to be concerned with themselves only.

TYPES OF GROWTH GROUPS

Although the rationale for working with people in a group setting may be somewhat similar across the variety of group approaches and modalities, different types of groups differ with respect to goals, time orientation, setting, role of the facilitator, and group membership. In Figure 1.1, Types of Growth Groups (Pfeiffer & Jones, 1972, p. 146), is presented a simplified description of the characteristics of training,

Group Type

Dimension	Training	Encounter	Marathon	Therapy	Counseling
Goals	To develop awareness and skill building	To develop awareness and genuineness	To break defenses	To increase coping	To develop effective planning skills
Time Orientation	Here and Now	Here and Now, Plus	Here and Now, Plus	Past and Present	Present and Future
Setting	Education, Business	All over	All over	Clinical	Educational
Role of Facilitator	Model and Scan	Model and Confront	Confront Aggressively	Treat	Facilitate group helpfulness
Clientele	"Normals"	Anyone	Anyone	Persons deficient in coping	"Normals"

Figure 1.1. Types of growth groups

encounter, marathon, therapy, and counseling groups on these dimensions.

In addition to the similarities noted in Figure 1.1, growth groups also are characterized by spontaneous interpersonal and intrapersonal interaction, freedom of expression, the development of trust in the group, fairly intense interaction, an absence of organizational structure and usually an emphasis on some kind of feedback. These groups also encourage creative use of self and an opportunity for members to truly be themselves in the group.

LIMITATIONS OF GROUP COUNSELING

Although group counseling has many inherent advantages and is often the preferred mode of counseling, the beginning group facilitator should be aware of the natural limitations to the effectiveness of counseling groups. Every person does not feel safe in a group and consequently certain individuals may not be ready to invest emotionally in the group experience. To think that everyone will profit from group counseling would be a mistake. Some individuals just naturally feel more comfortable and safe in one-to-one relationships and will readily explore very personal issues they would be most reluctant to even mention in a group. Other individuals may be too angry or hostile to benefit from the therapeutic factors in a group.

Age also must be considered to be a limitation in that wide age ranges usually should be avoided when determining group composition, especially for groups involving children and teen-agers. Children below age 5 usually do not possess the social and interactive skills necessary for most typical counseling groups to be effective. Even the most experienced play therapist often finds working with this age group in group play therapy to be a very trying experience.

Some individuals may use counseling groups as a place to hide. They go from emotional high to emotional high in various groups and seem not to be able to generate openness and emotional intensity outside the group in day-to-day relationships involving spouse, children, friends, or working relationships. They experience being cared for and appreciated in the group and instead of transferring such experiences outside the group, they seek out other groups and begin the process again. For such individuals, the group is primarily a place to ventilate with no real focus on change or growth.

Vander Kolk (1985) suggested a particular type of counseling group may be appropriate for one person, but not for another. He listed potential members who may not be ready for or suited to groups, such as those who show extremes in behavior that will sap the group's energy and interfere with forming close emotional relationships. Individuals who are verbal monopolizers, sociopaths, overly aggressive, extremely hostile, or narcissistic should probably be placed in individual counseling. Individuals who are out of touch with reality are not likely to benefit from counseling groups.

BASIC ELEMENTS OF GROUP FACILITATION

Know

The basic principles of a group discussion approach are essential in conducting counseling groups. The extent to which the group facilitator is sensitive to the needs of group members will be reflected in what the facilitator does to help members achieve a place of esteem for themselves in the group. Individuals value themselves more when they are responded to in ways which grant responsibility, convey respect for the person, and a valuing of potential contributions. Whether the topic or focus of the group is content or feelings or both, a group discussion format allows individuals to experience the power of their own unique contribution in the peer relationship.

Individuals learn best when they become involved as participating and contributing members to the group. The question for the facilitator of the group then is, "How can I help and encourage members to participate in the discussion?" Too often members do not express their thoughts and questions simply because they are not encouraged to do so. If the topic selected by the facilitator or the group is to have personal meaning to the members, they must be encouraged to interact with the discussion or material and helped to make a practical application to their own personal world.

The key to this approach is the utilization of personally focused questions or reflections by the facilitator that helps members of the group to relate points brought out in the discussion to themselves. If what is being discussed and a responsive, responsible way of life are to become relevant to members, they must be assisted in their struggle to explore their own personal world rather than a hurry up approach with *the* answers supplied by the leader. Questions or reflections that help group members to explore and to derive new meanings also help them to learn how to explore critically when they are outside the group. For the majority of members, the process of learning how to do something for themselves may be just as important as learning what the answers are supposed to be.

Contrary to popular opinion, most individuals are seeking a better understanding of themselves. When allowed to express their concerns, they reveal a desire to understand their own beliefs and attitudes. Understanding however isn't something that can be given. Understanding results from the individual's own unique struggle to discover, to derive meaning.

How, though, can the facilitator know what the members of the group need to know or about what they are puzzled? The answer to these questions will emerge and the dynamics of a discussion approach will be facilitated by helping individuals to fulfill the following seven needs as group members.

Each member needs to feel important and worthwhile.

The facilitator can help by making certain everyone gets a chance to talk, to state ideas, and to be heard. Some members can be helped to participate by calling on them when they look as though they would like to talk but have not, or when other members keep interrupting or will not let the member "get in." The important action is for the facilitator to show interest in each member. Each member's contribution deserves equal consideration. The facilitator might respond to these situations by saying, "Norma, you seem to be thinking about something; could you share it with us?" or "Bob has something to say but he keeps getting cut off. Let's give everyone a chance."

Each member needs to experience a sense of belonging and acceptance.

No place exists for "favorites" in group counseling. Each member wants to be wanted. The facilitator should avoid depending on certain members for answers or suggestions. Each member wants to feel needed. The facilitator can help by showing genuine interest in what each member has to say. Members know they belong when others show they are wanted in the group.

Each member needs to feel understood.

The facilitator can help by restating or repeating what a member or several members have said when the group seems to be confused. Understanding another person implies that you give that person your full attention and listen so carefully that you can restate what that person has said to his/her satisfaction. Listen with the speaker and try to understand how he/she "sees" the problem or situation. Even when the facilitator does not understand completely, to try to restate as much as possible so the speaker can fill in the gaps is helpful. Another approach would be to ask another member to explain what he/she thinks the speaker has said. Through observing the facilitator, other group members can learn how to listen, to understand, and to let the speaker know they understand. We only know someone understands us when they communicate their understanding to us. Therefore, a rule of thumb for the group might be that a member who speaks is always responded to by someone in the group.

**Each member needs to understand the
purpose of the group or topic of discussion.**

The facilitator's role is to help group members to
understand "what we are here for." The facilitator can help
members to understand more fully by asking them to state
what they think is the purpose of the group. The facilitator
could ask, "What do you think the purpose of the discussion
is for us?" "How could learning more about this be helpful to
you?" Wait for responses to such questions. At times the
facilitator may need to call on a member who has not spoken.
However, for everyone to participate verbally each session is
not necessary. As members hear other's ideas, new purposes
that they had not thought of will begin to emerge.

**Each member needs to share in the
decision making of the group.**

What the group does should involve every member in
some way. Sometimes the group may need the facilitator's
help in resisting one or two members who try to push their
ideas and force the group to agree with them. In such
situations the facilitator can help by saying, "Marilyn, you
and Beth are pushing hard to get the group to agree with
you, but some members don't really seem eager to do so. How
do the rest of you feel about this?"

**Each member needs to feel that the group or topic
will be helpful—that it is worth the effort.**

The facilitator can help by asking members to tell the
person on their right one specific way in which they think
the group or topic could help that person or something they
think would be helpful for that person to learn about self.
The idea is to help each other to discover something
worthwhile in the experience.

**Each member should be able to see
the face of other members.**

An effective group discussion can not be carried on if
everyone is seated in rows. Arrange the chairs in a circle.

Allowing people to face each other is psychologically conducive to interpersonal interaction and is, therefore, basic to the group-discussion approach. Such an arrangement stimulates participants to communicate with other members of the group and not just to the authority figure at the front of the room.

SUMMARY

Group counseling offers the unique advantages of providing members with the opportunity to discover that their peers also have problems and to learn new ways of resolving problems by observing other members in the group deal with those problems and issues. Unlike individual counseling relationships, a group provides the individual the opportunity to give as well as to receive help. This can be a powerful therapeutic variable for individuals who have poor self-esteem. In the group they can discover they are capable of understanding, accepting, and helping their peers; that they can contribute to another person's life. In turn members find that in spite of their faults, they are accepted for being the unique person they are. This process of understanding and acceptance frees members to express their own real feelings about themselves, about others, and about what they believe. Thus, members gradually begin to understand and accept themselves. The emerging trust in self and others facilitates the sharing of ideas and behaviors in a safe testing ground before applying those ideas and behaviors in relationships outside the group. Support within the group can be a powerful force and the impetus needed to resolve a given problem.

REFERENCES

Ackerman, N.W. (1955). Group psychotherapy with mixed groups of adolescents. *International Journal of Group Psychotherapy, 5*, 249-260.

Bach, G.R. (1954). *Intensive group psychotherapy.* New York: Ronald Press.

Blakeman, D., & Day, S.R. (1969). Activity group counseling. In G. Gazda (ed.), *Theories and methods of group counseling in the schools.* Springfield, IL: Thomas.

Blocher, D.H. (1966). *Developmental counseling.* New York: Ronald Press.

Cohn, B. (1967). *Guidelines for future research on group counseling in the public school setting.* Washington, DC: Guidance Association.

Corey, G., & Corey, M.S. (1987). *Groups: Process and practice.* Monterey, CA: Brooks/Cole.

Durkin, H.E. (1964). *The group in depth.* New York: International Universities Press.

Ellis, A. (1969). Statement made at North Texas State University Conference on rational psychotherapy.

Gazda, G.M. (1978). *Group counseling: A developmental approach.* Boston: Allyn and Bacon.

Hansen, J.C., Warner, R.W., & Smith, E.M. (1976). *Group counseling: Theory and process.* Chicago: Rand McNally.

Hobbs, N. (1951). Group-centered psychotherapy. In Carl R. Rogers, *Client-centered therapy.* Boston: Houghton-Mifflin.

Krumboltz, J.D. (1968). A behavioral approach to group counseling and therapy. *Journal of Research and Development in Education. 1*(2), 3-18.

Lecky, P. (1945). *Self-consistency: A theory of personality.* New York: Island Press.

Lifton, W.M. (1972). *Groups: Facilitating individual growth and societal change.* New York: Wiley.

Muro, J.J., & Freeman, S.L. (1968). *Readings in group counseling.* Scranton, PA: International Textbook.

Ohlsen, M.M., Horne, A.M., & Lawe, C.F. (1988). *Group counseling.* New York: Holt, Rinehart, Winston.

Pepinsky, H.B. (1953). The role of group procedures in the counseling program. In R.F. Berdie (Ed.), *Roles and relationships in counseling.* Minneapolis: University of Minnesota Press.

Pfeiffer, J.W., & Jones, J.E. (1972). *Annual handbook for group facilitators.* La Jolla, CA: University Associates.

Rogers, C.R. (1970). *Carl Rogers on encounter groups.* New York: Harper and Row.

Rogers, C.R. (1969). Statement made at North Texas State University Group Counseling Institute.

Slavson, S.R. (1955). Group psychotherapies. In James L. McCary (Ed.), *Six approaches to psychotherapy.* New York: Dryden Press.

Super, D.E. (1949). Group techniques in the guidance program. *Educational and Psychological Measurement, 9,* 496 510.

Vander Kolk, C.J. (1985). *Introduction to group counseling and group psychotherapy.* Columbus, OH: Merrill.

Varenhorst, B.B. (1969). Behavioral group counseling. In George M. Gazda (Ed.), *Theories and methods of group counseling in the schools.* Springfield, IL: Thomas.

Warters, J. (1960). *Group guidance.* New York: McGraw-Hill.

Wolf, A., & Schwartz, E.K. (1962). *Psychoanalysis in groups.* New York: Green & Stratton.

Yalom, I.D. (1985). *The theory and practice of group psychotherapy.* New York: Basic Books.

SUGGESTED READING

Gazda, G.M. (1982). *Basic approaches to group psychotherapy and group counseling.* (3rd ed.). Springfield, IL: Thomas.

In chapter one of this book, Gazda deals with the definition and heritage of group psychotherapy and group counseling. He provides short personal sketches of significant contributions to the development of group work beginning with the early period (1905-1932) and continuing through what he calls the period of expansion (1932 to the present). He distinguishes between group psychotherapy and counseling and guidance and points to various professional movements contributing to the increased development of group intervention systems.

CHAPTER 2

THE HISTORY OF GROUP COUNSELING

GROUP GUIDANCE, GROUP COUNSELING, AND GROUP PSYCHOTHERAPY

Throughout this text, the authors take the position that group counseling is a unique intervention system that differs significantly from those procedures that can be described as guidance and those therapy processes commonly referred to as psychotherapy. Much of the difficulty in clearly delineating the functions of these processes stems from the fact that considerable overlap exists in training of group leaders, methodologies employed, and client population served.

Another problem is that during the process of professionalization within the fields of guidance, counseling, and psychotherapy, the terms—particularly among lay persons—have been used somewhat interchangeably. Added to this problem has been a plethora of popular literature appearing regularly in widely read national weeklies concerning all kinds of groups, hence one readily can see the possibilities for misinformation. Condensed "quicky" versions of various therapeutic intervention systems that focus mainly upon "therapies" that range from highly experimental to bizarre are presented to the lay public often accompanied by visual reinforcers in the standard three-column synopsis.

More or less on a regular basis through the media the public is treated to nude therapy groups, massage, E.S.T., sensitivity training (a generic term covering the widest range of activities from "gamey" offensive nonsense to well-planned, systematic self-awareness laboratories), and primal screams. The height of this cultural grab for instant intimacy caused Shostrom (1969) to caution loudly through a professional prism that "the buyer should beware."

Major professional organizations are continuing in their attempts to define, delineate, and professionalize the counseling/therapeutic functions. The American Association for Counseling and Development, The American Psychological Association, and the Association for Specialists in Group Work have position papers and ethical guidelines that address the many problems of small group work.

On November 11, 1980, the ASGW Executive Board approved the 1980 Revision of the _Ethical Guidelines for Group Leaders._ To quote from the Preamble of that document, "Ethical standards consist of those principles which have been formally and publicly acknowledged by the membership of a profession to serve as guidelines governing professional conduct, discharge of duties, and resolution of moral dilemmas" (ASGW, 1980, p.1). This document and the considerable strength represented by ASGW membership constitutes a major step forward in the professionalization of group work in the United States.

A common problem with professional organizations is, of course, the latent spectre of "turfmanship" in carving out territoriality. A cautious eye needs to be kept on too rigid guidelines and rules lest they inhibit creativity and experimentation.

In an attempt to help clarify what we see as counseling in a small group, we offer the following definition that has served us over the past several years:

Know

> Group Counseling: a dynamic, inter- and intra-personal process whose content is generated out of the feelings and behavior of the individual group members. The leader is a professionally trained counselor who is capable of creating a climate of trust, openness, responsibility, and interdependency through the therapy processes of understanding, caring, and conflict management. The group is comprised of persons functioning within the normal ranges of adjustment who are seeking increased awareness of self and others so that they may better deal with developmental situations. (Berg & Johnson, 1971, p. x.)

In "fine-tuning" professional discriminations regarding the differences between guidance, counseling, and psychotherapy in groups, the reader is asked to study Figure 2.1 in which is presented a graphic illustration of the differences and similarities involved in these three processes.

Delineating clearly between functions on any one variable is difficult because of the overlap. The reader is asked to consider three variables—leader, methodology, and helpee or client population—in an attempt to discern degrees of similarity and difference. The guidance, counseling, psychotherapy continuum proceeds essentially from a preventative, proactive constellation of activities to increasingly more refined therapy functions that are primarily remedial or reconstructive in nature.

EARLY INFLUENCES

Group counseling is typically conducted with a small number of people, usually seven to ten. The individuals in the group provide the subject matter for discussion by sharing their personal thoughts, feelings, and behavior. Group members are expected to be involved in the process by reacting to other members through feedback, support, and problem solving.

The leader most usually has had special training in group counseling techniques and strives to create an atmosphere of trust, openness, responsibility, and interdependency. The leader typically models his or her behavior and guides group members through the processes of

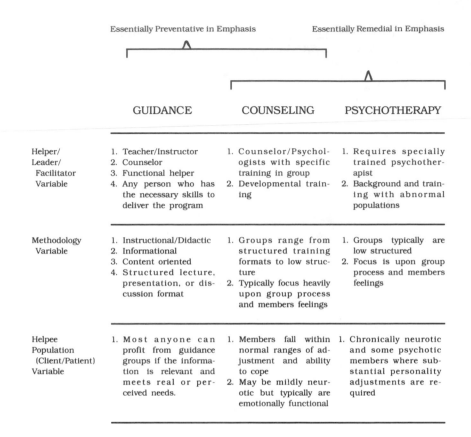

	Essentially Preventative in Emphasis		Essentially Remedial in Emphasis
	GUIDANCE	COUNSELING	PSYCHOTHERAPY
Helper/ Leader/ Facilitator Variable	1. Teacher/Instructor 2. Counselor 3. Functional helper 4. Any person who has the necessary skills to deliver the program	1. Counselor/Psychologists with specific training in group 2. Developmental training	1. Requires specially trained psychotherapist 2. Background and training with abnormal populations
Methodology Variable	1. Instructional/Didactic 2. Informational 3. Content oriented 4. Structured lecture, presentation, or discussion format	1. Groups range from structured training formats to low structure 2. Typically focus heavily upon group process and members feelings	1. Groups typically are low structured 2. Focus is upon group process and members feelings
Helpee Population (Client/Patient) Variable	1. Most anyone can profit from guidance groups if the information is relevant and meets real or perceived needs.	1. Members fall within normal ranges of adjustment and ability to cope 2. May be mildly neurotic but typically are emotionally functional	1. Chronically neurotic and some psychotic members where substantial personality adjustments are required

Figure 2.1. Distinguishing among kinds of groups in guidance, counseling and psychotherapy.

understanding, caring, and conflict management. The members function within relatively normal ranges of adjustment and seek increased awareness of themselves and others so as to deal better with developmental situations.

Differences between group counseling and group psychotherapy center on the composition of group membership, the degree of personality change expected, and the nature of the group leader's training. Methods and procedures used in counseling and therapy groups are quite similar.

Members of a counseling group can come from virtually any walk of life and typically fall within the normal ranges of adjustment and ability to cope with life situations. They join counseling groups to gain deeper personal insights and to develop their personal potentials. Therapy group members bring more severe personality problems to the group and may be mildly to chronically neurotic, with limited ability to deal with life problems. They usually require more intensive personal work in restructuring basic personality patterns.

Both counseling and therapy group leaders require special training in the conduct of groups. Counselors typically focus their training on normal life-span development. Psychotherapists usually spend more training time with abnormal populations and in the study of psychopathology.

Group counseling owes its historical roots to the influence of group dynamics and to the more established procedures used in group guidance and group psychotherapy. The virtual explosion of counseling-related groups since the mid-1960s has caused professionals within the field to struggle with defining and professionalizing the concept of counseling people in groups. Some argue that intensely personal problems are better dealt with in individual counseling.

Nevertheless, groups are a natural phenomenon in human history. Forerunners of organized groups include various religious movements, drama, and morality plays. Some historians cite Mesmer's work as a precursor of group treatment. After reviewing numerous influences on the development of group work, Corsini, (1957, p.9) described group psychotherapy as "a conglomerate of methods and theories having diverse multiple origins in the past, resulting inevitably from social demands and developed in various forms by many persons."

Most, however, note the "class method" work of J.H. Pratt, a Boston physician, as the beginning of scientific group treatment in the United States. In 1905, Pratt used a directive-teaching methodology with his tubercular patients as he instructed them in hygiene. His original intention was to boost their morale through more effective cleanliness. The method more closely resembled what we think of as guidance today. It is doubtful whether Pratt fully understood the psychological impact of his group methods, particularly in the early stages. It soon became clear that his patients were deriving more benefit from the supportive atmosphere of the group than from the information imparted in the lectures.

Somewhat later, Alfred Adler and J.L. Moreno began using group methods in Europe. Adler would counsel children in front of a group, with the primary purpose of instructing other professionals in individual counseling. Again, the observation was made that, far from interfering, the group or audience, as they asked questions and interacted, had a positive impact on the counseling. This methodology continues to be used by present-day Adlerians with the dual purpose of teaching and counseling.

Before leaving Europe to practice in the United States, J.L. Moreno used group techniques with the street people of Vienna. He worked with children, displaced persons, and prostitutes as he found them in their environments. According to Gazda (1982, p. 10), Moreno was "very likely the most colorful, controversial and influential person in the field of group psychotherapy . . . . Moreno introduced psychodrama into the United States in 1925; in 1931 he coined the term *group therapy* and in 1932, *group psychotherapy*."

Others who have had great influence on group therapy in the United States include S.R. Slavson who in the 1930s introduced methods later to become known as activity group therapy. His methods were developed with socially malad-justed children. Rudolph Dreikurs applied Adlerian principles in his work with family groups and children in Chicago. Carl Rogers (1951) and his client-centered or phenomenological approach helped popularize group work following World War II. A shortage of adequately trained personnel and a great need for reconstructive and supportive therapy accelerated the adaptation of Rogerian principles to group work with veterans.

The exact origins of group counseling are somewhat obscure, owing to influences of group psychotherapy and group dynamics. Furthermore, many of the early writers used the terms "guidance," "counseling," and "psychotherapy" interchangeably. R.D. Allen (1931) appears to have been the first person to use the term *group counseling* in print. Close inspection, however, indicates that the methods and proce-dures he described are what would be referred to as group guidance today.

While practitioners attempted to clarify the terms "group guidance" and "group counseling," considerable controversy raged during the late 1930s and 1940s. Noted writers like C.G. Wrenn (1938) and S.R. Slavson (1959) continued to argue that counseling was intimate and personal and should be done individually. With the proliferation of group counseling procedures during the 1960s and 1970s, the argument over terminology seems to be subsiding. The professionalization of school counselors and counselors in public agencies and private practice has added credibility and acceptability to group counseling procedures.

George and Dustin (1988) wrote about the influences of group dynamics and the NTL movement.

In the mid 1940s, a training group in Bethel, Maine, devised a method to analyze its own behavior. The leaders of this group had worked with Kurt Lewin, a psychologist at the Massachusetts Institute of Technology who had developed the idea that training in human relations skills was an important, but overlooked, type of education in modern society. Forming shortly after Lewin's death, the group focused on experience-based learning, that is, analyzing, discussing, and trying to improve their own behavior in the group situation. Observing the nature of their interactions with others and the group process, participants believed, gave them a better understanding of their own way of functioning in a group, making them more competent in dealing with interpersonal relations. The warm, caring relationships that developed among the participants led to very deep personal change in individuals.

As a result of these group experiences and the learning that resulted, those individuals organized the National Training Laboratories, which quickly became a model for training leaders in industry and education. The major impact of NTL was a new emphasis on the **process** by which a group operates, rather than on content. Group leaders placed far more importance on **how** something was said and the effects this had on other individuals than on the words themselves. Thus, participants in the group experience were not interested in learning content, but were focusing on how to learn, especially within the area of interpersonal relationships. (George & Dustin, 1988, pp. 2-3)

In 1971 Gazda, Duncan, and Sisson conducted a survey of the membership of an Interest Group in Group Procedures of the American Personnel and Guidance Association. One of their purposes was to clarify the distinctions among various group procedures. Gazda (1982, p. 23) summarized:

Group guidance and certain human potential-type groups are described as primarily preventive in purpose; group counseling, T-groups, sensitivity groups, encounter groups . . . are described as partially preventive, growth engendering, and remedial in purpose; group psychotherapy is described as remedial in purpose. The clientele served, degree of disturbance of the clientele, setting of the treatment, goals of treatment, size of group, and length and duration of treatment are, accordingly, reflected in the emphasis or purpose of each of these three distinctly different groupings.

Finally, G.M. Gazda, J.A. Duncan, and K.E. Geoffroy founded the Association for Specialists in Group Work, a division of the American Personnel and Guidance Association. In December 1973 Gazda was appointed its first president. Corey and Corey (1987, pp. 10-11) offered an explanation of group counseling that characterizes it as generally practiced at present:

The counseling group usually focuses on a particular type of problem, which may be personal, educational, social, or vocational. It is often carried out in institutional settings, such as schools, college counseling centers, and community mental-health clinics and agencies. This type of group differs from a therapy group in that it deals with conscious problems, is not aimed at major personality changes, is generally oriented toward the resolution of specific and short-term issues, and is not concerned with treatment of the more severe psychological and behavioral disorders.

Group counseling has both preventive and remedial aims. The group involves an interpersonal process that stresses conscious thoughts, feelings, and behavior. The focus of the group is often determined by the members, who are basically well-functioning individuals who do not require extensive personality reconstruction and whose problems relate to the developmental tasks of the life span or finding means to cope with stresses of a situational crisis. The group is characterized by a growth orientation, with an emphasis on discovering inner resources of personal strength and helping members to constructively deal with barriers preventing optimal development. The group provides the support and the challenge necessary for honest self-exploration.

The group counselor's job is to structure the activities of the group, to see that a climate favorable to productive work is maintained, to facilitate member interaction, and to encourage the members to translate their insights into concrete action plans. To a large extent group leaders carry out this role by teaching the members to focus on the here and now and to establish personal goals that will provide direction for the group.

Participants in group counseling often have problems of an interpersonal nature, which are ideally explored in a group context. Members are able to see a reenactment of their everyday problems unfold before them in the counseling group. The group is viewed as a microcosm of society, in that the membership is diverse. The group process provides a sample of reality, with the struggles people experience in the group situation resembling their conflicts in daily life. Members are encouraged to see themselves as others do through the process of receiving feedback. They have a chance to experience themselves as they did in their original family, reliving conflicts they had with significant people in their life. There is also the chance to practice new ways of behaving, for the empathy and support in a group help members identify what they want to change and how to change. Participants can learn to respect cultural and value differences and can discover that, on a deep level, they are more alike than different. Although their circumstances may differ, their pain and struggles are universal. (Corey & Corey, 1987, pp. 10-11)

CURRENT STATUS

Yalom (1985) addressed what he termed curative factors that operate in every type of therapy group. These curative factors are divided into 10 primary categories. Historical influences from group guidance, dynamics, and psychotherapy can be observed in the various factors.

1. **Imparting of information.** Included in this function is didactic instruction by the counselor, as well as advice, suggestions, or direct guidance about life problems offered by either the counselor or other group members.

2. **Instillation of hope.** Pregroup high expectations for success, and hope and faith in the treatment mode, have been demonstrated to be related to positive outcomes in groups.

3. **Universality.** The participation in a group experience often teaches people that they are not alone or isolated with the "uniqueness" of their problems which are shared by others. This knowledge frequently produces a sense of relief.

4. **Altruism.** Group members help one another by offering support, suggestions, reassurance, and insights, and by sharing similar problems with one another. It is often important to group members' self-image that they begin to see themselves as capable of mutual help.

5. **The corrective recapitulation of the primary family group.** Groups resemble families in several significant ways. Many group members have had unsatisfactory experiences in their original families; the group offers an opportunity to work through and restructure important family relationships in a more encouraging environment.

6. **Development of socializing techniques.** Although methods may vary greatly with the type of group, from direct skill practice to incidental acquisition, social learning takes place in all groups. The development of basic social or interpersonal skills is a product of the group counseling process that is encouraged by member-to-member feedback.

7. **Initiative behavior.** A group member often observes the work of another member with similar problems. Through "vicarious" therapy the group member can incorporate or try out new behaviors suggested or modeled by the group leader or other members.

8. **Interpersonal learning.** Man is a social animal living in communities. The group functions as a social microcosm providing the necessary therapeutic factors to allow corrective emotional experiences. Group members, through validation and self-observation, become aware of their interpersonal behavior. The group, through feedback and encouragement, helps the member see maladaptive social/interpersonal behavior and provides the primary supportive environment for change.

9. **Group cohesiveness.** Cohesiveness is defined as the attractiveness a group has for its members. More simply it is "we-ness," "groupness," or "togetherness." Cohesiveness in a group is analogous to the rapport or relationship between individual counselor and client. The acceptance and support demonstrated by the group, after a member has shared significant emotional experiences, can be a potent healing force.

10. **Catharsis.** The group provides members with a safe place to ventilate their feelings rather than holding them inside. The process encourages learning how to express feelings in general and to express negative and/or positive feelings toward the leader and other group members.

While these curative factors are cited by most authors as advantages for the use of groups as a treatment method, also several risks and limitations are involved. Corey and Corey (1987) cautioned that groups are not "cure-alls" and that not all people are suited for groups. Some potential members may be too suspicious, hostile, or fragile to gain benefits from a group experience. Additionally, a subtle pressure to confrom to group norms often is present. Members sometimes unquestioningly accept group expectations for norms that they had acquired in the same way originally.

When a group member accepts the process of the group, the possibility of some psychological hazard also must be accepted. As members open up, they may become vulnerable. As this vulnerability is carried back to the significant people in their lives, adequate support resources must be present to cope effectively.

Absolute confidentiality is difficult to ensure; some members may talk about what they have heard outside the group. Also, scapegoating may occur, especially if the group leader is not effective in intervening when several members attack a particular person. When a number of members join a confronter in an unjustified attack, it can leave the victim feeling ravaged. Any intervention system as potent as a group can cause a major disruption in one's life. Changes can occur in life-style and values, and in loss of security. When old values and ways of behaving are challenged, major life-style disorganization can occur—at least temporarily. Potential group members should be aware of these risks and limitations.

Dies (1985) reviewed the literature on group work with an eye toward generating some hypotheses regarding future group work research directions. He pointed out that group research in the 1950s was primarily concerned with remedial and educational groups while addressing methodological issues. In the 1960s, the thrust was toward attempts to link group process to treatment outcome. This trend continued into the 1970s with the emergence of human potential groups, personal growth groups, and the treatment of children and adolescents.

In the 1980s, researchers continued to try to correlate such variables as curative factors, group stages, leadership style, and member roles to treatment outcomes. There was and is a recognition of the limitations posed by the lack of large scale, multivariate research designs and of the need for stronger collaboration between researchers and practitioners.

MAJOR THEORETICAL APPROACHES

As group counseling has grown in acceptance and arguments regarding definitions have been resolved, so too have theory and group methods been refined. Four models can be used to represent some of the major theoretical approaches.

Know

Client-Centered Model

This group model developed by Carl Rogers (1951) and his proponents is based upon the assumption that human beings have an innate ability to reach their full potential. This includes the potential to solve their own problems, given a free and permissive atmosphere. The group leader is seen as a facilitator who is unconditional and genuine in his relationship with group members. The leader/facilitator creates a threat-free group climate and assists in clarifying communication among members through active listening. Rather than interpret, the facilitator will reflect or mirror back behaviors so that members can see them more clearly. From the client-centered point of view, the group will progress through predictable stages of development without the interference of the leader. Client-centered leadership is closely related to the humanistic-existential viewpoints, with emphasis on understanding one's subjective world, moving toward self-actualization, and facilitating the person-to-person encounter.

Gestalt Model

Frederick S. Perls (1951) and his followers are responsible for the development of Gestalt therapy in groups. The group experience focuses upon increasing a member's awareness of self through an intensive here-and-now orientation. The experiencing of the present moment provides insight into personal behavior and creates the insight upon which new decisions for behavior change can be made. Group members are taught to take personal responsibility for all of their feelings and behavior.

Group leaders focus much of their attention on body language and suggest various techniques to intensify experiencing the present moment. Leaders attempt to identify member behaviors that interfere with their present functioning and to facilitate the working through of historical unfinished business. The leader is a central figure in the group, and much of what goes on resembles individual therapy in a group setting.

Transactional Analysis (T.A.)

Published in 1964, Eric Berne's *Games People Play* brought together in one volume his conception of ego states, which he termed the Parent, the Adult, and the Child. In groups, the goal is for members to become aware of the ego state that they most usually function within. To develop this awareness, members will examine their early programming, the messages they received from their parents, and their early decisions as to their personal worth and position in life. A central concept in T.A. groups is that whatever has been decided can be redecided.

While a T.A. group is interactional and makes use of behavioral contracting, and the theory is designed to provide both intellectual and emotional insights, there is a strong emphasis upon rationality in the group. The group leader functions much like a teacher, frequently using didactic approaches to help members gain insight and control over their lives.

Rational-Emotive Therapy Model (RET)

The RET approach developed by Albert Ellis (1962) basically uses an educational rather than a medical or psychodynamic model. Direct behavioral action taken upon one's belief in irrational ideas that result from verbal self-indoctrination forms the bases for behavior change.

The group leader uses direct and persuasive techniques to help the member become aware of self-defeating behaviors based upon illogical thinking. The goal of therapy is to assist group members in internalizing a more rational philosophy of life and thus to behave and live life more fully. A major feature of an RET group is the use of homework to be done outside the group, ensuring that members keep their progress moving. Also a heavy use of behavior therapy techniques is utilized.

Other Models

Other theoretical approaches that have gained some measure of acceptance, but that may be limited to certain distinct settings, include the *psychoanalytic model*, the *reality therapy model* developed by William Glasser, the *behavior therapy model*, the *development approach* credited to George M. Gazda, and an *eclectic human resource development model* developed by Robert R. Carkhuff.

SUMMARY

Because group guidance, counseling, and psychotherapy are unique intervention systems, a clear delineation among the various functions, leader qualifications, and client populations is needed to understand the appropriate strategies used in each modality. Viewing guidance, counseling, and psychotherapy on a continuum that begin with preventive measures to more remedial inventions, leader training, methods and the helpee population will each differ.

J.H. Pratt, a Boston physician, employed the "class method" in his work with tubercular patients and his work is generally cited as the beginning of scientific group treatment in the United States. European pioneers in group work such as Adler, Moreno, and Dreikurs found their methods adapted in the U.S. The work of Rogers, Slavson, the impetus of the Human Potential Movement and the professionalization of group work through the efforts of people like Ohlson and Gazda helped define group work as we know it today. Rogers' *Client-centered Model*, Perl's *Gestalt Model*, Berne's *Transactional Analysis*, and Ellis' *Rational-Emotive Therapy Model* represent some of the major theoretical approaches used in group work.

REFERENCES

Association for Specialists in Group Work. (1980). *Ethical guidelines for group leaders.* Falls Church, VA: Author.

Allen, R.D. (1931). A group guidance curriculum in the senior high school. *Education, 2,* 189.

Berg, R.C., & Johnson, J.A. (Eds.). (1971). *Group counseling: A source book of theory and practice.* Fort Worth, TX: American Continental.

Berne, E. (1964). *Games people play.* New York: Grove.

Corey, G., & Corey, M.S. (1987). *Groups: Process and practice (3rd ed.).* Monterey, CA: Brooks/Cole.

Corsini, R.J. (1957). *Methods of group psychotherapy.* New York: McGraw-Hill.

Dies, R. (1985). Research foundations for the future of group work. *Journal for Specialists in Group Work, 10,* 68-73.

Ellis, A. (1962). *Reason and emotion in psychotherapy.* New York: Lyle Stuart.

Gazda, G.M. (Ed.). (1982). *Basic approaches to group psychotherapy and group counseling (3rd ed.).* Springfield, IL: Thomas.

George, R.L., & Dustin, D. (1988). *Group counseling: Theory and practice.* Englewood Cliffs, NJ: Prentice-Hall.

Perls, F., Hefferline, R., & Goodman, P. (1951). *Gestalt therapy: Excitement and growth in the human personality.* New York: Dell.

Rogers, C.R. (1951). *Client-centered therapy.* Boston: Houghton-Mifflin.

Shostrom, E. (1969). Group therapy: Let the buyer beware. *Psychology Today, 2,* 36-40.

Slavson, S.R. (1959). Parrallelisms in the development of group psychotherapy. *International Journal of Group Psychotherapy, 9,* 451.

Wrenn, C.G. (1938). Counseling with students. In G.M. Whipple (Ed.), *Guidance in educational institutions, Part I.* Bloomington, IN: Public School Publishing.

Yalom, I.D. (1985). *The theory and practice of group psychotherapy (3rd ed.).* New York: Basic Books.

SUGGESTED READING

Gazda, G.M. (1982). *Basic approaches to group psychotherapy and group counseling (2nd ed.)* Springfield, IL: Charles C. Thomas, Publisher.

For the student interested in the historical development of group work in the United States, Gazda presents a complete chronology of the various major and minor influences that have impacted the field. In addition, he addresses himself to the available research and proposes tentative guidelines for ethical practice.

The remainder of the book presents overviews of several basic theoretical orientations to group counseling and psychotherapy. The sections dealing with theory have been written by leading theorists in the fields of psychodrama, psychoanalysis, behaviorism, client-centered therapy, reality therapy, RET, and Gestalt.

CHAPTER 3

OUR THEORIES OF GROUP COUNSELING

GARRY'S GROUP CENTERED THEORY

The group-centered approach is a function of the facilitator's attitude toward self and each group member. It is both an acceptance of self and each group member and a deep and abiding belief in the capacity of each group member to be responsible for self in the process of exercising self-direction resulting in more positive behaviors. This attitude of commitment to the group member is expressed by Hobbs (1964, p. 158) as ". . . putting aside tendencies to evaluate what is good and right for other people. It requires a respect for their integrity as individuals, for their right to the strength-giving act of making and living by their own choices. And it requires, perhaps above all, a confidence in the tremendous capacities of individuals to make choices that are both maturely satisfying to them and ultimately satisfactory to society." A significant objective, therefore, of the group facilitator is to help group members feel safe enough to change or not to change, for only when the person is free not to change will genuine change be possible.

A unique aspect of this group-centered approach is the belief that "man's behavior is exquisitely rational moving with subtle and ordered complexity toward the goals his organism is endeavoring to achieve" (Rogers, 1957, p. 202). Therefore, what a person knows, some intellectual knowledge, or some "important" information that the facilitator can provide is not what is important; how a person feels about self is what makes a significant difference in behavior. Each individual possesses a personal perceptual view of self and the world that is for him/her reality and thus provides a basis for functioning in the daily experiences in which the person finds self.

Personality Development

The group-centered theory of personality development is based on three central concepts: (1) the organism, (2) the phenomenal field, and (3) the self (Rogers, 1951). The organism is all that a person is: thoughts, behaviors, feelings, and physical being. The phenomenal field is everything the person experiences, whether or not at a conscious level, internal as well as external, and forms the basis of internal reference for viewing life. Whatever the person perceives to be occurring is reality.

A basic proposition is that every person "exists in a continually changing world of experience of which he is the center" (Rogers, 1951, p. 483). As the person reacts to this changing world of experience, he/she does so as an organized whole so that a change in any one part results in changes in other parts. Therefore, a continuous dynamic intrapersonal interaction occurs in which the person, as a total system, is striving toward actualizing the self. This active process is toward becoming a more positively functioning person, toward enhancement of self, indepen-dence, and maturity as a person. The person's behavior in this process is goal directed in an effort to satisfy personal needs as experienced in one's phenomenal field which, for that person, constitutes reality. Personal needs, then, influence the person's perception of reality. Therefore, the person's perception of reality must be understood if the person and his/her behavior is to be understood. Thus, the facilitator avoids judging the person's behavior and works hard to try to understand the internal frame of reference of the person (Rogers, 1951).

The third central concept of the group-centered theory of personality development is the self. Through interactions with significant others in the environment and from the total phenomenal field, the person, as an infant, gradually begins to differentiate a portion as the self. According to Patterson (1974), the individual can only become a person and develop a self in a society or group. The self grows and changes as a result of continuing interaction with the phenomenal field. Rogers (1951) described the self structure as

> an organized configuration of perceptions of the self which are admissible to awareness. It is composed of such elements as the perceptions of one's characteristics and abilities; the percepts and concepts of the self in relation to others and to the environment; the value qualities which are perceived as associated with experiences and objects; and the goals and ideals which are perceived as having positive or negative valence. It is, then, the organized picture, existing in awareness either as figure or ground, of the self and the self-in-relationship, together with the positive or negative values which are associated with those qualities and relationships, as they are perceived as existing in the past, present, or future. (p. 501)

Awareness of self ushers in the development of the need for positive regard from others. This need for positive regard is reciprocal in that as a person satisfies another person's need for positive regard, the person fulfills the same need. Satisfaction or frustration of the need for positive regard in association with self-experiences contribute to the development of a need for self-regard. This "sense of self-regard becomes a pervasive construct influencing the behavior of the whole organism and has a life of its own, independent of actual experiences of regard from others" (Meador & Rogers, 1984, p. 154).

Rogers' (1951) propositions regarding human personality as paraphrased and summarized by Boy and Pine (1982) view the person as

1. being the best determiner of a personal reality,

2. behaving as an organized whole,

3. desiring to enhance the self,

4. goal directed in satisfying perceived needs,

5. being behaviorally influenced by feelings that affect rationality,

6. best able to perceive the self,

7. being able to be aware of the self,

8. valuing,

9. interested in maintaining a positive self-concept,

10. behaving in ways that are consistent with the self-concept,

11. not owning behavior that is inconsistent with the self,

12. producing psychological freedom or tension by admitting or not admitting certain experiences into the self-concept,

13. responding to threat by becoming behaviorally rigid,

14. admitting into awareness experiences that are inconsistent with the self if the self is free from threat,

15. being more understanding of others if a well integrated self-concept exists, and

16. moving from self-defeating values toward self-sustaining values. (p. 47)

The Therapeutic Relationship

If I am to be helpful to each group member, I must make contact with each person of the group at all levels of experiencing in our shared time together. I would like to gently touch each member's emotional world and also to hear as fully as I can his/her expressed thoughts and descriptions. I would like the total response of my person to convey to the group member the depth of my yearning to know and understand, to the extent to which I am fully capable, his/her experiential inner world of feelings and thoughts as known, experienced, felt, expressed, and lived out at the moment. I also want to hear that the other person has a longing to share what may be perceived by the person as a frightening part of his/her life, or confusion, but may fear doing so because I or others may reject. And so they venture forth in this relationship in ways which may seem to lack focus or direction as they experience this inner conflict of wanting to be heard and fearing evaluation and criticism. At such times a tentative and perhaps an almost imperceptable desire exists to share this vulnerable part of self in what may be an obscure or oblique manner which could easily go unnoticed because the message is so inconspicuous or veiled.

In many relationships the person seems to me to be perhaps at that moment only vaguely aware at some deeper level of this underlying part of self or experience which he/she would like to share, perhaps not even at a conscious level in the immediacy of our experiencing relationship. At other times, I have sensed at an immediate conscious level a deep longing on the part of the person to have this vulnerable part of self heard and accepted. The person seems to be crying out, "Does anyone hear me? Does anyone care?" At these moments in our sharing together a developing relationship, I would like by my attitude, words, feelings, tone of voice, and facial and bodily expression—by the total person I am—to communicate my hearing, understanding, and acceptance of this deeper message in a way that will help the person to feel safe, accepted, and appreciated. Sometimes to me by my response in such moments, I seem to be very gently opening a door the person has come to stand in front of in our journey together and by that jesture to say to the person, "I'm really not sure either, what is on the other side of the door. I understand that whatever is there may be frightening to you or something you had rather not face, but I am willing to walk through that door *with* you. I am not willing to lead you through the door not will I push you or follow you through the door. I will be fully present beside you and we will discover *together* what is there. I trust you in this process to be able to face and cope with whatever we find there." A young lady with whom I worked in a counseling relationship expressed her reaction to this kind of caring by writing, "One thing I have come to really appreciate about you is that you will allow me to be frightened, even though you and I both know there is no reason for me to be. You trust me, and I am coming to trust myself. Thanks for that." This kind of relationship is described by Rogers (1952, p. 70) as ". . . the process by which the structure of the self is relaxed in the safety of the relationship with the therapist, and previously denied experiences are perceived and then integrated into an altered self."

The beginning of this movement toward a different self is facilitated when the warmth, interest, caring, understanding, genuineness, and empathy I experience are perceived and felt by the group member. Other members of the group are just as capable of experiencing these conditions, and when they are communicated, may have an even greater impact when perceived by the member of focus. In this climate of facilitative psychological attitudes (Rogers, 1980), group members come to rely on their own vast resources for self-directed behavior and for altering their self-concepts and basic attitudes. Thus the power to change resides within the group member and is not a result of direction, advice, or information I might have to offer. As expressed by Roger (1961, p. 33), "If I can provide a certain type of relationship, the other person will discover within himself the capacity to use that relationship for growth and change, and personal development will occur." The relationship then can be described as therapeutic and a function of basic key attitudes of the group-centered facilitator who is willing to know the group member(s) and to be known in the process of the developing relationship. According to Rogers (1967), the following conditions are necessary and sufficient for personality changes to occur:

1. Two people are in psychological contact.

2. The group member is in a state of incongruence, being vulnerable or anxious.

3. The facilitator is congruent or integrated in the relationship.

4. The facilitator experiences unconditional positive regard for the group member.

5. The facilitator experiences an empathic understanding of the member's internal frame of reference and strives to communicate this experience to the member.

6. The group member perceives, at least to a minimal degree, the facilitator's empathic understanding and unconditional positive regard.

In this approach, the person and not the problem is the point of focus. When we focus on the problem, we lose sight of the person. The relationship that develops in the group and the creative forces this relationship releases in the group member is the process of change and growth for the group member. It is not preparation for change. Rogers (1959, p. 221) expressed this view as, "Psychotherapy is releasing an already existing capacity in a potentially competent individual." Although at times, the past may be described by the group member in light of certain experiences, the present is considered to be more significant. In this process, the group member is responsible for himself/herself and is quite capable of exercising that responsibility through self-direction resulting in more positive behavior.

BOB'S ECLECTIC APPROACH

Perhaps because of the complexity of human nature and the problems encountered in life, most group leaders of my acquaintance eventually evolve to an eclectic system of group facilitation. I chose the word evolve quite carefully because I believe that beginning counselors and group leaders need to select a single theory that fits their personality and style and master it first. Through the process of mastery, the group leader can try interventions that are time tested and eventually select what makes the most sense and what works best for him/her. I am not convinced that an inexperienced group leader should choose eclecticism as an initial intervention mode. My personal bias is that the eclectic group leader needs to have good solid reasons that are grounded in established theory in order to make consistent choices regarding what works best in groups.

My personal beliefs about how people learn and what motivates them to change have been most directly influenced by the following theorists and schools of thought. The influences of Carl Rogers (1951 through 1980's) and Robert Carkhuff (1969), the neo-psychoanalytic school and particularly the work of Karen Horney (1945), the gestaltists and most recently the conceptualizations of Harville Hendrix (1988) will become apparent as I discuss my views on the development of human personality and the therapeutic process.

Personality Development

One of the most difficult arguments to settle is the age old nature/nurture issue. We continue to learn more about the ways in which genetics influence the human organism. Studies with twins and increasingly sophisticated research with chromosomes indicate that heredity may influence disposition and behavior much more than previously thought.

I believe that heredity and environment are intricately interwoven and most probably in a fashion that will remain somewhat mysterious. I continue to be impressed with the powerful role that learning plays in the development of human personality and in the choices people make as they journey through life.

Learning begins at least at birth. Some would suggest that a very primitive kind of learning may even begin during gestation. The human brain is capable of processing hundreds of sensory inputs per second. The most complex and intricate computer in existence pales in comparison to the enormous capacity of the human brain. Naturally, we do not consciously process each piece of data that impacts the brain. That would literally be overwhelming. Nevertheless, some brain researchers believe that every experience we have is stored somewhere in the brain.

I chose to begin my discussion of human personality with the brain because I believe that all of our developmental experiences shape who we are and who we become. I think that early experiences are the most significant because they are being charted and stored in emotion that is uncontaminated by the higher processes of thinking and evaluating that develop later as the cerebral cortex and it's functions become more prominent. The older and more primitive limbic system of the brain is the repository of feelings and emotions. In this portion of the brain our memories of early and unevaluated experiences are stored—both positive and negative.

This primitive part of the brain is relatively uncritical and is most interested in having needs met: safety and security, warmth and nurturance, excitement and sex. The cerebral cortex is a more highly evolved part of the brain that gives rise to our ability to think logically and critically, evaluate, decide, and organize our lives. It also, for better or for worse, helps us control the more impulsive nature of the limbic or primitive brain.

As we "learn" about what culture considers appropriate behavior we also learn to moderate our primitive wishes and desires. Since most of us have difficulty remembering in exquisite detail some of our early experiences before age five or so, my belief is that many of our personality shaping experiences have been sublimated or repressed so that they are no longer part of our conscious awareness. Nevertheless, they remain, at an unconscious level, powerful influences upon our current perception of ourselves and our world.

Our uniqueness as individuals has to do with the delicate interplay between that naturally affective part of self and the way in which we choose to manage our lives—our perception of ourselves in our world. How we perceive ourselves is the sum product of our internalized experiences, both those of which we are aware and, perhaps more importantly, those that have been filed away in our brains but are no longer available to us consciously.

Our most demanding early needs also are the most influential in setting the course of our eventual development and feelings about self. The basic needs for safety and secruity can be clinically observed throughout the lifespan! They are powerful motivators and at some level probably play a part in most of the major decisions we make in life—from choices of occupation or career to the selection of our mate.

To me the recognition that infants enter the world crying and howling is no wonder. We have excised it from one of the most warm and nurturing environments imaginable—the womb. In that desirable place, all needs were met instantly and continually. It was warm, safe, and secure, a condition that will never be duplicated again. We sometimes return to that comfortably protective fetal position while sleeping or when experiencing pain. This regressive behavior also can be observed in severely withdrawn mental patients and in some ways can be interpreted as adaptive behavior. I use the example to illustrate the importance that I believe feelings of security play in the development of healthy personalities.

If we are wise enough to choose our primary caretakers carefully and to have been reared by warm and nurturing parents, we will have a decided advantage in developing in a healthy and positive direction. However, since even the most sensitive of caretakers could not possibly ever meet all of our needs, life becomes a process of learning the skills necessary to deal with and adapt to frustration. The manner in which the human organism perceives the world through those early and needy experiences will heavily influence it's perception of the world as a secure, warm, and nurturing environment that can be trusted, or as a world that is distant and cool, perhaps even a hostile one that need to be guarded against.

These early experiences with frustration of our needs give rise to an anxiety that will govern whether we move toward other people in a dependent manner, move away in a distant and isolated or independent way, or move against others with a hostile or aggressive personality orientation.

Horney (1945) first talked about these basic personality styles, and they are similar to what Hendrix (1988) later labeled *fusors* and *isolators* in relationships. The theory is that dependent or fusor personalities will move toward others in an attempt to ward off the anxiety associated with early childhood wounds. Perhaps as a child the fusor did not receive enough nurturance from the significant caretaker and therefore grew up literally craving an unusual amount of affection, reassurance, and physical contact. Fusors typically fear abandonment so they will seek and demand closeness, togetherness, and teamness.

Counterdependent or isolator personalities may have been overprotected or rejected as children and therefore adopt an independent, "I don't need anybody," personality. Isolators become extremely uncomfortable and anxious in relationships that they perceive to be too demanding of their time and energy. They frequently will state that they need personal space, freedom, and their own individuality in a relationship. What they fear most is being overwhelmed, suffocated, or engulfed by another person.

Basic personality styles, while acted out in an unconscious manner, have important implications for current relationships and the group. Adults have most likely developed many layers of defense in order to avoid things that they fear most—abandonment or engulfment. Ironically, when fusors and isolators grow up they tend to seek each other out as romantic partners. This can be seen as an attempt to heal those early childhood wounds. Paradoxically, while an isolator may be initially attracted to the fusor who seemingly possesses the natural warmth and acceptance that he/she was denied in childhood, as it later becomes apparent that the fusor also has strong needs for closeness and intimacy, the isolator will begin to experience an inner panic because the fusor has become so demanding and clinging!

The converse is also true, as the fusor moves forward with insistent affiliation needs, the isolator, in response, begins to distance. Thus begins an intriguing dance played out through the unconscious needs of the two confused participants. In effect, fusors become isolator phobic and isolators become fusor phobic.

What we need in order to get better is a healing of those childhood wounds. In essence, we need that which we most fear! Those childhood wounds are the result of unfinished business with our primary caretakers. We go through life attempting to get closure on those situations that have been left in our background but which continue in a very real sense to influence current behavior. When we enter relationships that have the potential to become powerful and significant in our lives, they are measured against the background of our experiences. That is, we project our unconscious agenda onto the person or the group. "This person can make me whole" or "This group of people can help me grow."

Against this theoretical backdrop of individual personality, I do group work. I tend to conceptualize groups as reconstructed families where early wounds can be reexamined and in some cases played out. A person's basic personality style will be apparent in the group because issues of boundaries, trust, power, and intimacy will activate the same defenses and roles as will the "real" world.

The Therapeutic Relationship

My own personality best suits me for the "good father" role as a group facilitator. I believe that Rogers was essentially correct regarding the core interpersonal conditions and while I feel they are necessary, my own personal role in the group tends to be broader than that and will vary with the levels of maturity and insight available in the group members. My inclination is to respond to group members with immediacy and gentle confrontation to both members' strengths and weaknesses. I attempt to remember, though, that old wounds are best healed with nurturing and gentle care. People can get plenty of aggression, anger, and confrontation in the streets and even in their families. The group should be, I believe, above all a safe place. Through my manner of acceptance and respect, I try to help create an atmosphere that is secure and safe so that members can trust me, other members, and primarily themselves.

I believe that group members deserve the best of me so I attempt to be well rested and fully available to them emotionally. I attend to their messages as carefully as I can. Being fully available means, however, that I am going to do more than just listen and nurture. Carkhuff's (1969) research into the interpersonal conditions and the concept of wholeness (See Chapter 2) is the model I use for personal availability in the group. While I will not be intrusive with my personal values—at least not consciously—I give myself permission to be fully human in the group. That means that sometimes I will share my likes as well as dislikes, my personal biases, prejudices, and opinions. In my work with group members, I will be respectfully confrontational and immediate with my reactions.

Since, in most cases, I am functioning at higher interpersonal levels and depth of insight than are my group members, I will assume somewhat more responsibility for helping to create a therapeutic climate in the group. I am mindful, however, that I am still only one person in a collection of individuals and so my impact is limited. The climate or atmosphere in the group is an ongoing concern of mine and so "how we are together" is always an issue that is available for inspection by the group.

Finally, I would like to say that all of my life experiences have in some way prepared me for group facilitation. That includes all of the laughter and tears, the highs and lows, wins and losses, elations and sorrows—all are part of me. In many ways, the most significant concentrated learning experience has been my own personal therapy. Actually experiencing the process that my group members go through has aided me most in being able to create for them a trusting and growing atmosphere.

ADVANTAGES OF CO-LEADERSHIP
FOR LEADERS AND MEMBERS

While most of the benefits of co-leadership acrue to the group members, a few are quite helpful to the leaders. The primary advantage is that another professional is in the group who can assist in observation of ourselves and promote growth and stretching in the other leader. As co-leaders work through their own feelings about each other in an intimate setting, they must, by the nature of things, come to grips with their own personal issues. We find this give and take reciprocity and the chances to learn about ourselves both exciting and enriching.

Another advantage to leaders is related. None of us is perfect. In fact, it would be folly to attempt to be so and we often instruct our group members in this area. As co-leaders, we can be aware of our partner's weaknesses, shortcomings, and blind-spots and compensate for them much as partners or teammates do in other situations. When one of the co-leaders makes a mistake in managing the group, the other is there to help right the course.

Groups are not always lively and stimulating. Some will even become boring for periods of time. When the limits of one of the leader's attention span has been reached, the other can likely fill in the gap. No group leader can possibly be on top of everything at all times. Even under the best of conditions we will miss opportunities or simply not hear as well as we can. Two leaders reduce the possibility of losing significant moments and data in the group.

One leader is usually verbally involved while the other may be quietly observing. This can result in a much more accurate appraisal of what is happening in the group or with individual members. In effect, it will provide a much clearer and highly developed picture of the group process and individual member growth.

Co-leaders are able to share some of the responsibility in the group and can reinforce each other's position. Often, group members will hear messages from two different sources, thereby increasing the possibility that it will be heard and acted upon.

Of course, all of these co-leader benefits ultimately flow to the group and its members. In addition, other advantages result in more value for the member from co-leadership. Pragmatically, more leader stimulation is available in the group resulting in less "down time" and a higher work to rest ratio. Theoretically, two leaders will bring double the energy to the group.

Related to this is the possibility that the group will profit from increased resources. Each leader will bring his or her own background and frame of reference to the group, thusly expanding the possibilities for learning. Also, because each leader will have a unique personality, group members will have a choice as to whom they will relate to best in a primary way. One leader may be more assertive and appeal to some group members while the other may share personal values that are attractive to other group members. Co-leaders provide richer opportunities for group member identification.

Lastly, an advantage that co-leaders have over the leader who works alone is that they can model effective interpersonal relationships in the group. Demonstrating respect, genuineness, and caring is a much more potent source of learning than simply talking about it. The co-leader relationship with each other is open and available to the group. This can be particularly enriching as a group becomes fairly stable and secure and tolerant of differences in the leaders. Leaders may even choose to work out their differences in the presence of the group as an example of how conflict and disagreements can be resolved in a constructive manner.

SIMILARITIES AND DIFFERENCES IN BOB AND GARRY'S APPROACH AND STYLE

We have been co-leading groups, team teaching, and involved in writing projects together for twenty years, and during those experiences, we have learned a great deal about each other's uniqueness. One factor that contributed significantly to our compatibility in the early stages of our working relationship was an appreciation for and acceptance of our differences in values, personality, theoretical beliefs, and counseling approach or style. We have not felt the need to challenge or question each other in these areas. We both seem to have little personal ego involvement in looking good or being the most important leader. To submerge our own personal ego needs for the betterment of the group has been rather easy for us. Although there have been few such instances, personal conflicts have been quickly and consistently worked out as needed in outside relationships. We are basically very tolerant of each other.

Our respect for each other's differences has helped us to be open to learning from each other and to trust each other's inclination and direction at the moment in the group even though we may have no idea where the other person is headed at the moment. We believe these characteristics are crucial in the development of an effective co-leadership approach. Our personality differences and differences in counseling approach compliment each other and thus add new dimensions to the counseling relationships in the group.

For both of us, to be as fully real as possible in the group is important. We would like to be known for who we are and so are willing to share ourselves with the group. This seems to come about most naturally in the immediate relationships of the group rather than delving into our past experiences. We trust ourselves in these encounters in the group. We also trust the members of the group and want them to experience our trust as fully as is possible under the circumstances. This issue of trust also extends to the group. We feel quite comfortable in placing great trust in the group and the group process. We do not always have to know where the group is going or how it is going to get there. We believe wisdom exists in the group, and we trust the inherent movement of the group toward that wisdom.

Perhaps the best way to describe our relationship in the group is to say we feel comfortable with each other. We like each other and have a healthy appreciation for each other based on mutual respect. That extends not only to the area of trust but also to helping each other with personal feelings that develop in the group. At times, we facilitate or clarify feelings about self for each other or this may be done in relationship to a group member.

Our differences in counseling approach are perhaps most noticeable in the initial session of the group experience. Bob focuses on modeling helpful responses in the first session, and Garry focuses on facilitating group member interaction. Thus Bob is teaching members how to be helpful to each, and Garry is helping members to discover their contribution is most important to other members.

Bob models a wider range of behaviors in the group. He tends to be more confrontive which sometimes stimulates testing behavior from members. He uses humor more and is more immediate in exploring what is happening between himself and a member. Garry is more immediate with member's intrapersonal issues and is more willing to stay with a member longer in exploring underlying feelings. Garry also tends to respond verbally more quickly and has at times held back to let Bob get in.

REFERENCES

Boy, A.V. & Pine, G.J. (1982). *Client-centered counseling: A renewal.* Boston: Allyn & Bacon.

Carkhuff, R.R. (1969). *Helping and human relations: A primer for lay and professional helpers. Vol. 1.* New York: Holt, Rinehart and Winston.

Hendrix, H. (1988). *Getting the love you want: A guide for couples.* New York: Holt, Rinehart and Winston.

Hobbs, N. (1964). Group-centered counseling. In C. Kemp (Ed.), *Perspectives on the group process.* Boston: Houghton Mifflin.

Horney, K. (1945). *Our inner conflicts: A constructive theory of neurosis.* New York: Norton.

Meador, B., & Rogers C. (1984). Person-centered therapy. In R. Corsini & D. Wedding (Eds.), (4th ed.), *Current psychotherapies* Itasca, IL: F.E. Peacock.

Patterson, C. (1974). *Relationship counseling and psychotherapy.* New York: Harper & Row.

Rogers, C. (1951). *Client-centered therapy: Its current practice, implications, and theory.* Boston: Houghton Mifflin.

Rogers, C. (1952). Client-centered psychotherapy. *Scientific American, 187,* 70.

Rogers, C. (1957). A note on the nature of man. *Journal of Counseling Psychology, 4,* 202.

Rogers, C. (1959). A theory of therapy, personality, and interpersonal relationships, as developed in the client-centered framework. In S. Koch (Ed.), *Psychology: A study of a science.* New York: McGraw Hill.

Rogers, C. (1961). *On becoming a person.* Boston: Houghton Mifflin.

Rogers, C. (1967). The conditions of change from a client-centered viewpoint. In B. Berenson & R. Carkhuff (Eds.), *Sources of gain in counseling and psychotherapy.* New York: Holt, Rinehart & Winston.

Rogers, C. (1980). *A way of being.* Boston: Houghton Mifflin.

CHAPTER

THE GROUP LEADER: SKILLS AND TRAINING

TYPES OF GROUP LEADERSHIP

Although the development of group theory and leadership intervention styles have been refined and differentiated greatly over the past 25 years, the early and classical leadership studies conducted by Kurt Lewin, Ronald Lippitt, and Ralph White (1939) and White and Lippitt (1968) provide a generic framework from which to evaluate group leadership. Essentially, they were looking at the dimension of group member participation in decision making. They identified three types of leadership for their studies: ***authoritarian, democratic, and laissez-faire.***

> ***The authoritarian leader:*** This type of leadership style is autocratic and places a great deal of emphasis on leader power and authority. The leader frequently behaves in an arbitrary and dictatorial manner. The group is not consulted in decision making and goals and plans are determined by the leader.

The democratic leader: This type leader as the term reflects, is egalitarian in orientation. Group climate and cohesiveness are stressed and participation by all group members in establishing goals and directions is encouraged. The democratic leader welcomes process input from the group and serves as more of a knowledgeable resource person.

The laissez-faire leader: The leader takes a very passive role in the group. The group itself becomes responsible for its own direction and purpose. The leader serves as a technical consultant who will offer process interpretations and assistance if requested.

From their studies, some interesting differences emerged particularly as related to group member satisfaction, aggressiveness, and group-task efficiency. Authoritarian and democratic groups were noted as tending to stay with their tasks about equally, but laissez-faire led groups were much less conscientious. When the leaders absented themselves from the groups, authoritarian groups wandered from the task, democratic groups continued at about the same pace, and the laissez-faire groups tended to *increase* their work.

As might be expected, authoritarian groups fostered more dependency upon the leader, were more discontented and openly critical, and made more aggressive demands. Friendliness and cooperation were characteristic of the democratic groups and, in general, group members expressed a preference for democratic leaders above the other two styles.

Luft (1984) addressed the issue of low structure groups:

> In a laboratory on group dynamics, where heterogeneous groups begin to function in an unstructured setting, problems of leadership invariably arise. It remains a significant issue throughout the life of the group, but particularly in the opening phases when the nominal leader clearly indicates that he or she will not assume the traditional leader role. Group members may experience considerable frustration when their reasonable expectations are not met. They soon find, however, that they can function when thrown on their own resources, and they are able, in addition, to experience and to observe leadership phenomena emerge. Soon the situation with respect to power and leadership becomes sufficiently stabilized so that members find they can work quite adequately and at the same time increase their understanding of leadership behavior.
>
> This understanding would not be so easy to gain in a structured group with an assertive leader. (pp. 116-117)

A close relationship exists between leadership style and group efficiency and satisfaction. Fiedler (1953) demonstrated that effective leaders tend to maintain a slightly greater "psychological distance" than do less effective leaders. This seems to indicate that while a democratically oriented group with shared responsibility is most desired and effective, the leader should be identifiable as opposed to being an "equal" member of the group.

Each group leader must explore and define for self what is the most effective and congruent style for him/her. The process of determining a "proper-fit" in terms of leadership style is one that requires experience and practice. We recommend that the leader in training experiment with several different approaches while under supervision. The most effective and satisfied leaders are those who find a relatively comfortable style that blends their own personality with a solid base of theory.

Kottler (1983) wrote about the group leader as a "fully functioning model." His group leader is a person who projects an image of a formidable individual who is fully in charge of his/her personal world. The leader exudes self-confidence, expertise, worldly experience, and serenity. Kottler defined "personal mastery" as the development of skills necessary for a happy existence. He further explained:

> Personally masterful therapists are busy persons, intensely concerned with their well-being and that of their fellow humans. They are action-oriented truth seekers who pursue the unknown and take productive risks in the search for a more satisfying life. Most important, they are in a continual state of improved change, ever working to become more personally masterful.
>
> In addition, there are some corollary assumptions implicit in the personal mastery model.
>
> 1. The more personally skilled group leaders become, the more professionally effective they become.
>
> 2. The group leader is in a constant state of change, as are all group members. Each client concern and interaction conflict forces the leader to look inward, asking the question, Have I worked this problem through for myself? While using group time to work through personal struggles is clearly unethical,

the group leader cannot help but use the time between sessions to personalize relevant struggles to bring them toward successful closure.

3. The more effective group leaders become at solving personal problems, the better teachers they can be at facilitating such outcomes in clients. The group leader should have learned ahead of time how to work through any concern with which a group member may have difficulty.

4. No mere human has ever reached perfection. Every group leader ought to be engaged in a rigorous self-training process aimed at teaching higher levels of personal mastery. Identifying behaviors in need of improvement is the first step in making constructive changes. (Kottler, 1983, pp. 92-93)

He concluded with a list of group leader characteristics to aid in self evaluation. They include self-confidence, risk taking, humor, flexibility, creativity, internal discipline, flow (being immersed in the present), free of negative emotions, honesty, energetic enthusiasm, and compassion.

Techniques and strategies in the group are frequently associated with specific theoretical approaches. Gestalt, T.A., and psychodramatic approaches all utilize techniques that are unique to that particular theory. Group functions, on the other hand, particularly in process-oriented groups, are more broadly based and comprise issues with which all group leaders need to be concerned. Group climate, cohesion, levels of trust, and interaction patterns fall into this category.

Finally, the accomplished group leader will engage in an on-going assessment of his/her own relationships with individual group members and the group as an entity. The concept that leader relationships are a critical dimension in an effective group leads to the following discussion of *interpersonal skills.*

INTERPERSONAL SKILLS

Interpersonal skills are constellations of behaviors that define and may circumscribe the quality of person-to-person relationships. The concept of looking carefully at how people behave with one another qualitatively is a relatively new dimension in psychology. Most often, interpersonal skills are defined as communication skills, and most systematic study has been devoted to the verbal and nonverbal communication transactions. The study and quantification of interpersonal skills has been impacted most directly by psychotherapy and communication theory.

The concept of interpersonal skills development and subsequent training implies that these skills are acquired rather than latent. Because of this focus on learning, consequently, the impact of culture, environment, social expectations, and societal and personal values are of interest to the therapist and communication theorist.

Historically, the groundwork for incorporating an inter-personal dimension into therapy was laid by the neo-Freudians who departed from Sigmund Freud's heavy reliance upon innate biological explanations for behavior. Alfred Adler, a social democrat, was the first to view humans as essentially social beings whose behavior is purposive and goal-directed. The later work of Karen Horney (1945), with her emphasis upon the cultural impact in the formation of neurotic conceptions of self, and—most important—the interpersonal theory of Harry Stack Sullivan, provided pathways for future theoreticians to explore the more subjective worlds of their patients.

The work of F.C. Thorne and his eclectic approach to psychotherapy further broadened attempts to provide a more balanced and integrated method of looking at human behavior. With the publication of Carl Rogers' *Client-centered Therapy* (1951) and its almost total focus upon the subjective, phenomenological world of the client, the relation-ship between the therapist and client became primary, and the process of relationship development came under more intense scrutiny. A major historical contribution was Rogers' attempt (1957) to identify the necessary and sufficient conditions of therapeutic personality change. In addition to his concern with a client as a "whole person," Rogers gave impetus to the concept that there is a central core of "facilitative" conditions crucial in developing a constructive relationship between therapist and client. He identified these conditions as therapist-offered empathy, warmth, and genuineness.

Citing ideas that "have their roots in the antiquity of man," Charles B. Truax and Robert R. Carkhuff (1967, p. xiv), utilizing the extensive resources of the Arkansas Rehabilitation Research and Training Center in Hot Springs, focused intensive research efforts toward identifying new knowledge of the ingredients of effective counseling and psychotherapy that result in client benefit. The primary methodological breakthrough from this impressive volume of research was the development of a reliable series of scales for the measurement of the identified interpersonal conditions of accurate empathy, nonpossessive warmth, and the therapist's self-congruence.

Concurrently, communication theorists such as D.K. Berlo (1960) and Samovar and Rintye (1970) were synthesizing the complex information available from a number of interdisciplinary fields into a set of principles that can be applied to interpersonal communication. Samovar and Rintye emphasized that human speech exhibits common elements and that human attention is highly selective. They posited that humans actively seek consistency between their self-image, behavior, and perceived information, and that they maintain perceptual consistency by distorting information or avoiding data they cannot change.

They contended that active listening on the part of the receiver of information produces better retention. Social roles and statuses influence communication in organizations, and no symbol or word has a fixed referent—that is, the "meaning" of the word is attached to the sender or receiver rather than to the word itself. They also addressed the issue of how nonverbal language contributes to human communication. They consider these principles basic to the study of interpersonal communication.

Building upon the work of Rogers and Truax, Robert R. Carkhuff refined the interpersonal rating scales and expanded the list of interpersonal communication dimensions.

Carkhuff (1983) and his associates developed an interpersonal helping model primarily for use in therapeutic settings, but theoretically applicable to all human interactions. Their model, which is essentially training- and learning-oriented, focuses initially on the skill of discrimination or the ability of the person to fully understand the message sent both in content and process. The ability to receive a message fully depends upon the receiver's level of attention. They have demonstrated techniques to improve a person's attending skills.

How a person responds to a message is critical to the continuance of constructive communication and lays the foundation for initiative action. Six interpersonal conditions impact on the effectiveness of communication: three facilitative and three action conditions.

Facilitative Conditions

When these conditions are offered in communication at observably high levels, they tend to facilitate one's effort to explore and understand oneself.

1. **Empathy.** This is the ability to merge temporarily with another person and see the world through that person's eyes. It is the ability to understand the experiences and feelings of the other person.

2. **Respect.** This is the ability to communicate caring for and belief in the potentials of another person.

3. **Concreteness.** This is the ability to assist another person to be specific about the feelings and experiences that person is talking about. *helping their feelings become clearer to them + me*

Action Conditions

When these conditions are offered in communication at observably high levels, they tend to lead one to initiate and take action upon one's own ideas. *Lead to Action*

4. **Genuineness.** This is the ability to be one's real self in a relationship with another person.

5. **Confrontation.** This is the ability to tell the other just the way it is and to point out discrepancies between words and action and perceived realities

6. **Immediacy.** This is the ability to understand the feelings and experiences that are going on between oneself and another person.

Multiple Impact Training

Perhaps the most complete adaptation is the nontraditional therapy model developed by George M. Gazda (1989) called *Multiple Impact Training* (MIT). An educational rather than a medical model, the theory is based upon the need for development of living skills within the psychosocial, physical-sexual, vocational, cognitive, moral, ego, and emotional areas of human development. The model is based on the teaching/training of "life skills," and historical credit is given to Robert Havighurst, Milton Erikson, Donald Super, Arnold Gesell, Jean Piaget, Lawrence Kohlberg, Jane Loevinger, and H. Dupont. The model is designed to focus specifically on life-skill deficits and to provide training modules to remedy those deficiencies.

Basic Assumptions in Helping

Interpersonal Skills Development can really be seen in the total design as an essential first step in the maximizing of each person's potential capacity toward what Carkhuff (1983) termed *Human Resource Development.*

The obligation of each person in helping situations is to accept the *right* to intervene at the critical points in the life of another person and, at the same time, take full *responsibility* for the level of help that we are willing to offer. When we have decided that we want and intend to be more than a mere "sounding board" off which others can bounce feelings and meanings, we also must accept the awesome responsibility for mobilizing all of the helping skills we have available to us in order to insure a successful completion.

This statement means that we will make a commitment to becoming as effective in helping as is in our power to become. It means that we will do the things necessary—incorporate the essential skills—physical, intellectual, and emotional—that will allow us to offer potent and functional help and to serve as efficient models and teachers—through our actions as well as our words.

Let us examine two basic assumptions underlying the helping process.

1. Helper-Helpee: The Universal Relationship

Essentially all transactions between two or more human beings can be broken down into helper-helpee roles. One person in the transaction will tend to be the helper (or the "more knowing" person) and the other will be the helpee (or the "less knowing" person). The critical factor in the helper-helpee relationship is the sum of interpersonal effectiveness brought to bear in the situation, as measured by a person's total impact—physical, intellectual, and emotional. An additional dimension is that the roles are not necessarily fixed or static and that they may change or reverse according to the kind of help that is sought and the relative "knowingness" of the persons involved.

The helper in a transaction will be the more knowing, whether in any one or a combination of two or more of the three areas: (a) *physical*—in that, through general physiological conditioning, the helper is able to demonstrate high levels of energy and endurance; or (b) *intellectual*—in that, having the appropriate and relevant information, the helper can creatively apply it to the situation; or (c) *emotional*—in that the helper is fully aware of his/her own personal feelings and interpersonal impact and can act compassionately and decisively as the situation and circumstances require.

2. Relationships Are "for Better or for Worse"

The second major assumption in human transactions is that they can be "for better or for worse"—constructive or destructive. The primary question is where do we fit in as helpers? When a person seeks our help does he/she leave the transaction in better shape—or worse? Ultimately, in our efforts to assist have we helped the other person grow, or have we retarded growth? The relationship that we provide for the other person will be, as a result of the level of the interpersonal skills we offer, either additive or subtractive in the helpee's life.

In summary, the helper-helpee is a universal relationship that can assume many configurations; i.e., parent-child, doctor-patient, leader-follower, friend-friend, and so forth. In addition, the level of the relationship or "help" offered will influence individual growth—either "for better," in a healthy, constructive fashion; or "for worse," in an unhealthy, deteriorative, destructive direction.

Philosophical Foundations For Interpersonal Skills Development

This model envisions a person as a developing, striving, growing organism who ultimately is a product of the levels of "help" received from the environment. That is, a person will respond to and grow in either a "for better" or "for worse" direction according to the effectiveness of the models to whom he/she assigns *significance* in life. Most usually, this model is the parents or significant primary caretakers. Later on, as a child's world expands, it will include significant teachers, coaches, counselors, aunts and uncles, peers, and others. Given inherent biological determiners, the child-adolescent-adult will, in effect, model behavior and learn appropriate or inappropriate skills from the people in his/her personal world.

Such a theory of personality focuses upon conscious growth and integration as the central motivating force. Putting this idea more concretely:

1. The most potent example of a person's total effectiveness is one's level of functioning in the world—not wishes, desires or self-reports—but observable behavior.

2. The person is mainly a product of the skills and behaviors that are learned from the world.

3. The person's ego (or that part of personality structure which sorts out and integrates internal needs with the reality of the world) is seen as moving toward fulfillment of potential and growth.

The central thesis of this model is that the life of the "whole person" is made up of actions that fully integrate the emotional, intellectual, and physical resources in such a way that these actions lead to greater and greater self-definition or integration. In a sense, then, the fully-functioning "whole person" is the person who can say and understand the implications of "I know who I am; and I know what I can do."

The Whole Person. The Carkhuff philosophy is committed to the fully-functioning, integrated, whole person as illustrated in Figure 4.1.

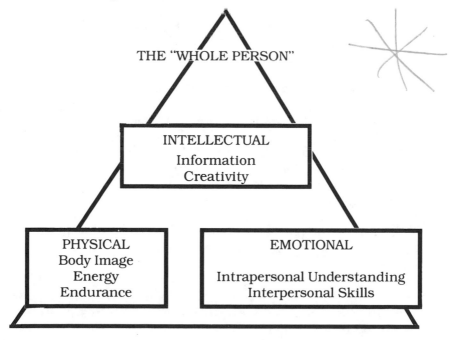

THE "WHOLE PERSON"

INTELLECTUAL
Information
Creativity

PHYSICAL
Body Image
Energy
Endurance

EMOTIONAL

Intrapersonal Understanding
Interpersonal Skills

Figure 4.1. Fully functioning, integrated, whole person.

In terms of "helping," the fully integrated, whole person will be able to better generate and sustain high levels of help because of superior capacities, as demonstrated by the three areas: physical—high energy levels and the ability to tolerate and endure hardships; intellectual—synthesizing relevant date and creatively applying it to the circumstance; and emotional—being able to offer appropriate dimensions of interpersonal responsiveness and initiative.

Perhaps the best way to capsulize the whole person or effective helper is with the following paragraph:

> The effective helper is a person who is living effectively himself and who discloses himself in a genuine and constructive fashion in response to others. He communicates an accurate empathic understanding and respect for all of the feelings of other persons and guides discussions with those persons into specific feelings and experiences. He communicates confidence in what he is doing and is spontaneous, intense, open and flexible in his relationship with others and committed to the welfare of the other person (Carkhuff, 1983).

The Growing Person. Latent forces seem to be available in an advanced technological society that are constantly at work to encourage and promote mediocrity. In a highly specialized and institutionalized society, the reward system seems designed to regulate human behavior in such a way as to stifle imagination and creativity. The fully-functioning helper recognizes these latent forces and becomes involved in a continual program of learning, relearning, and acquiring new and more effective skills. The helper understands that to stand still or to "play a pat hand" is not really standing still at all—but moving backward. No such thing as a holding pattern exists.

Growing persons accept the proposition that staying "fully in the moment" is an ability that requires continual upgrading of skills. Being full and complete means accepting the challenge of depending fully on oneself when situations develop, as opposed to manipulating or controlling people and events. This behavior means dealing with people honestly and in an "out front" manner, rather than by cunning and guile.

The key to confidence in the situation is the development of a wide range of abilities or, put another way, increasing our repertoire of responses. The person with the widest range of response to any situation stands the greatest probability of success. As we increase our repertoire of responses, we multiply the number of options available to us.

Concerning functionality, the truly integrated person knows that in critical situations we want the most skillful person in the driver's seat. That is, we must learn to concede to functionality where it exists and encourage its growth where the potential exists.

By way of illustration, let us say you are confronted with choosing between two players (A and B) to be the quarterback for your team. All other things being relatively equal, you find that A is a mechanically sound and adequate quarterback. In addition to being mechanically sound, however, player B seems able to infuse the team with a greater desire to perform well. He is an exciting leader. Choosing player B to quarterback the team will increase the probability of winning because he has *additional skills* to insure a successful delivery. The most functional person in the situation should play quarterback.

An Overview Of Interpersonal Skills Development

We begin our exploration of interpersonal skills with a schematic presentation of the overall model as presented in Figure 4.2. As suggested in the Figure, when we begin to examine carefully the kinds of things that happen between two people in an interpersonal relationship we need to focus upon **discrimination** (or the ability to listen) and **communication** (or the ability to respond to what we have heard). In addition Carkhuff has isolated six dimensions that occur to some extent (or at some level) in all human transactions. These dimensions are **empathy** (E), **respect** (R), **concreteness** (C), **genuineness** (G), **confrontation** (Co), and **immediacy** (I).

DISCRIMINATION and *COMMUNICATION*

of the

Facilitative/   and   Action-oriented/
Responsive   Initiative

Dimensions

1. Empathy
   (understanding
   someone)

2. Respect/warmth
   (caring for someone)

3. Concreteness
   (being specific)

4. Genuineness
   (being honest and
   open)

5. Confrontation
   (pointing out discre-
   pancies or "telling it
   like it is")

6. Immediacy
   (being in the here
   and now)

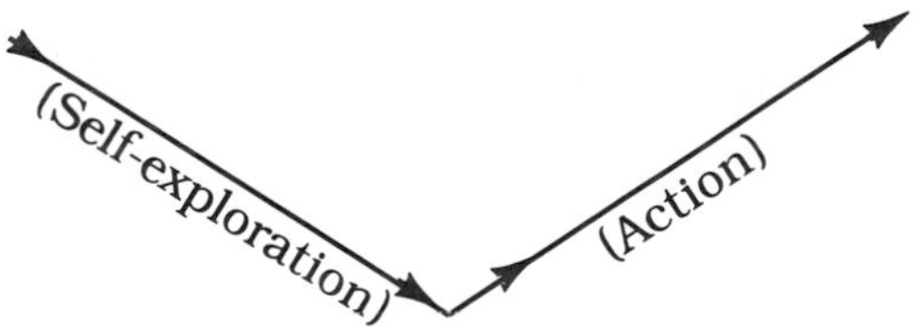

(Self-exploration)   *(Action)*

(Self-Understanding)

Preferred Mode of Treatment OR
Effective Course of Action

Figure 4.2. Schematic Model for Interpersonal Skills.

Carkhuff and his associates have systematically re-searched each of the dimensions and have found that persons (therapists, counselors, teachers, parents, students, and lay helpers) who offer high levels of the interpersonal conditions tend to create an atmosphere or climate for helpee growth. Conversely, persons who offer low levels of these same conditions tend to retard or inhibit helpee growth. This process has been demonstrated in the physical, intellectual, and emotional areas, but here we will primarily be concerned with the quality of verbal responses that the helper is offering the helpee.

Let's look at what we mean when we say "high" or "low" levels. In determining whether a response is high or low we use a five-point scale where each of the responses can be scaled by trained raters for content and feeling. The scale to evaluate overall helping effectiveness is provided in Figure 4.3.

Responses that fall below level 3.0 on the scale are judged to be subtractive, deteriorative, or destructive to the person who is seeking help.

Responses that are at the 3.0 level are called inter-changeable responses in that they (the stimulus statement from the helpee and the response from the helper) can be laid side by side and could have been said by either the helper or the helpee. The helper at level 3.0 attempts to simply restate or reflect back to the helpee as accurately as possible his/her *expressed* feeling and meaning.

The higher levels (3.0 and above) are termed additive empathic responses—when the helper goes beyond what the helpee has expressed in an attempt to add to the exploration and self-understanding.

The area of additive empathic responses between levels 3 and 4 on the scale is where the majority of good helping occurs. This is the area where the skillful helper will spend most time and energy facilitating the deeper self exploration of the helpee. It involves going beyond what the helpee has presented. To be additively empathic, the helper assists the

Helpfulness	Scale	Level of Communication
ADDITIVE RESPONSES	5.0	All conditions are communicated fully, simultaneously, and continually.
	4.0	Some conditions are communicated at a minimally facilitative level, some fully
AREA OF ADDITIVE EMPATHY		
INTERCHANGEABLE	3.0	All conditions are communicated at a minimally facilitative level
SUBTRACTIVE RESPONSES	2.0	Some conditions are communicated and some are not
	1.0	None of the conditions are communicated to any noticeable degree

Figure 4.3. Scale to evaluate overall helping effectiveness.

helpee in taking personal responsibility for his or her part in the problem. In effect this means that the helpee cannot put the meaning off onto someone or something else. It involves ownership or internalization of his or her position in the problem.

No value occurs in problem solving until the focus person internalizes and "owns" responsibility for self. This frequently involves letting go of some of the more primary ego defense mechanisms such as denial, blame, projection, and rationalization.

Subtractive responses on the five-point scale are "for worse" and according to Carkhuff's research, the overall average for various samples of the population is below 3.0, or the minimally facilitative level, i.e., lay helpers 1.49, general public 1.58, graduate students in psychology 2.35, classroom teachers 2.10, high school counselors 1.89, and experienced therapists 2.13 (Carkhuff & Berenson, 1977, p. 31), we can see that we are paying a heavy price in our interpersonal relationships.

INTERPERSONAL SKILLS FOR THE GROUP LEADER

Most of us find ourselves in "helping" situations several times each day. Some of us literally make a living from helping. Others are less directly involved with providing professional help but most people are engaged in some form of service to other people. The range of possible helping situations in which we find ourselves is almost infinite. That is, counselor-client, teacher-student, nurse-patient, parent-child, police officer-citizen, airline flight attendant-upset traveler, ad infinitum.

We believe that the critical determiner as far as the help we offer to others is ourselves. When we are called upon for help, the impact we have on the helpee or the effectiveness of the helping transaction will be related directly to the level of interpersonal skills we offer to the other person.

More concretely, we might ask ourselves the question: "If I didn't have the uniform, or the professional role, or the set of procedures, or the guidelines, what would I be able to offer to another person?" The answer is always the same—me.

Our major focus is on an exploration of the personal qualities that each of us have available to us and the level, or degree to which we offer these personal qualities to others in helping situations.

We could summarize by saying that each of us finds ourself in multiple situations where we are called upon to help. Further, let us assume that each of us wants to maximize our potential as potent and effective helpers. From this base we can proceed to further explorations.

Discrimination

What can we, as helpers, do to increase our levels of response and make a significant difference in the lives of our helpees. The first skill we need to examine is **discrimination.** Developing high discrimination (or attending) skills means that we will tend fully to the message that is being sent and all of its parts. Not only do we listen to the content, or *what* is being said, but also to the feeling, or *how* it is being said. To do this we need to listen to another person not only with our ears, but with our eyes. We need not only to hear the words (verbal), but also the feeling (non-verbal).

The first step in improving the quality of our responses is to make a good discrimination of what and how something is being said to us. The key is to attend fully to all of the cues—content, feeling, verbal, and non-verbal.

Our basic cue comes from some people in our world who tend to be naturally high discriminators. This person would be the kind of individual who tends to be quiet and observant of the behavior of others. This individual is what we might call a highly responsive personality-type—one who carefully watches others and then acts according to his/her perceived expectations. As a predominant mode of behavior, this could be dangerous if carried to its neurotic extreme because it results in behavior that is initiated only in response to others—loss of personal definition; or incorporation of a self-concept from the "outside in," so to speak.

By practicing our attending skills, we can train ourselves to be better, clearer, finer discriminators by listening and fully being with the other person.

Communication

Discrimination, while it is the foundation for higher level interpersonal relationships, is relatively of little value in helping if it stands alone. In other words, discrimination, while it is a necessary and even crucial step in helping, is not enough. After the careful discrimination has been made comes the next, and most important step—that is **communication.** This is the step where we respond to our helpee in terms of what our best discrimination tells us he/she is saying—or asking for. In a sense, we can make a judgment on how good our discriminations have been by evaluating the level of response that we communicate back to the helpee—or the other person in the transaction. At this point the five-point scale is meaningful. Now we can look at the stimulus (S) (for the statement presented by the helpee) and also look at the response (R) (or the statement given back to the helpee by the helper) and determine its effectiveness on the scale— its additiveness or subtractiveness.

Overall, helping involves discrimination and communication. Both of these skills can be trained, practiced, and improved. As you might expect, discrimination is somewhat easier to train because it is a relatively passive behavior. Discrimination involves *sensing* and *knowing*—fully attending to another person to determine as accurately as possible what is being said. Communicating back to the helpee is a more active behavior and, as such, demands a certain amount of risk on the part of the helper. We can never be a truly effective helper until we accept the risks of deep, active involvement with our helpees.

Summarizing, discrimination involves total *alertness* and communication involves *acting.*

The implication is clear. Helpees first want to know that their helper indeed can help them—that the helper is more functional, "more knowing" and able to deliver the appropriate help. We relate back to what was said earlier about functionality. The initial discrimination that the helpee will make is physical. They will want to know if the helper respects self enough to present a competent, ordered, and attractive physical picture. A book we once read talked about an adolescent girl who was heavily involved in the drug scene and who was taken to a psychiatrist for help. Her evaluation after two sessions was "Why should I listen to that fat S.O.B., he cannot even take care of himself." A few months later, she was dead from an overdose. The point is, a paid professional with an opportunity to intervene at a crisis point, was not able to deliver the needed help.

Let's assume that the helpee has decided to stay and run a few more tests. The next question asked or felt, however vaguely, is "Will I be understood—can he or she understand me?" Helpees frequently feel confused and upset—not able to sort our their thinking and feeling. This very fact often makes them anxious and fearful. At this point, the helpee is not interested in judgments, advice, or "being told what to do." He/she is interested in being cared for and understood as fully as possible. Being understood by another human being, at this particular point, helps to answer the question, "Am I still O.K.?" They want the helper to respond in a non-judgmental, unconditional way. They want to feel understood (empathy) and cared for (respect).

When offered to the helpee at interchangeable levels, these two conditions, empathy and respect, are called "the building block dimensions," in that they communicate and promote deeper and deeper levels of mutual trust. As empathy and respect are communicated, the helpee will learn to trust at deeper levels and feel free to explore self and problems more intensely.

The helpee also will progress toward deeper self-exploration and self-understanding as the helper focuses sharply upon what is being said—and not said—and guides the helpee into personally relevant material in specific terms.

At the point where trust has been established and self-exploration has been facilitated, what might be called self-understanding frequently occurs. This is often a cognitive or intellectual understanding of self or the problem. In Carkhuff's model, this level of understanding is achieved when the helpee can respond to self just as the helper would. In other words, the helper and helpee have become verbally interchangeable. Some therapists refer to this point as "insight."

The Carkhuff model goes beyond most "insight" therapies to an action or initiative stage. What is being said, in effect, is, "There is no understanding without action." Put another way, we could say that it is possible to "understand" ourselves or our problems, but the real proof of our understanding is how we put our insights into action through appropriate and constructive behavior.

Also, at this point the helper, after having demonstrated understanding and caring and developing a bond of trust, can become increasingly conditional or initiating with the helpee. At this point, the helper is established as a strong reinforcer for the helpee and can become increasingly genuine, confrontive, and immediate—more interchangeable or reciprocal as the helper/helpee team begins to work together to develop plans, programs, and effective strategies to reintegrate the helpee with his or her thinking, feeling, behavior, and world.

HELPING FROM THE POINT OF VIEW OF THE HELPER

From our previous discussion, we can see that the process of helping is essentially seen in two major phases—discrimination and communication. These two phases also relate directly to the interpersonal conditions that are emphasized in each phase.

Facilitative or Responsive Dimension

The facilitative or responsive dimension includes the conditions of empathy, respect, concreteness, and, to a somewhat lesser extent, genuineness. These "core" conditions, when offered at high levels, tend to meet the helpee's initial need for nurturance or unconditionality and aid in the process of trust-building and self-exploration.

The responsive dimensions, as the term implies, tend to take persons where they are and communicate to them that we understand their frame of reference or "where they are coming from." Let us look at each of the responsive conditions briefly.

Empathy (E). *The communication of empathy involves the helper communicating back to the helpee that he/she knows and understands both the **feeling** and **meaning** of the helpee's expression and experience.*

By focusing intently upon the content that the helpee is presenting and the manner in which the content is communicated, we can begin to respond to both parts of the message. At level 3, or the interchangeable level, we will want to communicate back to the helpee that we understand the expressed feelings and meaning. In a sense, we are asking the helper to **reflect** back to the helpee, as accurately as possible, what the helpee is meaning and feeling. At higher (or additive) levels, the helper will go beyond the helpee's expression and add noticeably in communicating understanding in a way that the helpee is not able to do for himself/herself.

Here are some further guidelines for judging empathic accuracy. At the responsive, level 3, or interchangeable level, the helper reflects

1. the helpee's verbally expressed feeling,

2. the helpee's obvious feeling experience, and

3. an understanding of the environmental stimulus or content.

Additive levels of empathy draw upon the helper's ability to integrate this information and experience and guide the helpee in

1. identification of the helpee's behavior pattern,

2. the helpee's feelings about self as a result of interaction with the environment,

3. the helpee's expectations of self,

4. the helpee's basic beliefs about self, and

5. incorporating the new feelings or reactions to new meanings.

Empathy Illustration

Helpee Stimulus:	"It's gotten so that I get nervous whenever we get an invitation to a party. I start to worry and fret a whole week in advance.
Interchangeable Response:	"Just the anticipation of going to a party makes you feel anxious and tense."
Additive Response:	"The anticipation of a party really makes you uptight and sort of scared. Like you won't be able to handle it all and that leaves you feeling confused and frustrated."

Respect (R). *The communication of respect involves the helper communicating back to the helpee a concern and regard for the helpee—his or her feelings, potentials, and experiences.*

The helper communicates respect at level 3 by indicating a positive regard and caring for the helpee's feelings, experiences, and potential to grow. The helper communicates an appreciation of the helpee's ability to express self and deal constructively with life experiences.

At higher levels, the helper's responses enable the helpee to feel free to be himself/herself and to experience being valued as an individual.

Respect communicates that the helper cares and values the helpee's ability to work through problems in a constructive way. At the highest levels of respect, the helper will initiate communication that causes the helpee to realize his or her full potential for growth.

Respect illustration

Helpee Stimulus:	"It makes me so darn mad. I know I'm a better basketball player than most of the guys on the team and every Friday night I buy a ticket to get in to watch them play."
Interchangeable Response:	"You get pretty angry when you feel that you could be playing and contributing instead of sitting in the bleachers."
Additive Response:	"You're pretty angry at yourself for sitting around and letting a good opportunity pass you. You've got a lot more than you're using right now and you want to find a way to test that ability."

Concreteness (C). *In communicating concreteness the helper guides and directs discussion into personally relevant material in specific and concrete terms.*

At the minimally effective level, or level 3, the helper, at times, enables the helpee to discuss personally relevant material in specific terms. The helper may not always develop the area of inquiry fully. The communication of concreteness requires that the helper make a fine discrimination in terms of the helpee's cognitive and affective readiness to discuss personally relevant material in increasingly specific and concrete terms.

These are the major responsive or facilitative dimensions and are usually communicated first in helping relationships. They assist the helpee in self-exploration and understanding and in laying the groundwork for the helper to become increasingly initiative and conditional in the relationship as the helper/helpee team beings the upward-outward process of reintegration with the real world.

Concreteness illustration

Helpee Stimulus:	"I suppose I'm not so different—I guess most people get pretty uptight and nervous when there's a lot of work to do."
Interchangeable Response:	"You're really hoping that your own uptightness won't get out of hand—that most people feel about the same as you do."
Additive Response	"On the one hand you still hope that your anxiety will just go away and at the same time it's pretty frightening to think that it might get out of control—overwhelm you."

Initiative or Action-Oriented Dimension

The initiative or action-oriented dimension includes the conditions of genuineness, confrontation, and immediacy. After the helpee has experienced the feeling of being understood and cared for and has demonstrated an increased self-awareness by becoming more and more interchangeable with the helper, he/she is ready to translate self-understanding into a concrete plan of action.

At this point, the implications for the helper are to become more "conditional" and, in a sense, more of a reciprocal person in the helping relationship. Let us look at the specific conditions that can be offered at higher levels during this later stage in helping.

Genuineness (G). *The communication of genuineness consists of the helper expressing his/her honest feelings to the helpee in a constructive manner.*

Perhaps a good way to illustrate what we mean by genuineness is to think about the opposite of being genuine—that is, being unreal or phoney. Being honest and open with real feelings in helping requires a good discrimination of the helpee's ability to handle your openness. An individual can be highly genuine and real with feelings and meanings and yet the total impact of an interchange can be destructive to the helpee. The key to helpful genuineness is being appropriate and constructive with feelings. At the lowest levels of genuineness, the helper often responds defensively or in a "professional" manner or role. The helper offering low levels of genuineness may sound rehearsed or pre-planned.

At level 3, or the minimally facilitative level, the helper provides no "negative" cues or, for that matter, "positive" cues to indicate a truly honest response. In other words, the helper indicates attentive listening, but responses do not reflect that he or she is either *insincere* or, on the other hand, *deeply involved.*

At higher levels of genuineness, the helper indicates honest responses (either positive or negative) in a non-destructive way. The helper is being honest, spontaneous, and constructive.

Genuineness Illustration

Helpee Stimulus: "It's almost surprising to me. I know it's what I've been working toward but I can really care for someone, and someone cares for me."

Interchangeable Response: "You weren't really sure it could happen to you. That you could care for me and allow me to care for you."

Additive Response: "It's really an amazing and awesome feeling to know that I care for you deeply and for you to care for me. It really makes me feel good to know that you understand and accept my caring."

Confrontation (Co). *Confrontation involves the helper focusing upon helpee discrepancies.*

Types of confrontation include

1. *real versus ideal self,*

2. *insight versus action, and*

3. *helper versus helpee experiences.*

Modes of confrontation include

1. *experiential,*

2. *didactic,*

3. *confrontation to strength,*

4. *confrontation to weakness, and*

5. *encouragement to act.*

Unfortunately the domestic violence of the 1960s and early 70s helped create an emotional response to the word "confrontation." Too frequently it is *equated* with anger and violence. As can be seen by the definition here, confrontation involves focusing upon *discrepancies* in ideas and behavior and is not necessarily accompanied by any particular affect. As we inspect the definition, we see that there are three major types or kinds of confrontation and five major modes or methods.

At the minimally facilitative level, the verbal and behavioral expressions of the helper, while open to helpee discrepancies, do not relate directly or specifically to these discrepancies. For instance, the helper may simply raise questions without pointing to the diverging directions of the possible answers.

At higher levels, the helper attends directly and specifically to helpee discrepant behavior and confronts the helpee directly and explicitly in a sensitive and perceptive manner whenever discrepancies occur.

Confrontation Illustration

Helpee Stimulus:

"I've been on diets a hundred times. Tried about everything. I can lose weight but then I gain it back. I don't seem to have the willpower to stick to anything."

Interchangeable Response:

"You've proven you can take the weight off—it's keeping it off that bothers you. This pattern raises some questions about your ability to stick with a program.

Additive Response:	"This, 'on-again, off again' pattern raises some real basic questions about yourself. It's a question of whether you can only work for short periods of time— but whether you can persist and endure. Whether you can make a commitment to real and lasting change."

Immediacy (**I**). *The communication of immediacy involves the helper focusing upon the "here and now" ongoing relationship between the helper and helpee.*

At the lowest levels of immediacy, the helper's responses disregard helpee expressions that have the potential for relating to the helper. The helper may disregard, remain silent, or just not relate the content to self.

At the interchangeable level, the helper remains open and alert to interpretations of immediacy but does not relate what the helpee is saying to the immediate moment. The helper may make literal responses or reflections that are open-minded but that refer to no one specifically.

At additive levels, the helper relates the helpee's responses to self either in a tentative manner, or, at the highest levels, in a direct and explicit way.

Immediacy Illustration

Helpee Stimulus:	"I don't know, I've seen two other counselors and it didn't seem like it helped much. Maybe I'll just have to learn to live with this. Nobody seems to have the answers."

| Interchangeable Response: | "It's pretty discouraging to you. You've tried before, you're trying again but you're just not sure that anyone can help you." |
| Additive Response: | "You're pretty discouraged at this point, partly with yourself and partly with me. You were hoping that I would be different than the others but right now you're just not sure." |

SUMMARY OF HELPER'S STRATEGY

And so, in summarizing the helper's strategy through the implementation of the dimensions in an interpersonal relationship, we see a helper who is aware fully of self and his/her personal impact on the helpee. The helper is able to make fine discriminations of the helpee's needs and is able to respond to those needs at an appropriate level.

The helper sees self both as a person who can be nurturing and facilitative and as a person who can initiate new material and add directionality to move the helpee to higher and higher levels of growth and self-fulfillment. The overall plan is to facilitate self-exploration and understanding and to strategize with the helpee in devising effective programs or courses of action to remedy destructive behavior patterns and encourage the incorporation of new and effective modes of living. A helper accepts the responsibility for becoming a potent force to the helpee and is willing to "go the extra mile" in order to maintain potency and increase his or her own personal growth.

Through a personal philosophy of being real and offering him or herself in a relationship at the highest levels, the helper discloses self as a person.

LEADERSHIP TRAINING

Experiential Component

Tamminen and Smaby (1978) initially identified the need for group counselors in training to crystalize a systematic set of skills that would prepare them to make effective interventions in a group setting. They recommended a mini-laboratory approach that focuses upon verbal intervention skills appropriate to a number of critical developments within the group process.

In response, Landreth and Berg (1979) suggested that in order to deal more effectively with the anxiety most novice group leaders feel regarding the initiation of an actual group, a more direct experiential approach can be helpful in addition to skill training. Dameron (1980) and his colleagues listed a direct, hands-on, group leadership experience as a master's level counselor competency.

The Standards Committee of the Association for Specialists in Group Work has developed a statement of competencies for master's level group leaders that contain both knowledge and skill competencies. Eventually, those competencies will be extended to include standards for group leaders at the specialist and doctoral levels.

We will attempt to share the kinds of directed experiences presently in use at the master's level in the group counseling courses at the University of North Texas.

The master's level course in group counseling is the second course in the group counseling sequence. The beginning course is offered to undergraduates through the Counselor Associate Program. The master's level course occurs late in the curricular sequence and, in fact, is the first formal exposure to study in group counseling for about 90% of the students.

The course is considered a laboratory course and is divided about equally between traditional didactic study in group dynamics and counseling and in more direct experiences. The experiential components include an actual counseling group where students participate as members and an out-of-class co-leadership experience.

Aside from the traditional study of group counseling, the experiential objectives and activities are designed so that the prospective group counselor will

1. gain an involved participant and leader understanding of group dynamics, group process, and group counseling;

2. develop sensitivity to the needs of group members with emphasis on listening and responding to feelings;

3. develop a first-hand awareness and understanding of the therapeutic and growth potential in a group; and

4. enhance his or her personal self-understanding through the group membership experience.

The Laboratory Group. Approximately one-half of the allotted class-time is devoted to group counseling, labeled a laboratory group. Norm class size is sixteen students so that, when divided, there are two laboratory groups of eight members each. Groups meet for 1½ hours weekly during the regular academic semester and twice weekly during summer sessions. The laboratory groups are led by senior doctoral students who receive partial internship or licensed supervision credit for their involvement. Since Texas has a counselor licensing law, students can accumulate 50 hours of supervised experience that counts toward the requirement for licensure.

The laboratory group component of the course is designed to be as non-evaluative as is possible in an academic setting. Students are encouraged to participate as fully as they can in helper and helpee roles and to test and explore their skills in a direct fashion. Grades are not assigned for laboratory group participation.

Pre-screening for group membership suitability is limited to acceptance into the master's degree program. Group counseling is a required course and all candidates participate. While most students are eager for the experience and graduates consistently rate the experience highly, it is probable that the laboratory groups would be even better were the course elective.

Group members are asked to keep detailed personal journals that focus upon their own in-depth self-exploration in addition to the process of the group itself. Particularly for some members, this assignment increases their personal awareness and facilitates the critical examination of the group process.

Finally, group members arrange for their group's own "extended session" during each semester. This group meeting typically lasts for about eight hours and provides members with a mini-marathon experience within the context of an ongoing group.

The "Out-of-Class" Group. This field-based leadership experience is typically rated as one of the most potent learning activities available to the students. Though there is usually the anticipated anxiety of a first group leadership experience, follow-up feedback has been exceptionally positive. While data has not been analyzed in a systematic way, written feedback is gathered anonymously at the conclusion of each course. Over the past ten years, students have consistently rated the "out-of class" group co-leadership experience as one of the top two learning experiences available to them through this course.

Students are asked to get to know their classmates early in the semester with the ultimate goal of selecting a person with whom they can work as a co-leader. Students who live in relatively the same geographical areas tend to choose each other initially simply out of convenience. To a large extent that seems to work but the course instructor reserves veto power over co-leader matches where personality types might conflict or in some way be unsuitable. Self-selection works rather nicely and the privilege of instructor veto power is seldom exercised.

When co-leader teams have been agreed upon, students are asked to go directly to the community to generate a group to work with for a minimum of six sessions. This requires the students to plan and organize their thinking and presentation to the people who are potential members. In some cases they must also "sell themselves" to the administrator of the school or agency where they hope to lead the group.

In a large metropolitan area there are many potential placement sites for graduate students to do groups. Typically, schools (public and private), churches, social agencies, college dormitories, and nursing homes provide intact populations from which to select group members. The instructor keeps a list of placement sites where personnel have been cooperative and helpful in generating groups.

While direct, on-site supervision is not provided by the university, student co-leaders are required to make audio-tapes of each session. The students have the availability of the doctoral level laboratory group leaders and the course instructor for help should they encounter difficulty in their groups. The audiotapes are used by the co-leaders to go back over their sessions and do self-evaluations of their leadership interventions.

The entire experience is time and energy demanding. Students find themselves motivated to read and attend carefully to class activities related to organizing and initiating groups. The pay-offs, however, are considerable. Student feedback has indicated that if they attend faithfully to administrative and organizational details, the vast majority of group co-leadership experiences are positive and growth producing. Also, once the initial anxiety of beginning a group has been overcome in a relatively safe environment, the chances are increased greatly that these counselors will continue to lead groups in their eventual professional settings.

At the conclusion of the co-leadership experience, each student is asked to submit a short, independently derived, summary of the group experience. This summary includes:

group member appraisal, a session by session analysis of content and process, and the conclusions they have drawn regarding organizational details and the insights they have developed into themselves as group leaders.

Through a combination of in-class skill practice and then applying the skills to a real live group, leaders have an opportunity to practice a number of group specific intervention skills.

Among the more prominent include:

1. To provide to potential consumers a clear and understandable definition of group counseling and a general description of methods, procedures, and expectations;

2. Practice in screening for readiness of prospective group members;

3. The opportunity to develop an effective working relationship with a co-leader; and

4. To operationalize procedures for closing individual sessions and terminating a fixed duration counseling group.

Regarding group process itself, the novice leader will have the opportunity to facilitate therapeutic conditions within the group; deal with various member roles and possibly disruptive members; intervene at crucial moments in the process of the group; intervene with group members' self-defeating behaviors; interpret non-verbal behaviors within the group; and practice appropriate linking, pacing, and interpreting skills during the group process.

Summary. The experiential component in the training of group counselors can add measurably to laboratory directed skills. With a minimum of organization, instructors can create a program design where students can have both a membership and co-leadership experience within a traditional group counseling course. These direct field experiences, while demanding time and energy of the students, have consistently been evaluated as beneficial and constructive.

ASGW Professional Standards

On March 20, 1983, the Executive Board of the Association for Specialists in Group Work approved a document (Figure 4.4 and 4.5) that had been in study and preparation for several years. A broad survey of trainers of group counselors throughout the United States was conducted in order to ascertain prevailing education practices. Then began a process of synthesizing the data received from all sections of the country into a practical and usable set of professional standards that can be used for guidance in establishing and maintaining a program for training professional group leaders. Individuals who had significant impact upon the final document include Jeffrey Kottler, George Gazda, Robert Cash, Robert Berg, Don Martin, Garry Landreth, and Marguerite Carroll.

CACREP Professional Standards

Counselor training programs in the future will most likely be guided by the training standards developed by the Council for Accreditation of Counseling and Related Educational Programs (CACREP). Incorporated in 1981, the Council is the primary accrediting body of the American Association for Counseling and Development. The independent Council was created by AACD and its various Divisions to provide guidelines for excellence in graduate level counselor training programs. While the scope of the Council's standards is broad and reaches into virtually every aspect of a counselor training program, they do, in Section II relating to Program Objectives and Curriculum, address in a general sense the components of a curriculum for group leader training.

GROUPS—studies that provide an understanding of group development, dynamics, and counseling theories; group leadership styles; group counseling methods and skills; and other group approaches.

(Continued on page 96)

PROFESSIONAL STANDARDS for TRAINING of GROUP COUNSELORS

PREAMBLE

Whereas counselors may be able to function effectively with individual clients, they are also required to possess specialized knowledge and skills that render them effective in group counseling. The Association for Specialists in Group Work supports the preparation of group practitioners as part of and in addition to counselor education.

The *Professional Standards for Group Counseling* represent the minimum core of group leader (cognitive and applied) competencies that have been identified by the Association for Specialists in Group Work.

DEFINITION

Group Counseling

Consists of the interpersonal processes and activities focused on conscious thoughts and behavior performed by individuals who have the professional credentials to work with the counsel group of individuals regarding career, educational, personal, social and developmentally related concerns, issues, tasks or problems.

Designated Group Counseling Areas

In order to work as a professional in Group Counseling, an individual must meet and demonstrate minimum competencies in the generic core of group counseling standards. These are applicable to all training programs regardless of level of work or specialty area. In addition to the generic core competencies, (and in order to practice in a specific area of expertise) the individual will be required to meet one or more specialty area standards (school counseling and guidance, student personnel services in high education, or community/mental health agency counseling).

Group Counselor Knowledge Competencies

The qualified group leader has demonstrated specialized knowledge in the following aspects of group work:

1. Be able to state for at least three major theoretical approaches to group counseling the distinguishing characteristics of each and the commonalities shared by all.

2. Basic principles of group dynamics and the therapeutic ingredients of groups.

3. Personal characteristics of group leaders that have an impact on members; knowledge of personal strengths, weaknesses, biases, values and their impact on others.

Figure 4.4. ASGW Professional Standards for Training of Group Counselors. (Reprinted by permission.)

Figure 4.4. Continued.

4. Specific ethical problems and considerations unique to group counseling.

5. Body of research on group counseling in one's specialty area (school counseling, college student personnel, or community/mental health agency).

6. Major modes of group work, differentiation among the modes, and the appropriate instances in which each is used (such as group guidance, group counseling, group therapy, human relations training, etc.).

7. Process components involved in typical stages of a group's development (i.e., characteristics of group interaction and counselor roles).

8. Major facilitative and debilitative roles that group members may take.

9. Advantages and disadvantages of group counseling and the circumstances for which it is indicated or contraindicated.

Group Counselor Skill Competencies:

The qualified group leader has shown the following abilities:

1. To screen and assess readiness levels of prospective clients.

2. To deliver a clear, concise, and complete definition of group counseling.

3. To recognize self-defeating behaviors of group members.

4. To describe and conduct a personally selected group counseling model appropriate to the age and clientele of the group leader's specialty area(s).

5. To accurately identify nonverbal behavior among group members.

6. To exhibit appropriate pacing skills involved in stages of a group's development.

7. To identify and intervene effectively at critical incidents in the group process.

8. To appropriately work with disruptive group members.

9. To make use of the major strategies, techniques, and procedures of group counseling.

10. To provide and use procedures to assist transfer and support of changes by group members in the natural environment.

11. To use adjunct group structures such as psychological homework (i.e., self monitoring, contracting).

12. To use basic group leader interventions such as process comments, empathic responses, self-disclosure, confrontations, etc.

13. To facilitate therapeutic conditions and forces in group counseling.

14. To work cooperatively and effectively with a co-leader.

Figure 4.4. Continued.

15. To open and close sessions, and terminate the group process.

16. To provide follow up procedures to assist mainten-ance and support of group members.

17. To utilize assessment procedures in evaluating effects and contributions of group counseling.

Training in Clinical Practice	
Type of Supervised Experience	Minimum Number of Clock Hours Required: Master's or Entry Level Program
1. Critique of group tapes (by self or others)	5
2. Observing group counseling (live or media presentation)	5
3. Participating as a member in a group	15
4. Leading a group with a partner and receiving critical feedback from a supervisor	15
5. Practicum: Leading a group alone, with critical self-analysis of performance; supervisor feedback on tape; and self-analysis	15
6. Fieldwork of Internship: Practice as a group leader with on-the-job supervision	25

Figure 4.5. Training in clinical practice in terms of type of supervised experience and clock hours required. (ASGW Professional Standards for Training of Group Counselors.)

Studies in this area would include, but not be limited to the following:

a.   principles of group dynamics including group process components, developmental stage theories, and group members' roles and behaviors.

b.   group leadership styles and approaches including characteristics of various types of group leaders and leadership styles.

c.   theories of group counseling including commonalities, distinguishing characteristics, and pertinent research and literature.

d.   group counseling methods including group counselor orientations and behaviors, ethical considerations, appropriate selection criteria and methods, and methods of evaluation of effectiveness.

e.   other types of small group approaches, theories, and methods. (CACREP, 1988, p.26)

The evolutionary status of accreditations standards for professional group leaders is evidenced by the relative thoroughness of the documents issued by professional accrediting agencies. At the spring 1988 meeting of the Council in Houston, CACREP voted to include a more comprehensive list of guidelines in the appendix of their accreditation manual. That more definitive list of group worker competencies are provided in Figure 4.6.

Group Counseling Competencies

In 1980, Dameron and his colleagues at the University of North Texas compiled a very comprehensive guidebook designed to present competencies, behavioral performance guidelines, and assessment scales in all the major counseling specialties. This widely used handbook was the forerunner of the initial counselor accreditation efforts and was published and sponsored by the Association for Counselor Education and Supervision (ACES). The handbook is presently under revision and an updated version that will reflect the growth of counseling as a profession is scheduled for publication in 1990.

In Figure 4.7 are the specific guidelines related to group leadership as given in the handbook by Dameron.

(Continued on page 104)

PROFESSIONAL STANDARDS FOR TRAINING OF GROUP COUNSELORS

Preamble

Whereas counselors may be able to function effectively with individual clients, they are also required to possess specialized knowledge and skills that render them effective in group counseling. The Association for Specialists in Group Work supports the preparation of group practitioners as part of and in addition to counselor education.

The Professional Standards for Group Counseling represents the minimum core of group leader (cognitive and applied) competencies that have been identified by the Association for specialists in Group Work.

DEFINITION

Group Counseling

Consists of the interpersonal processes and activities focused on conscious thoughts and behavior performed by individuals who have the professional credentials to work with and counsel groups of individuals regarding career, educational, personal, social and developmentally related concerns, issues, tasks or problems.

Designated Group Counseling Areas

In order to work as a professional in group counseling, an individual must meet and demonstrate minimum competencies in the generic core of group counseling standards. These are applicable to all training programs regardless of level of work or specialty area. In addition to the generic core competencies, (and in order to practice in a specific area of expertise) the individual will be required to meet one or more specialty area standards (school counseling and guidance, student personnel services in high education, or community/mental health agency counseling).

Group Counselor Knowledge Competencies

The qualified group leader has demonstrated specialized knowledge in the following aspects of group work:

- Be able to state for at least three major theoretical approaches to group counseling the distinguishing characteristics of each and the commonalities shared by all.

Figure 4.6. CACREP Professional Standards for Training of Group Counselors.

Figure 4.6. Continued.

- Basic principles of group dynamics and the therapeutic ingredients of groups.

- Personal characteristics of group leaders that have an impact on members; knowledge of personal strengths, weaknesses, biases, values and their impact on others.

- Specific ethical problems and considerations unique to group counseling.

- Body of research on group counseling in one's specialty area (school counseling, college student personnel or community/ mental health agency).

- Major modes of group work, differentiation among the modes and the appropriate instances in which each is used (such as group guidance, group counseling, group therapy, human relations, etc.).

- Process components involved in typical stages of a group's development (i.e., characteristics of group interaction and counselor roles).

- Major facilitative and debilitative roles that group members may take.

- Advantages and disadvantages of group counseling and the circumstances for which it is indicated or contraindicated.

Group Counselor Skill Competencies

The qualified group leader has shown the following abilities:

- To screen and assess readiness levels of prospective clients.

- To deliver a clear, concise and complete definition of group counseling.

- To recognize self-defeating behaviors of group members.

- To describe and conduct a personally selected group counseling model appropriate to the age and clientele of the group leaders' speciality area or areas.

- To accurately identify nonverbal behavior among group members.

Figure 4.6. Continued.

- To exhibit appropriate pacing skills involved in stages of a group's development.

- To identify and intervene effectively at critical incidents in the group process.

- To appropriately work with disruptive group members.

- To make use of the major strategies, techniques and procedures of group counseling.

- To provide and use procedures to assist transfer and support of changes by group members in the natural environment.

- To use adjunct group structures such as psychological home-work (i.e., self-monitoring, contracting).

- To use basic group leader interventions such as process comments, empathetic responses, self-disclosure, confrontations, etc.

- To facilitate therapeutic conditions and forces in group counseling.

- To work cooperatively and effectively with co-leader.

- To open and close sessions and terminate the group process.

- To provide follow-up procedures to assist maintenance and support of group members.

COMPETENCIES The counselor is a skilled professional who is able to:	PERFORMANCE GUIDELINES The professional counselor provides evidence of competence by demonstrating the ability to:	
1. Discern when individual or group counseling would be most facilitative to the problem presented by the client. (This implies recognition of the referral responsibility when the client can best be served in this manner.)	1.1	Specify the types of problems that are especially amenable to group or individual counseling.
	1.2	Structure specialized groups as to topic and purpose as well as membership composition.
	1.3	Specify the effectiveness of both peer and adult models on individual behavior.
	1.4	Coordinate and sequence a client's participation in both individual and group counseling sessions.
2. Use the dynamics of group counseling and the various group activities that can facilitate attitude and behavior change according to the age level of the client.	2.1	Display a working knowledge of group dynamics such as:
	2.1a	Content and process variables;
	2.1b	Typical stages of group development;
	2.1c	Various leadership styles;
	2.1d	The conditions under which groups promote healthy growth.
	2.2	Display a working knowledge of developmental tasks and coping behaviors of different age levels and the skill to use various group techniques appropriate for client level including:
	2.2a	Play group counseling;
	2.2b	Modeling—social learning techniques;
	2.2c	Role playing (sociodrama and psychodrama).

Figure 4.7. Competencies and performance guidelines for group counseling as specified in handbook by Dameron (Dameron, 1980, pp. 28-32). Printed by permission.

Figure 4.7. Continued.

COMPETENCIES The counselor is a skilled professional who is able to:		PERFORMANCE GUIDELINES The professional counselor provides evidence of competence by demonstrating the ability to:
3. Observe and record verbal and nonverbal interaction in groups, following predetermined cues and procedures for making such observations.	3.1	Use the anecdotal method of observation and recording to report the significant components of individual and group interaction.
	3.2	Chart group interaction through the use of an appropriate interaction tool.
	3.3	Rate the responsive and initiative dimensions of group interaction.
	3.4	Record the operant level and chart the baseline of selected operants as they emerge in a group (e.g., physiological phenomena, hostile statements).
4. Demonstrate a familiarity with the unique characteristics of the major group theories and the persons associated with their development.	4.1b	Human resource development training;
	4.1c	Adlerian psychology;
	4.1d	Rational-emotive therapy; *Ellis*
	4.1e	Development group counseling;
	4.1f	Reality therapy;
	4.1g	Behavioral group counseling; *Glasser*
	4.1h	Group psychodrama;
	4.1i	Client-centered group therapy; *Rogers*
	4.1j	Gestalt group therapy; *Perls*
	4.1k	Conjoint family therapy.
5. Demonstrate competency in dealing with terms specific to group counseling by discriminating among the various kinds of group activities.	5.1	Adequately define and explain the differences in orientation, methodology, procedures, leadership qualifications, and client population associated with:
	5.1a	Group guidance;
	5.1b	Group counseling;
	5.1c	Group psychotherapy;

Figure 4.7. Continued.

COMPETENCIES The counselor is a skilled professional who is able to:		PERFORMANCE GUIDELINES The professional counselor provides evidence of competence by demonstrating the ability to:
	5.2	Display a functional knowledge of the following terms and concepts and their application to groups:
	5.2a	Group dynamics;
	5.2b	T-groups;
	5.2c	Psychodrama;
	5.2d	Closed groups;
	5.2e	Open groups;
	5.2f	Esalen Institute;
	5.2g	Self-directed groups
	5.2h	Group-centered counseling;
	5.2i	Ground rules for groups.
6. Communicate familiarity with a number of group growth and intervention systems and advise as to the appropriate group activity.	6.1	Function as a member or leader in the following kinds of group experiences:
	6.1a	A sensitivity group with controlled physical contact;
	6.1b	An encounter group;
	6.1c	A family therapy group;
	6.1d	A play-therapy or an activity-therapy group.
	6.2	Co-lead ongoing group counseling sessions in conjunction

Figure 4.7. Continued.

COMPETENCIES The counselor is a skilled professional who is able to:	PERFORMANCE GUIDELINES The professional counselor provides evidence of competence by demonstrating the ability to:	
		with an instructor, supervisor, or selected colleague.
	6.3	Describe and/or experience various specialized methods and techniques in group counseling such as:
	6.3a	Focused feedback;
	6.3b	Systematic desensitization;
	6.3c	Psychodrama;
	6.3d	Sociodrama;
	6.3e	Modeling;
	6.3f	Role playing;
	6.3g	Extended sessions or marathon groups;
	6.3h	Assertiveness training.
7. Demonstrate personal behaviors that foster an appreciation of ethics in group work.	7.1	Relate critically to writings in relevant publications that address the topic of ethics in group work. (See suggested readings in selected references on group counseling.)

ETHICAL STANDARDS

The group counselor is expected to have a thorough knowledge and understanding of the ethical standards established by professional associations. These principles, which ". . . are those agreed-upon practices consistent with our broader ethical commitments (political, moral, and religious) that we think reasonable and which responsible practitioners and clients will generally support at a given point in time" (Gazda, 1982, p. 87), provide a framework for identifying the counselor's responsibility to group members and provide guidelines for clarifying what group members can expect from the counselor. The Association for Specialists in Group Work (ASGW) and the American Group Psychotherapy Association have established specific ethical guidelines governing the behavior of the group counselor and adherence to ethical standards is expected.

We believe one of the most effective ways of helping beginning group counselors to engage in the process of learning ethical decision-making involves four stages: (1) personal individual counseling; (2) specific course instruction and training; (3) participation as a member in group counseling; and (4) supervised experience in facilitating a group. Such training and experience is consistent with ASGW's (1980) central principle that "group leaders shall not attempt any technique unless thoroughly trained in its use or under supervision by an expert familiar with the intervention" (B-7).

Personal Standards

In addition to adhering to a generally accepted code of ethics, Gazda (1982) suggested guidelines for group leader qualities that could form the basis for personal ethical standards. They are as follows:

- The group leader should have a clear set of group rules that guide him or her in the leadership of his or her group.

- The group leader should be self-confident and emotionally stable.

- The group leader should possess high perceptual and communication skills.

- The group leader should have a well-conceptualized model for explaining behavioral change.

- The group leader should have evidence that he or she has received training commensurate with his or her group practice.

- The group leader should have evidence that his or her leadership is effective, i.e., posttreatment and follow-up data of group members illustrates that they have benefited from membership in the leader's group.

- The group leader should possess the necessary certification, licensure, or similar evidence of qualifications generally accepted by his or her discipline.

- The group leader who does not possess professional credentials must function under the supervision of a professionally qualified person.

- The group leader should attend refresher courses, workshops, etc., to upgrade his or her skills and obtain evaluation of others regarding his or her skills and/or level of functioning.(pp. 88-89)

The development of an effective objective position on ethics is largely dependent on the counselor's self-under-standing. Prospective group counselors should examine carefully their own needs that are being met by facilitating a group. A counselor who is unaware of his/her own emotional needs is very likely to use inappropriately the group to meet those needs and will thus be less emotionally available to group members. We consider this a basic ethical issue in that the primary purpose of the group is to meet the needs of group members. Such counselor variables are crucial, and personal limitations must be recognized. Yalom and Lieber-mann (1971) reported that aggressive, authoritarian, con-frontive leaders, and leaders who are distant and emotionally cool produce the most casualties in groups.

Abuses of Group Techniques

Since group techniques are so prevalently used and easily abused, we have chosen to deal with this issue in a separate section. Most group techniques are easily learned and can be utilized in the group with little or no training in the rationale for the technique, the underlying issues or how to handle expected and unexpected outcomes. Corey et al. (1988) pointed out that the counselor can use group techniques in unethical ways such as using techniques with which they are unfamiliar, as gimmicks, to meet their own hidden agendas, to create an explosive atmosphere, or to pressure members. They suggest the following guidelines to avoid abusing techniques in a group:

- There should be a therapeutic purpose and grounding in some theoretical framework.

- The client's self-exploration and self-understanding should be fostered.

- At their best, techniques are invented in each unique client situation, and they assist the client in experimenting with some form of new behavior.

- Techniques are introduced in a timely and sensitive manner, and they are abandoned if they are not working.

- The tone of a leader is consistently invitational, in the members are given the freedom to participate or not participate in a given experiment.

- It is important that leaders use techniques they have some knowledge about and that they be aware of the potential impact of these techniques. (pp. 349-350)

Group facilitators have a professional obligation and an ethical responsibility to be not only knowledgeable but thoroughly trained in the use of procedures before such procedures are tried out on an unsuspecting group. Reading about a group technique or seeing it demonstrated once at a conference or workshop will not suffice.

ASGW Ethical Guidelines

The ASGW Ethical Guidelines provide guidelines in the general areas of counselor competence; recruitment and informed consent; screening and orientation of group members; preparation of group members; voluntary participation; psychological risks; confidentiality; experimentation, research, and tape recording; protecting member rights; leader values and expectations; insuring member opportunities in the group; treating members equally; personal relationships; promoting member independence and development of personal goals; use of alcohol and drugs; providing help after sessions and follow-up. Guidelines as written in 1980 are provided in Figure 4.8. To note changes in one decade, see the 1989 edition in the Appendix.

SUMMARY

In their classic 1939 study of three generic leadership styles, Lewin, Lippitt, and White noted differences in group member satisfaction, aggressiveness, group-task efficiency, and dependency in response to *authoritarian, democratic,* and *laissez-faire* leadership.

The developmental work of Adler and Sullivan, in departing from classical Freudian psychoanalysis to a more interpersonal orientation, and the more recent work of Thorne, Rogers, Tmax, and Carkhuff is noted in the historical background to interpersonal group work.

Carkhuff's work with an interpersonal model that expands upon Roger's "necessary and sufficient" conditions to include an action dimension includes the philosophical foundations and a scale for measuring levels of interpersonal dimensions offered by the helper.

Training group counselors should include supervised practica, skill acquisition, and an experiential component typically conducted in the field.

The further professionalization of group leaders was assisted in 1983 with the adoption by the Association of Specialists in Group Work of the document entitled *Professional Standards for Training of Group Counselors.* The document provides a definition, leader knowledge, and skill competencies, and the minimum number of supervised clock hours required for entry level (Master's degree) group leaders.

PREAMBLE

One characteristic of any professional group is the possession of a body of knowledge and skills and mutually acceptable ethical standards for putting them into practice. Ethical standards consist of those principles which have been formally and publicly acknowledged by the membership of a profession to serve as guidelines governing professional conduct, discharge of duties, and resolution or moral dilemmas. In this document, the Association of Specialists in Group Work has identified the standards of conduct necessary to maintain and regulate the high standards of integrity and leadership among its members.

The Association for Specialists in Group Work recognized the basic commitment of its members to the Ethical Standards of its parent organization, the American Association for Counseling and Development, and nothing in this document shall be construed to supplant that code. These standards are intended to complement the AACD standards in the area of group work by clarifying the nature of ethical responsibility of the counselor in the group setting and by stimulating a greater concern for competent group leadership.

The following ethical guidelines have been organized under three categories: the leader's responsibility for providing information about group work to clients, the group leader's responsibility for providing group counseling services to clients, and the group leader's responsibility for safeguarding the standards of ethical practice.

A. RESPONSIBILITY FOR PROVIDING INFORMATION
   ABOUT GROUP WORK AND GROUP SERVICES

A-1. Group leaders shall fully inform group members, in advance and preferably in writing, of the goals in the group, qualifications of the leader, and procedures to be employed.

A-2. The group leader shall conduct a pre-group interview with each prospective member for purposes of screening, orientation, and, insofar as possible, shall select group members whose needs and goals are compatible with the established goals of the group; who will not impede the group process; and whose well-being will not be jeopardized by the group experience.

A-3. Group leaders shall protect members by defining clearly what confidentiality means, why it is important, and the difficulties involved in enforcement.

Figure 4.8. ASGW's Ethical Guidelines for Group Leaders.

Figure 4.8. Continued.

A-4. Group leaders shall explain, as realistically as possible, exactly what services can and cannot be provided within the particular group structure offered.

A-5. Group leaders shall provide prospective clients with specific information about any specialized or experimental activities in which they may be expected to participate.

A-6. Group leaders shall stress the personal risks involved in any group, especially regarding potential life-changes, and help group members explore their readiness to face these risks.

A-7. Group leaders shall inform members that participation is voluntary and that they may exit from the group at any time.

A-8. Group leaders shall inform members about recording of sessions and how tapes will be used.

B. RESPONSIBILITY FOR PROVIDING
   GROUP SERVICES TO CLIENTS

B-1. Group leaders shall protect member rights against physical threats, intimidation, coercion, and undue peer pressure insofar as is reasonably possible.

B-2. Group leaders shall refrain from imposing their own agendas, needs, and values on group members.

B-3. Group leaders shall insure to the extent that it is reasonably possible that each member has the opportunity to utilize group resources and interact within the group by minimizing barriers such as rambling and monopolizing time.

B-4. Group leaders shall make every reasonable effort to treat each member individually and equally.

B-5. Group leaders shall abstain from inappropriate personal relationships with members throughout the duration of the group and any subsequent professional involvement.

B-6. Group leaders shall help promote independence of members from the group in the most efficient period of time.

B-7. Group leaders shall not attempt any technique unless thoroughly trained in its use or under supervision by an expert familiar with the intervention.

B-8. Group leaders shall not condone the use of alcohol or drugs directly prior to or during group sessions.

Figure 4.8. Continued.

B-9. Group leaders shall make every effort to assist clients in developing their personal goals.

B-10. Group leaders shall provide between-session consultation to group members and follow-up after termination of the group, as needed or requested.

C. RESPONSIBILITY FOR SAFEGUARDING
    ETHICAL PRACTICE

C-1. Group leaders shall display these standards or make them available to group members.

C-2. Group leaders have the right to expect ethical behavior from colleagues and are obligated to rectify or disclose incompetent, unethical behavior demonstrated by a colleague by taking the following action:

   (a)   To confront the individual with the apparent violation of ethical guidelines for the purposes of protecting the safety of any clients and to help the group leader correct any inappropriate behaviors.

   (b)   Such a complaint should be made in writing and include the specific facts and dates of the alleged violation and all relevant supporting data. The complaint should be forwarded to:

         The Ethics Committee
         c/o The President
         Association of Specialists in Group Work
         599 Stevenson Avenue
         Alexandria, Virginia 22304

         The envelope must be marked "CONFIDENTIAL" in order to assure confidentiality for both the accuser(s) and the alleged violator(s). Upon receipt, the President shall (a) check on membership status of the charged member(s), (b) confer with legal counsel, and (c) send the case with all pertinent documents to the chairperson of the ASGW Ethics Committee within ten (10) working days after the receipt of the complaint.

   (c)   If it is determined by the Ethics and Professional Standards Committee that the alleged breach of ethical conduct constitutes a violation of the "Ethical Guidelines," then an investigation will be started within ten (10) days by at least one member of the Committee plus two additional ASGW members in the locality of the alleged violation. The

Figure 4.8. Continued.

investigating committee chairperson shall: (a) acknowledge receipt of the complaint, (b) review the complaint and supporting data, (c) send a letter of acknowledgement to the member(s) of the complaint regarding alleged violations along with a request for a response and relevant information related to the complaint and (e) inform member of the Ethics Committee by letter of the case and present a plan of action for investigation.

(d) All information, correspondence, and activities of the Ethics Committee will remain confidential. It shall be determined that no person serving as an investigator on a case have any disqualifying relationship with the alleged violator(s).

(e) This charged party(ies) will have not more than 30 days in which to answer the charges in writing. The charged party(ies) will have free access to all cited evidence from which to make a defense, including the right to legal counsel and a formal hearing before the ASGW Ethics Committee.

(f) Based upon the investigation of the Committee and any designated local ASGW members one of the following recommendations may be made to the Executive Board for appropriate action:

1. Advise the charges be dropped.

2. Reprimand and admonishment against repetition of the charged conduct.

3. Notify the charged member(s) of his/her right to a formal hearing before the ASGW Ethics Committee, and request a response be made to the Ethics Chairperson as to his/her decision on the matter. Such hearing would be conducted in accordance with the AACD Policy and Procedures for Processing Complaints of Ethical Violations, "Procedures for Hearings," and would be scheduled for a time coinciding with the annual AACD convention. Conditions for such hearing shall also be in accordance with the AACD Policy and Procedures document, "Options Available to the Ethics Committee, item 3."

4. Suspension of membership for a specified period from ASGW.

5. Dismissal from membership in ASGW.

REFERENCES

Berlo, D.K. (1960). *The process of communication.* New York: Holt, Rinehart and Winston.

Carkhuff, R.R. (1987). *The art of helping VI.* Amherst, MA: Human Resource Development Press.

Carkhuff, R.R. (1983). *Helping and human relations: A primer for lay and professional helpers* (Volumes I & II). Amherst, MA: Human Resources Development Press.

Carkhuff, R.R. (1983). *The development of human resources.* Amherst, MA: Human Resource Development Press.

Carkhuff, R.R., & Berenson, B.G. (1977). *Beyond counseling and therapy* (2nd ed.). New York: Holt, Rinehart and Winston.

Corey, G., Corey, M., & Callahan, P. (1988). *Issues and ethics in the helping professions.* Pacific Grove, CA: Brooks Cole.

Council for Accreditation of Counseling and Related Educational Program. (1988). *Accreditation procedures manual and application.* Alexandria, VA: AACD Press.

Dameron, J.D. (Ed.). (1980). *The professional counselor: Competencies, performance guidelines, and assessment.* Washington, DC: AACD Press.

Fiedler, F.E. (1953). *The leader's psychological distance and group effectiveness.* In D. Cartwright & A. Zander (Eds). Group dynamics: Research and theory (2nd ed.). New York: Harper & Row.

Gazda, G. (1982). *Basic approaches to group psychotherapy and group counseling.* Springfield, IL: Charles C. Thomas.

Gazda, G.M. (1989). *Group counseling: A developmental approach* (4th ed.). Boston: Allyn & Bacon.

Kottler, J.A. (1983). *Pragmatic group leadership.* Monterey, CA: Brooks/Cole.

Landreth, G.L., & Berg, R.C. (1979). Overcoming initial group leader anxiety: Skills plus experience. *Personnel and Guidance Journal, 58,* 65-67.

Lewin, K., Lippitt, R., & White, R. (1939). Patterns of aggressive behavior in experimentally created "social climates." *Journal of Social Psychology, 10,* 271-299.

Luft, J. (1984). *Group processes: An introduction to group dynamics* (3rd ed.). Palo Alto, CA: Mayfield.

Rogers, C.R. (1951). *Client centered therapy.* Boston: Houghton Mifflin.

Rogers, C.R. (1957). The necessary and sufficient conditions of therapeutic personality change. *Journal of Consulting Psychology, 22,* 95-103.

Samovar, L.A., & Rintyc, E.D. (1970). Interpersonal communication: Some working principles. In R.S. Cathcart & L.A. Samovar (Eds.). *Small group communication: A reader.* Dubuque, IA: Brown.

Tamminen, A.W., & Smaby, M.H. (1978). You can be a skilled group helper. *Personnel and Guidance Journal, 56,* 501-505.

Trotzer, J.P. (1989). *The counselor and the group: Integrating theory, training and practice.* Muncie, IN: Accelerated Development.

Truax, C.B., & Carkhuff, R.R. (1967). *Toward effective counseling and psychotherapy: Training and practice.* Chicago: Aldine.

White, R.K., & Lippitt, R. (1968). Leader behavior and member reaction in three "social climates." In D. Cartwright & A. Zander (Eds.). *Group dynamics: Research and theory (3rd ed.),* New York: Harper & Row.

Yalom, I & Liebermann, M. (1971). A study of encounter group casualties. *Archives of General Psychiatry, 25,* 16-30.

SUGGESTED READING

Shapiro, J.L. (1978). *Methods of group psychotherapy and encounter.* Itasca, IL: Peacock. Chapter 6, The Group Therapist

In this chapter focusing on leadership styles, Shapiro talks about types of leadership and presents an interesting continuum clarifying the differences in an intrapsychic/ intrapersonal approach to leadership from an interpersonal approach. He cites research in comparing leader roles and skills. Several different models are discussed.

Additionally, the issue of group leader characteristics is addressed with the ideal personality and the integration of personality and method presented in an interesting manner.

Carkhuff, R.R. (1987). *The art of helping VI. (6th ed.).* Amherst, MA: Human Resource Development Press.

This classic paperback traces the evolution of helping and presents a functional helping model—focusing on contributions of both the helpee and the helper. The book is a virtual self-help guide that teaches *specific* helping skills. Carkhuff concludes by looking at the future of helping and the growth and development of helpers.

CHAPTER **5**

THE
GROUP LEADER'S
INTERNAL
EXPERIENCE

We have been puzzled by the reluctance of counselors, even those who have had a course in group counseling, to organize and facilitate counseling groups. Why do counselors seem even more anxious about leading a group than can reasonably be expected? Why are they apparently so resistant to trying a group approach?

We agree with Tamminen and Smaby (1978) that a primary reason for the high degree of apprehension is that counselors have seldom been taught precisely what to do and how to do it in a group setting. Effective group facilitation is indeed much more than the application of individual counseling skills to a group setting. As is true of many counselor education programs (Hansen, Warner, & Smith, 1976; Muro, 1968), Tamminen and Smaby have not addressed the equally critical variable of a "real life" group practicum experience. To learn and practice helping skills in the safety of a supportive, effective helper led group is one thing. To be in a position of having sole responsibility for facilitating interaction and sharing among a group of strangers and at the same time attempting to deliver high level helping responses is quite a different matter. The experience of facilitating a counseling group is the catalytic agent necessary in the integrative process of melding theory, counselor self-understanding, and practical experience. Such an integration can result in reduction of anxiety as counselors begin to trust the person they are in the process of coping with a group.

THE PERSON OF THE GROUP FACILITATOR

If indeed true, as most writers in the field of counseling propose, that the person of the counselor is a significant variable in the counseling process (Corey & Corey, 1987; Gazda, 1984; and Yalom, 1985), then the prospective group counselor must be provided supervised experiences which allow the person of the counselor to be utilized as a therapeutic agent in the role of group facilitator. How else can the prospective group counselor experience fully the person he/she is as a group leader without being a group leader? While we agree that a sequential, skill-acquisition approach is a necessary and valuable first step, we question the effectiveness of counselor education programs that provide only didactic and/or laboratory group membership experiences for the prospective group counselor.

RATIONALE

High on the list of the unspoken fears of counselors is a lack of trust in the group and self-doubt regarding an ability to "handle" the group. Such reactions promote apprehension and reluctance to start a group and conceivably also could be detrimental to the success of the group if the counselor allows such feelings and reactions to persist without being verbalized, explored, and integrated. The logical place to deal with such feelings is in a setting similar to that which precipitates the feelings—a position of leadership in a group. To do otherwise is to be inconsistent with a basic rationale for group counseling.

LEADERSHIP STYLES AND GROUP APPROACHES

The authors take the position that the theoretical orientation of the leader seems to be less important to group outcome than is the nature of the relationship between leader and group members. A number of studies have focused upon the relationship variable demonstrating that successful leaders have many characteristics in common regardless of theoretical school of thought (Carkhuff & Berenson, 1977; Lieberman, Yalom, & Miles, 1973). This is consistent with the position taken by Tamminen and Smaby (1978) as they have emphasized interpersonal conditions in their skill acquisition program.

Accordingly, counselors in training are encouraged to test and experiment with a number of procedures and techniques generally considered to be within a broad humanistic frame of reference. Also, group size is kept purposefully small, seven to nine members, in order to promote interaction.

Within this general framework, group supervision focuses upon

1. the quality of relationships and responses, and

2. the appropriateness of intervention strategies within the group as they relate to both the group as a whole and individual members.

GROUP COUNSELING PRACTICUM

As early as 1961 supervised experience in group counseling was considered to be a minimal necessity for counselor preparation. As recently as July 1988, CACREP adopted accreditation standards for counselor education programs that specify supervised practice in group counseling.

In keeping with long standing recommendations in the field, counselors in our group counselor training program are required to organize and facilitate an on going counseling group in a setting similar to that in which they anticipate working. In addition to the supervised leadership experience, counselors are asked to keep a diary of their reactions to the experience and to write a self exploration paper. Our experience has been that the following diary excerpts resulting from initial group leadership experiences are typical of changes in attitudes, concepts, and perceptions of beginning group counselors.

LEARNING ABOUT SELF

The first excerpt is an example of the group leader's need to assume responsibility for the group members.

Excerpt 1: "I learned several things about myself and the way I lead a group. I felt all along that I was trying too hard to *lead*, or structure. This was especially true at the beginning of our first two or three sessions, because they were sitting there without talking much. This is something I need to work on because sometimes I didn't let the group go where it wanted to go. Another thing I tended to do was to respond too quickly myself, not giving the rest of the group an opportunity to act as helpers."

This feeling of pressure or anxiety is related to the counselor's need to "make something happen." Low-level structuring or ice-breaker activities are usually enough to help the group get going. After that, the counselor's best investment of energy is to actively facilitate interaction by encouraging, reflecting, listening, clarifying, and linking.

Group leader No. 2 perhaps best sums up the most healthy resolution to the problem of responsibility and control as this person found a direct relationship between self-trust and the ability to trust the group to provide its own direction.

Excerpt 2: "I have come a long way with my group, in learning to accept deep feelings in myself and others. More important I feel that for the first time I trust and accept myself. I have come to feel very comfortable in the group without feeling the need for establishing myself as the authority. I have learned to trust the group. There were a few times when I found myself questioning more than I should."

The next excerpt is provided by a group leader who is learning to trust self without the roles and symbols of status.

Excerpt 3: "I have learned that I must be myself in a group rather than concentrating on the role of group leader. When I started relaxing in my group, the members began to relax. I found myself to be much more facilitative when I quit worrying about what I was supposed to be doing as a group leader. When I relaxed my role, other members began to be more facilitative.

LEARNING ABOUT THE GROUP

In Excerpt No. 4 is addressed the issue of group member responsibility and how it was resolved in this case. The importance of patience in group work is fully evident.

Excerpt 4: "Overall my group was a good experience for me and, I think, for the group members. The thing that stands out most in my mind was my frustration because of what I thought was a lack of progress after the first group session. I had certain expectations that were not being met, and I blamed myself for the lack of success. I offered a minimum of structure for my high school seniors and after the first two sessions of very superficial kinds of talk, I was seriously considering initiating some kind of direct and forceful approach. I was going to try to push them into something that I considered serious and worth exploring. However, I did not use any more structure in the third session and much to my relief we made real progress. We got to some personal feelings and the group began to jell. I am glad I didn't push them as I was about to do. I have learned to have a little more faith in the group process."

Excerpt No. 5 is shared by a counselor who was in touch with the potential power of a group and the energy it takes to attempt to stay aware of all of the things going on. In the opening sentence are suggested at least some of the things that a group can be.

Excerpt 5: "Working with a group is scary, fun, and challenging. I was surprisingly comfortable. It was tremendously frustrating a lot of the time because so much material was presented—far more than could be dealt with in the time allotted. It was a draining experience. I learned that I prefer some structure in early meetings, and in later sessions I feel more free to allow the group to branch out in any direction. The potential within the group for disclosure sometimes frightened me afterwards, but I was never totally at a loss as to how to respond as I had feared would be the case."

Group leader No. 6 tended to see the group leader's function as more of a member—albeit a member with good facilitative skills. This counselor was able to take a personal dynamic (shyness) and through sensitive projection make it work to the advantage of some group members. In addition this counselor recognized the significance of group interactions.

Excerpt 6:   "Felt relaxed, easy in the group—fit in smoothly as a member—able to help establish climate of acceptance, comfort, safety—able to help those who were a little shy to begin to share themselves freely—felt good about that. I, too, am a little shy and quiet in new situations, and I really appreciate it when someone helps me to get into the swing of it. I'm learning more about tuning in on interactions not just individuals."

As these group leaders discovered, anxiety that results in trying too hard to make things happen, assuming too much responsibility for the group, and lacking faith and trust in the group inhibits the group process. Although frustrating to the beginning group counselor, these important learnings are possible only through experiencing and being personally open to learn about self in relationship to the group. Effective group facilitation is much more than knowing theories and techniques of group counseling. Counselors' recognition and acceptance of their personal needs are crucial to the group process. The more fully group counselors can be themselves in the group, the more effective they will be in attempting to help members to be themselves, and this can be discovered best by "getting your feet wet" in that first group counseling experience.

ENCOUNTERING CARL ROGERS: HIS VIEWS ON FACILITATING GROUPS

Carl Rogers' views on facilitating groups are presented as expressed in a telephone dialogue seminar with graduate students in the Department of Counselor Education at The University of North Texas.

QUESTION: *Dr. Rogers, there are 20 counseling graduate students, sitting in a circle here this morning, and we are all eager to interact with you about your approach to facilitating groups. Because each person is involved in facilitating a group, a current topic is the facilitator's own feelings. How do you keep in touch with your own feelings, Dr. Rogers, when you are facilitating a group? Also, how do you handle your feelings in the group?*

CR: I suppose I have the same kind of difficulty that everyone does in really keeping in complete touch with what is going on at the gut level in me. I think I have improved over the years; partly because that is something you can't accomplish in yourself overnight. Often with me, if I am not in touch with my feelings, I realize it afterward. I notice this particularly when I get angry, which always has been something of a problem for me. Sometimes after a group session, I begin to realize that I was very angry with a member, but I did not realize it at the time. Fortunately, in an encounter group, I usually have a chance to meet the person again and express that feeling. I am quite pleased whenever I can be aware of my anger right at the moment it occurs. Then as to what I do about it, I have kind of a "rule of thumb" that helps me. In any significant relationship, whatever persisting feelings I have, I had better express to the person toward whom they are directed.

In some strictly casual relationships, such as those with clerks in a store, it doesn't make much difference whether I express my feelings or not. In deep relationships, such as those often experienced in an encounter group, however, or in a persisting relationship with a staff member, a colleague, or a member of the family, I have found that I had better express persisting feelings, whether negative or positive, because they will leak out around the edges anyway. The other person will be aware that I am feeling something I am not expressing and won't be sure what because they are getting a rather confused message from me. So if it is anger, dislike, or whatever the persisting feeling might be, I think I had better express it.

One other thing that is important to me is that so often we pile up our feelings, and then they come out as judgments of the other person. If I let my anger pile up, then it might come out in calling the other person names or by making some judgment about the person and that, I think, is not helpful. If I express it as my feelings, that gives the person a chance to respond and we can enter into fruitful dialogue.

Confrontation

QUESTION: *Do you consider what you have just described to be a form of confrontation? If not, do you consider confrontation to be appropriate once the initial basis of trust and respect is established within a counseling relationship?*

CR: Let me explain my situation. I have learned a great deal about myself and about how to counsel with people because I have become more heavily involved with groups, but I am not doing any individual counselling now because my schedule just doesn't permit it. Part of what I will say is speculation. I am quite certain even before I stopped carrying individual counseling cases, I was doing more and more of what I would call confrontation. That is, confrontation of the other person with my feelings. I don't know what your definition of confrontation is, but mine is to confront the other person with my feelings in relation to their behavior or some specific thing they did.

For example, I recall a client with whom I began to realize I felt bored every time he came in. I had a hard time staying awake during the hour, and that was not like me at all. Because it was a persisting feeling, I realized I would have to share it with him. I had to confront him with my feeling and that really caused a conflict in his role as a client. It was my problem, but I was bringing it up to him. So with a good deal of difficulty and some embarrassment, I said to him, "I don't understand it myself, but when you start talking on and on about your problems in what seems to me a flat tone of voice, I find myself getting very bored." This was quite a jolt to him and he looked very unhappy. Then he began to talk about the way he talked and gradually he came to understand one of the reasons for the way he presented himself verbally. He said, "You know, I think the reason I talk in such an uninteresting way is because I don't think I have ever expected anyone to really hear me." He then told me some of his background to explain this reaction. Now that was a very valuable confrontation. We got along much better after that because I could remind him that I heard the same flatness in his voice I used to hear. Saying something like that would bring up some old issues again, he would become much more alive, and as a result I was not bored.

Cocounselor Group Facilitation

QUESTION: *How do you feel about using a cocounselor in a group, and do you feel it's best if this person has differing views? What type of person do you feel most comfortable with in a group as a cofacilitator or cocounselor?*

CR: A number of years ago, I preferred not to have a coleader in my group. I would rather form my own relationship with the group and handle it that way. Then when I tried working with a coleader, it was a very valuable experience for me and the group. For me some difference in approach between the two coleaders is very helpful. I wouldn't want to see a carbon copy of me being my coleader. I would like to work with a person of somewhat different approach. Then on the other hand, I suspect there are leaders I could not work with because their approaches would be so diametrically opposed we would not be comfortable working with each other. What I say to anyone who is coleading with me is, "Let's each of us work in the way that seems natural to us. If I don't like what you are doing, I will say so, and if I do something you don't like, you do the same." I think it does an enormous amount of good for a group to find the coleaders are human and can differ openly and work out their differences right in front of the group. That helps the group members to do the same sort of thing.

When I think about the kind of person I like to work with, I think about Bob Tannenbaum at UCLA. I have worked with him two or three times, and I like very much to work with him because he is better at stirring up people's feelings than I am. I think I work very well with a group that is already having some feelings they would like to express. With an apathetic group that really has nothing to say, or express, Bob is very good at sort of provoking relationships. If I knew exactly what he did to stir things up, I would tell you. He is just a sparkling person. People react to him and begin to express feelings if he is in a group. That helps a group to move further and more deeply. He happens to be the kind of coleader I like to work with, but for someone else it probably would be a different type of person.

I do think there are a number of advantages to working with a coleader. For example, I think of one incident where I got very angry with one member of the group. Although I am sure there was some irrationality in my anger, the coleader was very helpful in understanding my point of view and also the point of view of the group members. He handled us both as participants during that interchange and I think that is one of the advantages of having a coleader. We both received help in resolving the problem.

Nonverbal Group Exercises

QUESTION: *In various kinds of groups, nonverbal communication exercises are used a lot. Do you have any reactions to that?*

CR: Yes, I do. I have a lot of respect for the wide use of nonverbal communication, body contact, and that sort of thing, but I am not particularly good at nonverbal exercises myself. The environment I was brought up in was too inhibited and although I don't like to do anything that is not spontaneous, this part of me has experienced slow growth. In recent years, I have become a lot more spontaneous. I will go across a group and put my arm around someone who is in pain, but I don't do much to stimulate nonverbal communication. I just think it is a mistake for any group leader to try a procedure with which he is not comfortable. The group will pick the discomfort up in a minute and will know the leader is going beyond what is comfortable. I really regret I am not as skilled in that realm as I would like to be.

QUESTION: *Dr. Rogers, do you place any limits on nonverbal techniques when you evaluate some of the more experimental things being done?*

CR: My personal judgment is it is quite possible to be very cultish about body movements. The worst example is the nude marathon where the assumption is if you take off your clothes you are also removing your inhibitions. I think that is a lot of bunk. Publicity seekers have entered that field and gotten reams of publicity about it for all of us. I don't like anything that makes a cult out of groups. On the other hand, I have seen someone like Joyce Weir take a group and begin with them very gently doing different kinds of body movements. In her groups, anyone has a chance to opt out. In other words, you can choose not to participate if you wish.

I don't like the idea of limits where everyone must do the same thing. If members of a group began to do something I didn't like, I would feel very free to express my reaction. Then what the members do about it becomes a group consideration and is not just up to me. I have never had to face that situation; so I don't like to say exactly what I would do because I have never had a group run away with the idea of body movements.

Extended Group Sessions and Marathons

QUESTION: *Since we have such a limited amount of time to invest in counseling, how do you see this time best used if we are going to work with groups? For instance, would one 12-hour session or four 3-hour sessions be more profitable? What is the most appropriate way to use our time if we can use it as we want?*

CR: My answer to that keeps changing a little bit as time goes on. Personally, what I like and what I think is most effective is an intensive experience of approximately 12 hours, which I distinguish from a marathon, followed by briefer follow-up contacts of perhaps 2 or 3 hours. We have in the whole group movement tended to put too little emphasis on the follow up. I think sessions of shorter duration are very important and necessary in working with students, but I like the intensive longer sessions. First, I prefer a whole weekend, with evenings off for rest, if I can get it, then later follow-up contacts.

QUESTION: *Dr. Rogers, what is your reaction to marathon groups? Do you have any recommendations as to how a counselor might prepare to become a marathon leader or facilitator, and what is your reaction to marathon groups for couples?*

CR: If you are interested in marathon groups, the best thing would be to become a participant in some marathon and see what your reaction is. I don't particularly care for marathons but that is not a criticism. I think partly it is because I need some sleep and don't relish going 24 hours straight. I have tried marathons once or twice and it has not seemed to me to be preferable. An intensive 12 hours with a group is gruelling enough and seems to me to be as effective as a marathon.

You asked what I think about marathons for couples. I don't favor marathons for couples. In a couple's group, one of the good things that happens is in the hours between sessions or in the late evening or early morning hours, each couple begins to digest and assimilate what they have gained from the group. I would really prefer, especially in couple's groups, to meet with the group on an intensive, but not marathon, basis. On the other hand, if a group could only get away one day, then it might be better to have a marathon than to simply have a 10- or 12-hour session during the day. I have never really tried that. But I feel that if a group could only get away for one day and were eager to get as much out of the experience as possible, then they would enter the marathon with a very good attitude and that would make a great deal of difference in whether it would work.

Owning And Expressing Feelings

QUESTION: *Dr. Rogers, you said your reaction to the marathon is based on your becoming tired. Do you also feel this is a crucial issue for the participants you have been with?*

CR: One of the arguments that is often stated for the marathon is that people get so weary their defenses drop, and they express attitudes they otherwise would not have revealed. That may be an advantage, but it is also one of the disadvantages. I like for individuals to be responsible for what they express in a group. If the member can say to himself or herself afterward, "Well, I did not really mean that. I was so fatigued it just came out of nowhere" then I don't believe the experience is going to be helpful. Being responsible for the feelings expressed is one of the things that makes any type of counseling or group encounter helpful. For example, when I carried an active client load in counseling, I can think of one or two clients who would come in somewhat drunk and while drunk they might express attitudes and discuss things they wouldn't reveal in a sober state. But then in the next interview, they would back away and say, "That wasn't really me. I had a little too much" and so forth. So I don't think the expression of feelings can be helpful unless the person is willing to stand behind the expression of feelings.

QUESTION: *I really did appreciate your answer to that question, Dr. Rogers. How free do you feel to react to what group members do in the group? For instance, if you perceive that one member of the group is manipulating the group, would you bring this out or would you wait for one of the group members to react?*

CR: I would certainly wait for a time to see if a member of the group did object. If I felt the group was too fearful or was not strong enough to handle the member, then I am sure my feelings would begin to build up and I would express my feelings, I would not be trying to protect the group so much. It would just be that if I knew a person was manipulating the group, and no one was objecting, then I couldn't help but object. I would be guided by my own feelings. I think, ordinarily, I would like to give the group a chance to handle such a situation rather than give them the feeling I would handle it for them.

A Different Rogers In Groups?

QUESTION: *I would like to change the subject a bit, I have watched you work several times in groups and what I* *am seeing is a different Carl Rogers than the picture we have in an individual counseling session. Can you tell us how you are different in a group, why you are different in a group, and what kind of behavior you are trying to elicit that you don't in an individual session?*

CR: First, let me pick up on the last part of your question. I don't think in either individual counseling sessions or an encounter group I try to elicit something. You speak as though it were a conscious objective on my part and to me that makes a difference. If I was doing something with a member, thinking "this will cause her to react a certain way and to move in a particular direction," I would not like myself for that.

I do believe spontaneous reactions to be an influence on people, that is certainly true. I like myself best in a group when I am not using any planned procedure. One thing I don't like about myself in the film, "Journey Into Self," was that I was clearly anxious at the beginning of the group and I was not aware enough to just say so. Instead, I gave a much longer introduction to the group than I would normally do. I just talked and talked and I would have liked it much better if I had been more aware of my anxiety and said, "Oh boy, I am really somewhat scared, but I think we will get along." That, therefore, expresses my doubtful feelings better than the long speech I gave.

As to the differences in my behavior, yes, I do behave differently in a group than I did in individual counseling. I think if I went back to individual counseling, I would behave somewhat differently now than I did then. The main difference as I see it is that I would be more expressive of my own feelings. I would let things enter the relationship more than I used to. Let's see, what is that? I think it is that I have grown somewhat more free through my participation in groups. Then, too, there are some feelings that I have in a group that I must confess I have never been aware of in an individual counseling situation. I don't ever recall being really angry at an individual client. I am not bragging about that, I am just saying as far as I can recall, that is the truth. Yet in the more complex situations of a group, I can become quite angry at an individual's behavior. Usually the individual's behavior toward others is what stirs up anger in me; so perhaps that is why it didn't occur in the individual counseling situation. There is no doubt that work with groups and my own personal growth has made me realize my feelings have a perfectly good place in the relationship as well as my being very sensitive to the feelings and attitudes of the other persons. Let me put it this way, I think any expression of real feeling certainly has influence on another person.

The Counselor's Expression of Values In The Group

QUESTION: *Often in your writings you have stated or implied a counselor should not make personal evaluations or judgments in a counseling situation. When you are working with someone and you feel what that person is doing is wrong, how do you handle that?*

CR: Well, whether it is because of my personality or my experience in counseling, I am not judgmental in interpersonal relationships as many people are. The way I would say it is there are few things that bug me or shock me. While for some other people I know, there are many things that bug them and shock them or arouse strong feelings. If that is the person's attitude, then it is possibly better that it be out in the open than trying artificially to keep it covered up.

You used one word I don't think I have ever used, or at least I hope not, "The counselor should be nonjudgmental." I don't tell counselors what they should do. I describe the relationships that seem to me to have been the most productive of personal growth. To put it in more graduated terms, I would say the less judgmental a counselor is, the more likely he is to produce a climate in which growth will occur. But if in fact he is feeling judgmental and evaluative, then I would be inclined to say bring it out in the open as something in you. Say something like, "I think I should let you know to me that seems wrong," which is different from saying, "That is wrong." The latter really is basically a judgment on the other person, but to let that person know your values would be better than trying to keep it to yourself.

If you think it is wrong, the other person is going to pick up that attitude, I am sure.

The Future Of Group Work

QUESTION: *Dr. Rogers, we have seen a tremendous movement in personal growth through groups. Would you comment about what you see in the future for groups and what you would like to see?*

CR: The thing I would like to see happen in the whole group movement is to see it multiply in its various forms, I have been primarily involved in encounter groups aimed toward personal growth, but there are task-oriented groups, organizational development groups, and other varieties of groups or new forms that might emerge. One thing I would hope would occur in the lower levels of education is that an encounter group would become unnecessary because the whole climate of the classroom would be of a sort that both intellectual thoughts and highly emotional feelings both could be expressed; then the whole person could be attending class, not just his head. Those are two things I would like to see develop out of groups. I think the group movement has a lot of implications for our culture because it is a counter force against all the impersonal qualities of our technological civilization.

Thank you for sharing your thoughts with us, Dr. Rogers.

Carl Rogers (1902-1987)

Despite nagging minor illnesses and failing eyesight, Carl Rogers remained professionally active until the time of his sudden death following hip surgery on February 4, 1987 at age 85. Born in Chicago, he taught at the Universities of Wisconsin, Chicago, and Ohio State and served as director of the Child Guidance Clinic in Rochester. From 1963 until his death he lived and worked in LaJolla, California at the Center for the Study of the Person.

Rogers impacted virtually every corner of the fields of counseling and psychology with his then revolutionary ideas and theories, many of which now prevail in the Humanistic, 3rd Force movement in psychotherapy.

In his later years, Rogers pioneered the use of his person-centered methods in the encounter group movement. During the last 20 years of his life, he devoted almost all of his time exclusively to the development of group work in small and large social settings. It is likely that no other single individual has had the impact on group work that Carl Rogers did. His ideas and theories are far too numerous to list here. In spite of his enormous stature and eminence, he remained an almost simple man—an embodiment of his theories. He could listen. He will be greatly missed.

SUMMARY

This chapter focuses on the internal experience of the inexperienced group leader and suggests direct, supervised experience to overcome initial anxiety.

Carl Rogers presented some of his views on facilitation groups including the use of his own feelings, confrontation, co-leadership, non-verbal exercises, extended sessions and marathons, and owning and expressing feelings. Also Rogers told about how he differs in group from what he does in individual therapy, the expression of values in the group, and concluded by speculating about the future of group work. He was hopeful that interpersonal groups can provide a counter force to the talent impersonal qualities of a technological civilization.

REFERENCES

Carkhuff, R.R., & Berenson, B.G. (1977). *Beyond counseling and therapy (2nd ed.).* New York: Holdt, Rinehart & Winston.

Corey, G., & Corey, M.S. (1987). *Groups: Process and practice (3rd ed.).* Monterey, CA: Brooks/Cole.

Council for Accreditation of Counseling and Related Educational Programs. (1988). *Accreditation procedures manual and application.* Alexandria, VA: AACD Press.

Gazda, G.M. (1984). *Group counseling: A developmental approach (3rd ed.).* Boston: Allyn & Bacon.

Hansen, J.C., Warner, R.W., & Smith, E.M. (1976). *Group counseling: Theory and process.* Chicago: Rand McNally.

Lieberman, M.A., Yalom, I.D., & Miles, M.B. (1973). Encounter: The leader makes the difference. *Psychology Today, 6,* 69.

Muro, J.J. (1968). Some aspects of the group counseling practicum. *Counselor Education and Supervision, 7,* 371-378.

Tamminnen, A.W., & Smaby, M.H. (1978). You can be a skilled group helper. *Personnel and Guidance Journal, 56,* 501-505.

Yalom, I.D. (1985). *The theory and practice of group psychotherapy (3rd ed.).* New York: Basic Books.

SUGGESTED READING

Rogers, C.R. (1970). *Carl Rogers on Encounter groups.* New York: Harper and Row.

In this book, early in the sense of the total group movement, Rogers addresses such group issues as origin, scope and trends, group process, and the personhood of the group leader. Topics covered also include the applicability of encounter groups to person, relationships and organizations.

This book is important in content and because of Roger's intense personal involvement with groups in their early development.

Bednar, R.L. & Melnick, J. (1974). Risk responsibility and structure: A conceptual framework for initiating group counseling and psychotherapy. *Journal of Counseling Psychology, 21*, (1), 31-37.

The authors postulate that group-member exposure to levels of personal risk and responsibility are most conducive to group development and that these behaviors can be regulated by group structure.

While a form of structured group therapy is not advocated, they attempt to delineate the appropriate role of structure in initiating and maintaining group development.

CHAPTER **6**

GETTING A COUNSELING GROUP STARTED

Although theoreticians and researchers in group counseling have long demonstrated the efficacy of group procedures in many settings (Clack, 1971; Cull & Hardy, 1974; Mahler, 1973; Ohlsen, 1968), a continuing puzzlement to many counselor trainers, particularly those involved in group training, is that practicing counselors are not more involved in counseling groups. Many counselors have had specific group-counseling training and others would have little difficulty in transferring their individual skills to a group setting. Nevertheless, some hesitancy seems to exist about taking the initial step. Many counselors seem unwilling to "risk" beginning a group program. In private conversation, many counselors express themselves as accepting on an intellectual level that groups provide a therapeutic situation that cannot otherwise be achieved. At the same time, a hesitancy exists on the part of the counselor to begin such a program. Typical of the concerns raised are, "I'm not sure what to expect from a group," and "I'm not sure what my role should be in a group." Reluctance to attend the myriad of details involved in getting a group program started, also seems to be a major factor.

Those counselors who have begun group programs consistently report that they become committed to groups as a potent counseling vehicle and in many cases it becomes their preferred mode. Not unlike a client who is viewing a number of options with anxiety and trepidation, our hypothesis is that some counselors never begin group programs simply because too many potential roadblocks and details need to be attended.

With the available fund of knowledge relating to positive outcomes, procedures, and process, the practicing counselor must take the initial plunge into a first experience with group leadership. If the first group experience is a positive one, both for the members and the leader, more likelihood exists that the counselor will continue to use groups as an intervention method.

Most experienced group leaders report that the time spent attending to what might be considered minor details enhances the chance of a successful first experience. From numerous discussions with practicing counselors and trainers, the following guidelines were developed that conceivably could be used by the counselor as a checklist of activities to follow in getting a group started.

PRE-GROUP ACTIVITIES

Group processes, as such, are not automatically therapeutic. Just as in individual, one-to-one relationships, the group can be for better or for worse. One of the major variables, perhaps the most crucial, is the group leader himself/herself. The leader is primarily responsible for structuring the group and engineering the dynamics in such a way as to promote positive growth in group members. Any group leader who has taken the time to hone interpersonal skills so that he/she is a constructive helper has the right and responsibility to create the conditions before and during the group that will maximize the potential for a constructive, growing experience. Group leaders should do everything they can to insure a successful outcome. Several things can be done or attended to before the group meets for the first time. The following are some of the considerations that can be classified as pre-group activities.

Selection and Composition of Group Members

Until young adulthood is reached, college age and beyond, group members within a rather narrow age range is best. Throughout the school years, grade level seems to be a practical and sound method of selecting group members.

During the high school years grouping ninth and tenth graders and grouping eleventh and twelfth graders will work well. The developmental concerns common to ninth graders, however, are vastly different from those of twelfth graders and maturity levels will have an impact on group interaction.

Less need exists to be concerned about age homogeneity at college level and beyond. Usually by this age a sufficient level of maturity is available to foster an appreciation for the developmental concerns of those different than self. Differences and varied concerns can enhance an adult group and provide a wider range of opportunities to experience and facilitate new learning.

Preselection of group members is not always possible. When possible, however, it is the preferred condition. It may be necessary to work in groups with intact populations, for example, or time considerations may interfere with preselection procedures. While a pre-group screening interview is preferred, the group leader will not always be able to afford this luxury, so he/she should sharpen assessment skills and implement procedures to screen during the initial group meeting. Following is a list of essential tasks that should be accomplished either in a pre-group interview or during the initial meeting:

1. **Assess the potential member's readiness for a group experience.** The potential group member should have good motivation for change and an expectation of success.

2. **Select as group members persons who are maintaining at least one minimal primary interpersonal relationship.** This reservoir of successful experience will aid the group member in dealing with the impact of multiple relationships in the group.

3. **Select only persons who have relative absence of pathology or problems too extreme for group members to deal with.** This factor, combined with No.2, would indicate the need for a referral to individual therapy until such time as the helpee could profit from a group experience.

4. **Determine the potential member's "fit" in the group.** Ideally, the total group would be fairly heterogeneous in terms of personality dynamics. This will allow for greater creativity in problem solution and provide a wider range of interactional possibilities. This is especially important when groups are organized around common problems such as traffic violations, alcoholism, divorce, or drug abuse.

Physical Setting

The group setting should be a comfortable, attractive, inviting room that is small enough for intimacy without being crowded. Preferably, the room should be carpeted and provided with low, comfortable chairs and floor pillows so that group members can choose where and how they wish to sit. Low, soft, indirect lighting is preferred over harsh ceiling lights.

Freedom from outside distractions and complete privacy is essential. Coffee and soft drinks are acceptable, but food is usually distracting. For extended sessions when eating is required, the preferred procedure is to take a formal break for eating rather than incorporating the meal into group time.

When the group is meeting for many separate sessions, the same meeting room is recommended as a home base for security. This does not rule out an occasional variation when appropriate or even necessary in order to change a set or introduce new stimulation.

Finally, group members should sit in a circle so that each member can view everyone fully. No obstructions should exist between members such as a table or a desk. Members should be close enough to reach out and touch each other if they choose, but at the same time not so close that they cannot shift body position without bumping someone. The aim of paying attention to these physical arrangements is to provide options for the integration of both intimacy and privacy.

Media and Instructional Aids.

A wide range of techniques are available that are limited only by the creative ability of the group leader. The use of techniques of any kind ought to serve a very specific purpose, such as stimulating interpersonal communication, providing data for members' perceptions of self, or cognitive input designed to provide information to group members so they can consciously work on a given skill or skills.

Appropriate media for these purposes might include music, poetry and poetry writing, painting, dancing, videotape feedback, human development exercises, and simulation games. The key is that the group leader needs to be very careful and insist that the media used is worth the time invested, that it is constructive and conducive to further realization of human potential, and that the leader has full command of the technique employed. A major factor is that the media remain a stimulant or catalyst for interpersonal exploration rather than becoming an end in itself.

Meeting Times: Length and Duration

Weekly or semi-weekly sessions from 1 ½ to 2 hours in length over a specified period of time is preferred. Sessions of less than 1 ½ hours are too short for adult groups due to warm-up and transition periods. Longer sessions, unless planned for in the prearranged context of an extended session or marathon, can be counterproductive if they become tiring for the members. For children's groups, a 30 to 45 minute session is probably all they will endure before their concentration begins to wander.

Specified beginning and ending sessions are preferable to open-ended groups. This can range anywhere from 10 to 25 sessions but should have a definite duration. Just as in the 50-minute hour, duration tends to set up a series of expectations on the part of group members. If at the end of the specified time, work is still to be done, the group should be formally dissolved and reorganized. Most likely, not all of the members will want to continue.

An extended session, ranging from 8 to 15 hours, is a possible option for an on-going group. A marathon is recommended as an extended session that is part of the total group experience, rather than a free-standing, one-shot occasion. The marathon is usually scheduled after the group has had several regular sessions and has developed its own style. The extended session is best placed about three-quarters of the way through the life of the group so that adequate follow-up time is available if necessary.

Some groups also can be compacted into daily or twice daily sessions over a short period of time to increase impact. This "total impact" approach is best used in a distraction free setting where participants are in residence for a specified period of time and the group is used in conjunction with didactic training. This particular schemata is popular with school personnel, organizational development units, and other intact organizations where retreat type workshops are administratively convenient.

Preferred Group Size

To promote maximal interaction effectiveness in the group, the number of members should not exceed 9 or 10 for adolescent and adult groups. Groups for children would normally include 5 or 6 members. Also, the minimum number for adults should not be fewer than 5 members. This number provides enough people to tap the resources of the group dynamic while at the same time keeps the group small enough to allow closeness and intimacy. With numbers larger than 10, the group leader has difficulty in attending to all group members. Many transactions will be lost simply because time is not sufficient for all to become involved. An unrealistically small number in the group can create unwanted artificial pressures to respond and participate.

An effective configuration in a workshop or training setting is for large groups to be brought together in one assembly for the didactic or instructional phases of the program and then disbursed into small groups with an individual group leader for intra and interpersonal development.

Establishing Ground Rules and Primary Expectations

Unnecessarily rigid rules for groups should be used only to provide guidelines for members and to insure protection and safety while maintaining maximum freedom to explore and test new behaviors.

In a pre-group interview, a helpful procedure is to review some of the primary expectations with prospective group members. An efficient way to do this is to simply print a statement or list on a single sheet of paper so that the group member can look them over before the first meeting. Where an interview is not possible, this should be a primary agenda at the first meeting. Minimal rules and expectations would include the following:

1. **Attend sessions regularly and on time.** When accepting membership, the new group member should respect the time of the leader and the other group members by observing time frames carefully. The group leader also will find advantages in starting and stopping each group session promptly. This helps create an atmosphere of work and also allows the members to plan their out-of-group time efficiently.

2. **Maintain confidentiality.** This is absolutely crucial to group development and a concrete understanding needs to be obtained on the part of each group member. Talking outside the group in any form should be discouraged and talking about the group and its members to non-group participants should not be allowed. With this requirement, group members can at least have an assurance of bureaucratic type trust which opens the possibility of developing psychological trust at deeper levels.

3. **Listen carefully to other group members.** In order to earn the right to share oneself with the group, each member has the responsibility to tend carefully to other members while they are the focus of attention. This increases respect and allows for practice of tending skills.

4. **Be honest, concrete, and open in discussing problems.** The group member can expect to get back about what he/she is willing to invest in it. All groups offer the opportunity for members to function both as helpers and helpees. Groups tend to develop most helpfulness when a commitment is present on the part of members to be as genuine and frank as possible.

5. **Set concrete goals for self-growth.** The group member should demonstrate a willingness to profit from the group experience by actively seeking clearer focus on solutions to problems. These should be stated in terms of goals for self. Work toward growth increases dramatically, within and without the group, when individuals have set obtainable goals.

6. **Make a commitment to attend the first four meetings.** This expectation is based on the idea that it takes a minimum of four sessions for the individual member to do a realistic assessment of the group, the members, the leader, and the possible gains available for self. If at that time the member decides that his/her needs are not being met, he/she has fulfilled the initial obligation and is free to terminate.

Procedural Group Rules. While informal group rules and norms will grow out of the unique life of any group, some minimal procedural rules are sometimes helpful to assist the group in getting started. If the procedural rules are distributed by the leader to each member during the intake interview, they will have an opportunity to read and reflect upon them before the first meeting. These rules then can be used as a method of beginning the initial session. Discussion can ensue regarding the rules and additions and/or deletions can be made according to the needs of the particular group.

In Figure 6.1 is a list of minimal procedural rules (guidelines) that we use for our groups. These, of course, can be modified with regard to content and language to fit the particular age group involved.

RULES FOR GROUP PROCESS

Group counseling is a learning experience and members must learn how to work together to maximize the learning possibilities. The assumption cannot be made that group members already know how to work together as a group. Since the group counseling experience will be new to most members, often a helpful procedure is to provide a list in the first session of general guidelines of expected or suggested behaviors that other groups have found to be facilitative.

The following list of rules for the group could be copied and distributed to group members with instructions to select the rule they think they will have the most difficulty following. Members could then be encouraged to share the rule they selected and why they think it will be difficult for them. Other members could then offer suggestions about how they could help or what that person might do to help himself/herself.

1. **Let others know what your ideas are.** What every member has to say is important. Sharing your thoughts and reactions with the group will stimulate other members and will help them to share what they are thinking.

(Continued on page 145)

1. **Confidentiality.** This is the most binding group rule. You may share your *personal* pilgrimage and growth with your spouse and/or friends, but any personally identifying information about *anyone else* in the group is confidential. Personally identifying information is given in confidence and should be guarded as *private.*

2. **Goals, procedures and leader qualifications.** You have a right to know the general and specific purposes of the group. This is primarily important in the beginning stages but it will be your responsibility to talk about it any time that you have questions.

3. **Attendance.** Regular attendance is expected. Absences are rare. Group process requires time. Six weeks is a bare minimum to expect any lasting personal results. Results frequently depend upon relationships that are built and maintained over a period of time.

4. Participants are responsible for claiming time to work rather than relying on the leader to make sure each participant has time. No one is required to participate or share information about him- or herself, unless he or she chooses to do so. For maximum benefit from the group process, however, participants are strongly encouraged to get involved in all aspects of the group process, including discussion, sharing, participating in exercises and completing homework assignments.

5. **Alcohol and drugs.** The use of alcohol and illegal drugs is prohibited prior to and during group sessions. If you are taking prescription medication under the supervision of a physician, you should inform your group leader.

6. Freedom and Permission exist in the group. Any behavior, dress, expression, or action that you wish to try is acceptable.

   Exceptions:

       (a) direct physical violence; and
       (b) overt sexual activity

7. While groups can activate powerful sources of potential growth there can and may be some risk involved in the process. When people commit themselves to growth and change, they may expect some periods of turbulence in their lives. Growing might include significant life changes.

These group rules are based upon the 1980 Revision of the *Ethical Code for Group Leaders* as sponsored and adopted by the Association for Specialists in Group work.

Figure 6.1. Procedural group rules and guidelines.

Figure 6.1. Continued.

---

8. Any relationship developed in the group or as a result of associations from the group is the *property of the group.* Failure to share the outside group relationships and actions robs others of the full process.

9. **Leaving the group.** If you decide to terminate, please give the group leader and members one week notice. Frequently, persons who terminate all in one session act on impulse and fail to profit from the power of departure procedures. When you initially join the group, you will be expected to commit yourself to a minimum of four sessions.

---

2. **Ask your questions.** If you have a question or you want to know more about something, ask. No such thing as a stupid question exists in this group. Several other members probably want to know the same thing.

3. **Do not do all the talking.** Others want to participate also and they can not if you take too long to express your ideas.

4. **Help other members to participate.** If someone looks as though he/she wants to say something but hasn't, encourage that person to do so. You could say, "Karla, you look as though you'd like to say something." Silent members may especially need your support and encouragement to participate verbally. Don't overdo it though. A member doesn't have to talk to be involved in what is happening.

5. **Listen carefully to other members.** Try to listen so intently that you could repeat what the other member has said to his/her satisfaction. You aren't listening effectively if you are thinking about what you are going to say when you get the chance. Give the other person's ideas a chance and try to understand what he/she is saying. Listen to other members the way you would want them to listen to you.

6. **Group members are here to help.** Problems can be solved by working cooperatively together. In the process of helping others, you can help yourself. The information you have can be helpful to others. Suggesting alternatives or causes can help other members to make better decisions.

7. **Be willing to accept another point of view.** Don't insist that you are right and everyone else is wrong. The other person just might be thinking the same thing. Try to help other members to understand rather than trying to make them understand.

8. **Keep up with the discussion.** If the discussion is confusing to you, say so.

9. **In this group to talk about your feelings and reactions is acceptable.**

FACILITATING RESPONSIBILITY

Assumption of responsibility for one's own behavior is not something that occurs automatically in group counseling. The group counselor must be able to facilitate the kind of climate which not only allows but encourages group members to become involved in the process of determining what they will contribute and what they will get out of the group.

One of the major objectives of group counseling is to help members assume responsibility for themselves and their behavior. However, in initial group counseling experiences, counselors often feel they are solely responsible for almost everything that occurs in the group. Such an attitude may deprive group members of an opportunity to experience responsibility for many decisions they could make.

Depending upon the group counselor's theoretical and philosophical position, the perceived role is either to initiate, motivate, encourage participation, or facilitate involvement. The counselor is not however responsible for "running the show." Group members need to share in the responsibility for what happens in the group. Therefore, the focus of attention in the group should be on the members.

Keeping the Focus on Group Members

Group members cannot be helped to learn about responsibility through observation alone. If group members are to assume responsibility, they must be allowed to experience the process of decision making. If the group counselor makes most of the decisions concerning the group, even the seemingly minor ones, dependency is much more likely to be fostered than responsibility. A better group counselor's approach would be to enable members to become more aware of their own strengths and the strengths of other members.

Allowing and helping group members to accept responsibility are especially crucial in the first few group counseling sessions because the tone is being set for succeeding sessions. Therefore, an important activity is for the group counselor to demonstrate in the early sessions that members can be responsible to each other and for themselves. The following points may be helpful in facilitating responsibility:

1. Helping members learn how to work together effectively is a slow process and requires much patience on the part of the counselor.

2. Group counseling is a new experience for most members. The counselor must remember that members need time to learn how to work together effectively.

3. Due to the nature of group process, the counselor may think very little is being accomplished in the first few sessions. The counselor should recognize this as a personal need rather than the members' need to "get something done."

4. In most groups, initially a tendency exists on the part of the members to give their responsibility to the counselor. Members may ask the counselor to tell them what to do and how to do it. To avoid this trap

the counselor could respond, "I know you have had people tell you what to do before, but in here, in this group, you can work things out for yourself. I'll try to help, but I won't decide what you want to talk about."

5. The group counselor has a responsibility to help members to respond to each other. In most groups, members tend at the beginning to direct their responses to the counselor even when talking to another member. The counselor could respond, "Robert, you are talking to Jack, but you seem to be telling me. Could you tell Jack?

6. The counselor must be careful so as to avoid implying what answers should be. Often implications are given by tone of voice or facial expression.

7. By answering all questions with direct answers, the group counselor quickly becomes the answer source and thus deprives members of the responsibility for deriving solutions. Members do not always want an answer from the counselor even though they have asked. The counselor could reflect some questions to the whole group by asking, "What do the rest of you think?"

8. When the counselor allows the group to "set members straight," the group experiences the responsibility of their behavior.

PATIENCE: A PREREQUISITE

At times the group counselor may experience difficulty in restraining himself or herself in the group. This seems to be especially true during those moments when the counselor is experiencing a need to "get things going" or when the counselor suddenly "sees" what no one else in the group is perceiving. Group counseling requires patience and a willingness to allow members to discover for themselves. Patience is indeed a basic prerequisite to the developing of responsibility in a group. Grady Nutt (1971) has written of patience:

> Mushrooms grow to maturity overnight. Orchids take seven to twelve years to bloom. Your relationships can be mushrooms or orchids. The mature person waits for orchids but is patient with mushrooms! (p. 78)

Through waiting to see what will happen or restraining a response for a few seconds, the counselor provides the members of the group with an opportunity to take responsibility for "getting things going" or helping other members. Group members thus come to realize "this is our group" and the counselor learns that other helpers are in the group.

GROUP MEMBER RESPONSIBILITY

Acceptance of responsibility to help another person and experiencing the process of being helpful is for group members a profoundly positive and self-enhancing encounter. The extension of responsibility outward to touch the lives of others in a helpful way adds a unique depth dimension quality to the life of the helper. After just such an experience, a group member once wrote:

> Working in this group has helped me to form a stronger self-concept, and I'm liking myself better with each session. I really can be helpful to people. That's important to know. I'm thinking of myself in a new light now.

Group members are more likely to experience personal change when they are allowed to be responsible for that change. Members tend to resist even the possibility of new behaviors when the atmosphere is one of attempting to force change. The potential for change is greatly enhanced when group members are granted the freedom to be and at the same time are helped to accept responsibility for resulting behavior. The impact of this willingness to allow rather than force change is perhaps best expressed by a group member who wrote:

> One of your ways of helping me is letting me change. I trust that.
> I'm not afraid of exploring something or making a change. You let
> me grow. If I were to come up against something and be immensely
> afraid, you'd let me be afraid even though you and I both would
> know plenty of good reasons not to be.

When members experience the opportunity to accept responsibility, they discover that they trust themselves more fully and as a result are more willing to risk and to explore the inner depth which they possess. Personal growth then is facilitated by members' responsible involvement in their own behavioral change.

ACHIEVING GROUP STABILITY IN GROUP COUNSELING

Groups are inevitable and ubiquitous (Cartwright & Zander, 1960). People being social animals, the very omnipresence of the group setting is what is so appealing. Persons tend naturally and spontaneously to form groups. The counselor in an educational setting is in an advantageous position to make use of this principle for the formation of counseling or "growth" groups.

Membership and Group Stability

Any counselor who initiates a group has an obligation to create the kinds of conditions most conducive to success. Evidence seems to point to the fact that voluntary membership is preferable to involuntary or counselor-contrived groups. This does not necessarily doom involuntary groups to failure however because even more important than initial membership is the atmosphere or growth climate that the leader is able to facilitate once the group is underway.

Group stability, or the desire of the group to remain together and work toward commonly accepted goals, is related to the attractiveness the group holds for its members. In other words, the group will achieve its goals in direct proportion to the extent to which members perceive the group in a positive way.

If a group is to become attractive to its members, it must attempt to imitate the structural makeup of society in general. Single-sex or "single-problem" groups do not do this. When responding to the question "What does it take to start a group?" Carl Rogers (1969) replied, "Oh, six or seven people." He was at the time talking about a basic encounter group, but the implication is clear. The attractiveness necessary in achieving group stability probably is more attainable with heterogeneity.

Leadership and Group Stability

The primary function of the leader is to facilitate interaction between group members and to assist in clarifying situations that group members see as being problematic. The unstructured group leader will operate from a democratic base rather than as an authoritarian type of leader. They will not allow their own status needs to interfere as the group process produces emergent leaders. They will tend to see themselves as a member of the group, but at the same time as a member who is capable of sensitivity to changing and evolving group needs and to those individuals who comprise the group.

The leadership variable which is so important to effective group interaction seems limited only by the degree of personal flexibility of the leader. Perhaps another way of expressing this concept is by saying that the leader needs to remain open to the content and the process of the group as it manifests itself. The group leader, to an even greater degree than in an individual setting, must remain in tune and be sensitive to the total dynamics of the group. The number of possible interactions is multiplied greatly in a group setting, thus offering fertile ground for exploring new areas of concern and affording new avenues for testing behaviors.

Progress and Learning in Groups

The learning that takes place in the group is again relative to the individual members' perception of the attractiveness of the group. If the climate of the group is such that individuals are overly concerned with protection and maintenance of the self, the learning process will be inhibited.

The leader has the responsibility for being sensitive to and adjusting group and personal motivational factors that enhance the learning situation. The non-threatening, accepting, and empathic atmosphere will ease the need for self protection and maintenance and thus free the individual for new learning, exploratory, and self-enhancing behavior.

Cattell (1951, pp. 161-184) formulated the concept of "group syntality" which grows through participation and sharing by group members and the leader. Each group member has an opportunity to share responsibility, thereby providing a feeling of true involvement and emergent leadership. Subsequently, Friedlander (1970), Plutchink and Landau (1973), and many other writers have examined the concepts of group trust, interrelationships, dominance or power, and emotionality as they relate to total group progress and task accomplishment.

Lack of attractiveness or group stability will quickly lead to the dissolution of the group. On the other hand, a group that is attractive and meaningful to its members will have a powerful holding ability. This attractiveness, facilitated through meaningful interaction, should lead to group stability and its atmosphere of growth. Figure 6.2 conceptualizes the steps in producing a growth or learning climate.

Attractiveness will not be consistently uniform among group members. This will account for feelings of dissatisfaction that are expressed at different points as the group progresses. The leader will need to work with these dissatisfactions as they are presented and at all times will need to be attentive to the expressed needs of the group along these lines. Groups are intuitive about progress and the leader should be aware that groups will "run their course" at varying levels. If a climate of acceptance has been established, the group will be free to express their feelings with regard to perceived progress. In the unstructured setting, of course, the group will make the determination as to when it has fulfilled its function and should disband.

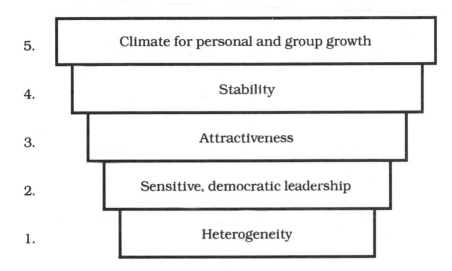

5. Climate for personal and group growth

4. Stability

3. Attractiveness

2. Sensitive, democratic leadership

1. Heterogeneity

Figure 6.2. Conceptualized steps in producing a growth or learning climate.

The group also will recognize when things begin to "bog down." At these points the leader will want to help clarify the reasons for slow downs in group progress.

USING DAYBOOKS TO FACILITATE SELF-EXPLORATION

Since most of the work by individuals in group counseling takes place between sessions, the group facilitator may want to consider avenues for encouraging continuation of the process that has been initiated during the session. The use of a diary or daybook by group members to record their feelings and reactions can significantly facilitate continued self-exploration outside the group sessions. Since in any group only a limited amount of time is available to any individual member, the daybook can be viewed as an opportunity to express and explore thoughts and reactions for which there was not an opportunity to do so in the group.

Daybooks are seldom used with groups below high school age and even at this level with considerable caution because school age adolescents may view writing in the daybook as homework or an assignment. In such cases, unnecessary resistance to the total group process may develop. A very simple approach to the daybook utilizing a list of feeling objectives and self descriptive phrases from which to choose could be quite effective with elementary school age children. Children also could be asked to draw pictures depicting what they learned in the group that day, how they felt, or something they experienced between sessions.

For members who find it difficult to express very personal feelings and reactions in the group, the daybook can be a safe place to begin. Our experience has been that such members then are better able to verbalize those same feelings and reactions in the group and usually in a more direct manner. Although it is possible that writing in a daybook could "drain off" or detract from the spontaneity of the expression, this is not usually the case.

The daybook also affords the group facilitator an opportunity to know and understand group members more fully. These additional insights can greatly enhance the facilitators sensitivity, understanding, and effectiveness in the group. A caution seems appropriate at this point, though. Material revealed in a diary should not be introduced into the group by the facilitator. That is the responsibility of the group member. Premature introduction by the facilitator could be viewed as a violation of confidentiality by the member, or at the least it could create dependency on the facilitator to "bring it up" and then deprive the member of the opportunity to learn from taking a risk.

The purpose and structure of the daybook should be discussed fully with the group and their wishes honored. The following two examples of structured guidelines for writing in the daybook could be utilized separately or parts of each combined to meet the needs of your particular group.

Example 1: Guide to Writing in the Daybook

The Daybook is like a diary but different in that it is not a simple chronicle of events and situations that occur in the laboratory group. Rather than summarizing what happened, your focus in writing should be upon your own feelings as you experienced them in the group. You may have feelings regarding other people in the group, the leader, yourself, or the 'group" in general.

Following are some guidelines:

1. Write in the Daybook as soon as you can following each group experience. This will make your recollection as current as possible.

2. Focus on your own affect; rather than upon other people or group process.

3. Be specific and concrete.

4. Try to make the Daybook an extension of the group experience rather than a summary. It should be an exercise in depth self-exploration.

5. The logical extension of "getting in touch" with your current feelings is to inspect them for motivation.

6. Treat the Daybook as you would any professional material that is highly confidential in nature. The Daybook will be read by your group facilitator.

The following four excerpts from Daybooks illustrate the kind of material that is most helpful to the writer.

Excerpt 1. . . . . . perhaps that's why I'm so interested in _____ —as an individual. I'm also wondering if significant people for me develop because of their approval, trust, and liking—it has a big part to do with it. I have enjoyed very few people who gave me negative feedback. Criticism is difficult for me to accept—but I find a deeper respect and eventual high regard for those who give me criticism in a building way.

Excerpt 2.   When Marilyn said we weren't totally strangers, it really hit me that that's exactly what I felt—a stranger, separate, and alone. While I was talking about myself the first time, I was glad because I wanted almost to be forced to be open, to reveal myself although it scared hell out of me to do it. I wanted the group to focus on me because I wanted to be reassured that they wouldn't let me get by with being phony, that they wouldn't just leave me as I was.

Excerpt 3.   So a woman is good, kind, open, and honest, and really has some basic strong points. But these are not selling points in today's market. Is what I am asking too much? I really can't believe that it is. But I find myself doubting me and even the strong points when I face the everyday world I live in. I almost want to shout "I have played the game fair and done everything I was taught to do and still it isn't enough. Why! Why! Why!"

Excerpt 4.   I winced a little as Frank suggested that Jim was not being open. It was obvious that Jim felt great pain at such a charge. I too felt the pain because even though I would like very much to be open, I don't seem to know how.

Example 2: Structure for Daybook Entries

1. **Group goals.** Were the group goals defined? Do they change from session to session?

2. **Personal goals.** Are your own goals well-defined, unclear or in the process of development? Do they change from session to session? Are they specific or general?

3. **Group process.** What was the level of interaction, intellectual, feeling oriented, additive? Is the group

stuck or moving? Are there sub-groups? What is the emotional climate of the group in general?

4. **Personal/individual.** (Names are O.K., but not necessary). (a) What are the attitudes, feelings, beliefs and reactions/behaviors of individual group members? *(b) Myself: How do I feel, respond and behave. Did anything get triggered in me? What avenue of self-exploration can I pursue to learn more about myself?

*This should be the area where you devote most of your attention.

5. **Session.** What did this session accomplish: (a) for the group, and (b) for me?

Entries in the daybook often are quite creative as is shown in the following poem written by a graduate student enrolled in the Master's level group counseling course.

> Group.
> Persons thrown together
> At random;
> By chance.
> The luck of the draw
> Bringing people together
> To communicate with others
> About what's important.
> We share hopes for marriage,
> The pain of broken relationships,
> Frustration caused by overload.
> We want to know how others
> See things important to us.
> Like God and family and work
> And dissertation topics.
> Sometimes our progress
> Isn't impressive or dramatic;
> Not easily measured
> Or apparent to a casual observer.
> When the intruder came by
> To sell miracle cleanser,
> He was politely informed:
> "You will have to come back later."
> "I'm involved in something important right now."
>   (Gunn, 1988).

SUMMARY

In summary, the preceding discussion of common organizational concerns will assist the counselor who is considering beginning a group program to avoid some of the most frequently encountered pitfalls. While attending to these details is not very glamorous, they will help enormously to insure a successful, smooth-flowing group.

The literature on group counseling and group dynamics is growing and indications are that when the group climate is appropriate to the task, positive growth can take place. The purpose here has been to identify some key elements that will enhance the counselor's chances of achieving positive growth and learning in a group setting.

For more complete treatment of some of the typical problems and procedures that the counselor may expect to encounter in a group counseling setting, he/she is referred to the very helpful texts by Yalom (1985) and Gazda (1982).

Listed here, in summary fashion, are some of the key elements of which the counselor should be aware when initiating a group for counseling.

1. Voluntary groups seem to be preferable to involuntary groups but more important than either is the climate that the counselor is able to achieve when the group has begun.

2. In order to achieve stability, the group must be attractive to its members. It must emulate society in general in terms of individual makeup.

3. Interaction among members is facilitated if the group is limited in size from six to nine members.

4. Leadership must proceed from a democratic base and at all times be sensitive to the evolving needs of the group. The leader will need to strive for flexibility and openness.

5. A non-threatening, accepting atmosphere is to be fostered so that protective and maintenance behaviors can be cast aside in favor of more growth-facilitating conditions.

6. The goals of the group involve growth and learning, but the group is to define its own growth and to decide how growth will be achieved. The counselor can and must help the group members to do so.

REFERENCES

Cartwright, D., & Zander, A. (1960). *Group dynamics: Research and theory (2nd ed.).* Evanston, IL: Row, Peterson.

Cattell, R.B. (1951). New concepts for measuring leadership in terms of group syntality. *Human Relations, 4,* 161-184.

Clack, R. (1971). Encouraging participation in group counseling. *School Counselor, 18,* 286-289.

Cull, J., & Hardy, R. (1974). Group counseling with adolescents in the school setting. In *Counseling high school students.* Springfield, IL: Charles C. Thomas.

Friedlander, F. (1970). The primacy of trust as a facilitator of further group accomplishment. *Journal of Applied Behavioral Science, 6,* 387-400.

Gazda, G.M. (Ed.). (1982). *Basic approaches to group psychotherapy and group counseling (3rd ed.).* Springfield, IL: Charles C. Thomas.

Gunn, P.W. (1988). *Group.* Unpublished poem. University of North Texas. Denton.

Mahler, C.A. (1973). Minimal necessary conditions in schools for effective group counseling. *Educational Technology, 13,* (2), 21-23.

Nutt, G. (1971). *Being me.* Nashville: Broadman Press.

Ohlsen, M.M. (1968). Counseling children in groups. *School Counselor, 15,* 343-349.

Plutchink, R., & Landau, H. (1973). Perceived dominance and emotional states in small groups. *Psychotherapy: Theory Research and Practice, 10,* 340-342.

Rogers, C.R. (1969). Statement made at North Texas State University, Group Counseling Institute. August.

Yalom, I.D. (1985). *The theory and practice of group psychotherapy (3rd ed.).* New York: Basic Books.

SUGGESTED READINGS

Berg, R.C. & Smallwood, K. (1974). *Effective personal integration: A guide for group leaders.* Fort Worth, TX: Institute for Studies in Effective Living.

This practical handbook provides a low-structure approach to group leadership with members who have little or no previous counseling group experience.

Based on the assumption that certain "group skills" are necessary to promote the full potential of the group, the authors suggest a step-by-step sequence that includes feedback, perception, and self-disclosure exercises plus methods of contracting for behavior change.

Additional topics covered include: characteristics of the leader, suggestions for getting the group started, and stages of group development.

Corey, G., & Corey, M.S. (1987). *Groups: Process and practice.* Monterey, CA: Brooks/Cole Publishing Company.

The Coreys have collaborated on a very practical book concerning a wide range of the major issues in group counseling. They present a balanced and complete discussion of the group members, the leader, basic issues in group work and a particularly helpful series of chapters dealing with stages of group development. They also present material relevant to working with special groups such as children, adolescents, college students, couples, and the elderly.

Yalom, I.D. (1985). *The theory and practice of group psychotherapy (3rd ed.).* New York: Basic Books, Inc., Publishers.

Yalom presents a cogent and comprehensive overview of the practical aspects of group work. In our opinion, this book is an indispensable addition to the group leader's professional library.

In highly readable form, the author covers such relevant areas as curative factors, learning, cohesiveness, therapist function, selection and composition, and several other topics crucial to group work.

SUGGESTED FILMS

Activity Group Therapy. Psychological Cinema Register, Audio-Visual Aids Library, University of Pennsylvania, University Park, PA (50 min.).

The film focuses on selected events from sixty activity group therapy sessions with a group of emotionally disturbed and socially maladjusted ten and eleven-year old boys. Dramatic changes in personality and behavior are shown.

Journey Into Self. Psychological Cinema Resiger, Audio-Visual Aids Library, University of Pennsylvania, University Park, PA; (45 min.)

This film won an Academy Award for the best feature-length documentary of 1969. The film focuses primarily on the experiences of four members of a sixteen-hour weekend encounter group facilitated by Carl Rogers and Richard Farson. An emotionally moving presentation of the power of the group process and the impact one member can have on another.

CHAPTER 7

PROBLEMS AND INTERVENTION TECHNIQUES IN GROUP COUNSELING

CHARACTERISTICS OF THE LEADER

A fundamental tenet of group leadership is that the group leader demonstrates the way he/she leads life and that he/she is a growing, accomplishing, and effective human being. Since much of what is done in groups is based upon the helpee modeling effective responses after the leader, an essential component is for the leader to have high level skills (Egan, 1982).

First of all, the leader must incorporate a basic and expanding knowledge of self. This includes an awareness of personal dynamics and major modes of behavior and also how he/she responds to many different kinds of people and situations. The expectation is for group leaders to have spent many hours themselves as group members and in a helpee mode. Obviously, we don't encourage people to spend their lives as helpees, but rather to stay fully in touch with the part of self that can become vulnerable and to ask for help when needed. The goal is to encourage mutually satisfying relationships that are interdependent in nature: relationships that are free enough from threat so that group members are allowed to demonstrate both strengths and weaknesses without fear of reprisal.

Secondly, the leader must demonstrate interpersonal skills that verify ability to tend fully to another person, with an intensity that allows him/her to understand as completely as possible what the other person is saying, feeling, and asking. In other words, the group facilitator needs to demonstrate interpersonal functionality by practicing and incorporating tending skills that help in understanding helpees.

From a group development point of view, the facilitator will serve as a primary, functional model of skills and behaviors that group members are expected to learn. Initially the facilitator will provide high levels of nurturant behavior: empathy, warmth, respect, and concreteness. His/her overall tone will communicate both an acceptance of where the group is and an intensity of purpose that points toward increased skill acquisition, intra- and interpersonal growth, and an expanded behavioral repertoire that will lead to increased effectiveness in living. An important step in this process is for the group leader and group member to mutually confront any feelings of dependency and trans-ference experienced by the helper and the helpee. The ultimate goal is for the helpee to move out of the group constellation toward a more self-motivated, inner-directed individual who accepts responsibility for his own behavior without undue recourse to external reinforcers.

Another responsibility of the group leader is a keen awareness of the process or developmental stages within the group itself. An appreciation of the dynamics, or "chang-ingness" of the group as it develops, is essential if the leader is to facilitate growth in the group.

To actively expect and encourage group members to demonstrate their new levels of interpersonal effectiveness is essential. Therefore, the group facilitator will probably find it necessary to intervene in certain nonproductive or destructive group member behaviors. The concept of a laissez-faire or strictly nurturant group leader seems incongruent and inefficient. The group leader has certain skills in his/her behavioral repertoire that are needed in facilitating member growth.

ASSESSING GROUP MEMBERS' STRENGTHS AND WEAKNESSES

A key function of group leadership is the assessment of individual group members. Self-assessment instruments can aid the group member in determining the level at which he/she is presently performing and the direction in which he/she would like to move in each of the emotional, physical, and intellective areas. Individual inventories can be easily profiled by each group participant and should allow the member to arrive at a concrete contract for growth.

Several advantages exist to these kinds of assessment instruments:

1. The group member is able to do a conscious evaluation of strengths and weaknesses, thereby approaching a realistic appraisal of self in relation to other group members.

2. The assessment process raises the level of functioning to conscious awareness, thereby allowing for a relatively systematic approach to growth.

3. The strengths of the individual are given equal valence with weaknesses. This allows the group leader and other members to proceed from a reasonable base of capabilities and potentials rather than to focus exclusively on crisis points or areas of dysfunction.

4. Assessment provides a base for translating growth into behavioral terms that can be checked and monitored in the group. Rather than speaking in vague generalities, individual group members can contract for growth skills and behaviors that are achievable, observable, measurable, and repeatable, in the group setting.

5. Assessment allows both group member and group leader to clarify directionality and to work in a mutually supportive relationship toward gaining the skills, understandings, and desired behaviors.

A possible criticism of this approach is that it might tend to inhibit freedom of self-exploration. To minimize this possibility, the scale suggested here is intended to be as comprehensive and yet as functionally succinct as possible. The experienced group leader should be aware of this possible limitation and while providing clear focus and directionality should also remain open and attentive to new and unexplored helpee directions.

The *Self-assessment Scale* shown in Figure 7.1 is a semantic-differential type procedure that allows the individual to make a personal evaluation of where he/she sees self *now* and *where he/she would like to be* (i.e., which direction he/she wants to grow and gain skills).

In the area of emotionality the *Self-assessment Scale* is broken into three major areas:

1. **Intra-personal awareness.** How well is the individual in touch with self and own dynamics? What are typical patterns of coping with stress?

2. **Self-concept.** How does the individual see self in relation to other people and to ideal self?

3. **Interpersonal skills.** How does the individual see self regarding the behavioral skills available in relationships with others?

The physical aspect of the Self-assessment Scale focuses on three major elements:

1. **Body image.** This area is primarily concerned with how a person sees self sexually and in what behaviors (dress, personal style, etc.) he/she engages as an outward manifestation of sexuality.

2. **Body shape and endurance.** The focus here is on physical energy variables that relate to work, play, and interpersonal potency.

In addition to the physical aspect of the *Self-assessment Scale*, an increasingly comprehensive inventory is used to quantify the type and duration of physical activity in which each group member engages during a specified period of time. Once again, this tends to raise activity levels to consciousness and allows for realistic self appraisal and goal setting.

The intellective aspects of the Self-assessment Scale attempt to assess a member's perception in two areas:

1. **Attitudes.** Individual belief and value systems.

2. **Intellective skill bundles.** The basic tools that are necessary to gain knowledge and understandings.

In summary, with a realistic appraisal of self that can be checked out for accuracy and honed to observable behaviors, growth can occur in a much more systematic and intensified way. Group time that might otherwise be spent in random exploration can be devoted to developing programs and courses of action that lead to increased personal effectiveness.

COMMON PROBLEMS IN GROUP PROCESS

Our experience has been that many potential problems in group process can be minimized if the group leader will give careful attention to detail during the organizational stages of

(Continued on page 171)

This instrument is designed to help determine how you see yourself in relation to the words and concepts listed. It will be used to work with you in developing programs of self-growth in those aspects of self you choose to emphasize.

In completing this instrument, you are asked to indicate your position in terms of what the scale-items *mean to you*—do not be concerned about different ways the descriptive items can be interpreted.

Here is how you are to complete the first part of the assessment process:

DIRECTIONS: Step 1

If you see yourself as *VERY* like one or the other descriptive terms at each end of a line, you should place an "X" as follows:

Strong   ___ : ___ : ___ : ___ : ___ : ___ : ___ : _X_   Weak

Strong   _X_ : ___ : ___ : ___ : ___ : ___ : ___ : ___   Weak

If you see yourself as *QUITE* like one or the other descriptive terms at each end of a scale, you should place an "X" as follows:

Fair   ___ : ___ : ___ : ___ : ___ : ___ : _X_ : ___   Unfair

Fair   ___ : _X_ : ___ : ___ : ___ : ___ : ___ : ___   Unfair

If you see yourself as *RATHER* like one or the other end-term of a scale, you should place an "X" as follows:

Wise   ___ : ___ : ___ : ___ : ___ : _X_ : ___ : ___   Foolish

Wise   ___ : ___ : _X_ : ___ : ___ : ___ : ___ : ___   Foolish

If you see yourself as only *SOMEWHAT* like one or the other descriptive term of a scale, you should place an "X" as follows:

Complex   ___ : ___ : ___ : ___ : _X_ : ___ : ___ : ___   Simple

Complex   ___ : ___ : ___ : _X_ : ___ : ___ : ___ : ___   Simple

IMPORTANT: (1) Place your marks in the middle of spaces, not on the boundaries. (2) Be sure you place an "X" mark on every scale—do not omit any.

Work fairly quickly through this part of the process. Do not puzzle or worry over individual scale items—just give your first impression, your immediate "feelings" about each item.

Figure 7.1. Self-assessment Scale.

Figure 7.1. Continued.

___ leader	___ : ___ : ___ : ___ : ___ : ___ : ___ : ___	follower
___ sloppy	___ : ___ : ___ : ___ : ___ : ___ : ___ : ___	neat
___ angry	___ : ___ : ___ : ___ : ___ : ___ : ___ : ___	peaceful
___ dull	___ : ___ : ___ : ___ : ___ : ___ : ___ : ___	bright
___ dogmatic	___ : ___ : ___ : ___ : ___ : ___ : ___ : ___	tolerant
___ open	___ : ___ : ___ : ___ : ___ : ___ : ___ : ___	closed
___ active	___ : ___ : ___ : ___ : ___ : ___ : ___ : ___	passive
___ out of style	___ : ___ : ___ : ___ : ___ : ___ : ___ : ___	in style
___ sad	___ : ___ : ___ : ___ : ___ : ___ : ___ : ___	joyful
___ good vocabulary	___ : ___ : ___ : ___ : ___ : ___ : ___ : ___	poor vocabulary
___ insensitive	___ : ___ : ___ : ___ : ___ : ___ : ___ : ___	sensitive
___ warm	___ : ___ : ___ : ___ : ___ : ___ : ___ : ___	cold, aloof
___ confident	___ : ___ : ___ : ___ : ___ : ___ : ___ : ___	unsure
___ clumsy	___ : ___ : ___ : ___ : ___ : ___ : ___ : ___	graceful
___ depressed	___ : ___ : ___ : ___ : ___ : ___ : ___ : ___	optimistic
___ read slowly	___ : ___ : ___ : ___ : ___ : ___ : ___ : ___	read fast
___ insincere	___ : ___ : ___ : ___ : ___ : ___ : ___ : ___	genuine
___ talk a lot	___ : ___ : ___ : ___ : ___ : ___ : ___ : ___	talk infrequently
___ independent	___ : ___ : ___ : ___ : ___ : ___ : ___ : ___	dependent
___ out of shape	___ : ___ : ___ : ___ : ___ : ___ : ___ : ___	in shape
___ helpee	___ : ___ : ___ : ___ : ___ : ___ : ___ : ___	helper
___ understand	___ : ___ : ___ : ___ : ___ : ___ : ___ : ___	don't understand
___ flexible	___ : ___ : ___ : ___ : ___ : ___ : ___ : ___	rigid
___ self-directed	___ : ___ : ___ : ___ : ___ : ___ : ___ : ___	other-directed
___ feminine	___ : ___ : ___ : ___ : ___ : ___ : ___ : ___	masculine
___ shakey	___ : ___ : ___ : ___ : ___ : ___ : ___ : ___	stable
___ write well	___ : ___ : ___ : ___ : ___ : ___ : ___ : ___	write poorly
___ specific	___ : ___ : ___ : ___ : ___ : ___ : ___ : ___	vague

---

Figure 7.1. Continued.

___

___ poor figure	___ : ___ : ___ : ___ : ___ : ___ : ___ : ___ good figure
___ loner	___ : ___ : ___ : ___ : ___ : ___ : ___ : ___ activity-oriented
___ poor researcher	___ : ___ : ___ : ___ : ___ : ___ : ___ : ___ good researcher
___ neutral	___ : ___ : ___ : ___ : ___ : ___ : ___ : ___ sexy
___ accept ideas	___ : ___ : ___ : ___ : ___ : ___ : ___ : ___ challenge ideas
___ listen well	___ : ___ : ___ : ___ : ___ : ___ : ___ : ___ listen poorly
___ verbal	___ : ___ : ___ : ___ : ___ : ___ : ___ : ___ non-verbal

Step 2

In the first part of the self-assessment process you have just completed, you indicated how you see yourself in terms of the series of descriptive scales on the preceding page. The second part of the process will consist of going back through each of the scales, and placing an "0" at the point on each scale you would like yourself to be.

IMPORTANT: (1) place your marks in the middle of the spaces, not on the boundaries. (2) Be sure you place an "0" on every line—*do not omit any.* (3) On a few scales, you may see yourself as being now where you would like to be. In that case, draw a circle around the "X" mark you entered on that line in the first place.

Step 3

When you have finished marking your "X"s and "0"s, look back over the descriptive scales, and pick out the four or five items which seem the most important to you in terms of your self growth. You should select those four or five descriptive items which, to you, seem to represent aspects of yourself on which you most want to work to change. Draw a line in the margin to the left of each of the items you feel are most important, and indicate on that line the *priority ranking* (1, 2, 3, 4, 5) you wish to assign to that concept, in terms of change.

For example:

___

___	1 (2, 3, etc.)	Fair	___ : X : ___ : ___ : ___ : ___ : O : ___	Unfair

___

Walters, 1975

170   *Group Counseling*

a group. Many of these administrative details, while somewhat time consuming, can pay benefits when the group actually begins. Many of these activities, which we term pre-group activities are covered in the chapter on getting a group started. Group member selection procedures, group composition, the use of structure in the group, formal operating rules and guidelines are examples of decisions that can be made prior to the group starting that will have an impact on the eventual success of the group (Corey & Corey, 1987).

We feel that the leader needs to have a reasonably good grasp of what constitutes normal group development and stages through which a group can be expected to progress. Developmental stages in process groups are discussed more thoroughly in the chapter on maintaining a group.

Silence

Silence at the beginning of a group is usually one of the most dreaded fantasies for the beginning group counselor. "What will I do if nobody wants to talk?" Probably a wise procedure is to understand that some periods of silence are to be expected at the beginning of the group. It represents a transition from the "outside" world and concerns to the work life of the group. It's frequently an opportunity for members to change gears and focus energy on the immediate surroundings. At the start of the initial group session the leader probably should not allow the group to sit for an extended period of time in silence. This simply adds to the group member's anxiety—unnecessarily. Since many group members will not know what to expect, they will respond to a prolonged period of silence with fear and sometimes anger. A much better procedure is for the group leader to help bridge that initial discomfort in a productive way while not sweeping the available anxiety totally under the rug. We never recommend that the leader provide any pseudo issue for the group to deal with such as shall we sit on the floor or in chairs. Decision making of that nature at the beginning of a group holds the potential to quickly polarize the members creating barriers that will later need to be overcome. Some more positive things that can be done include:

1. *Introducing a Discussion of Group Rules or Guidelines*

The leader will definitely want to reinforce the confidentiality aspects of the group. A good idea is to get a public concurrence with this rule. It begins to reassure members that they can disclose themselves in relative safety.

Other group guidelines also can be discussed if necessary. This has the advantage of providing content about which the group can verbalize. A goal of the leader would be to get as many members as possible involved verbally. Verbal involvement can signal commitment.

2. *Modeling Appropriate Self-disclosure*

Frequently, members are reluctant to begin to participate simply because they're not sure how to start or about what to talk. We have had a good deal of success with starting groups by sharing with members our own affective states at the particular time. A slight case of anticipation anxiety is usually something with which most members can identify and this disclosure frequently sets the tone for talking about one's feelings. Members tend to feel less isolated and unique and frequently will say "Yes I'm kind of nervous too. My stomach has butterflies—cause I don't know these people." This has the added benefit of usually eliciting empathic responses from some group members. Most usually, this kind of beginning is followed by one or several members coming forth with some problem or aspect of themselves that they are willing to share and work on.

3. *Using Some Low Threat Interpersonal Exercise*

These activities or techniques are frequently called "ice-breakers" and, used judiciously, can help ease the transition to group productivity, particularly for group members with little prior group experience. A number of these activities are available whose primary goal is to get members interacting with each other. Activities that focus on personality characteristics, attitudes, values, beliefs, and perceptions tend to be better than those that are content, topic, and data oriented. Exercises designed to work with first impressions tend to break the ice.

In the normal development of a group many first-time occurrences in the group can be termed critical incidences (Cohen & Smith, 1976). The manner in which the group leader handles the incident is important because group members are focusing their attention upon leader behavior. Initially, they prefer to see the leader as flawless.

Subgroups

What quickly becomes apparent in the initial stages of a group is that verbal participation will be unequal. Several of the more verbally powerful members may unconsciously form an alliance that excludes some of the more passive members. They can quickly monopolize group time as resentment builds among the less assertive members. Structured activities and in some cases a timer can be used to prevent this. As the group becomes more trusting and self-responsible, these issues can be dealt with directly in the group.

The leader will want to remain sensitive to the possibility of subgroups developing around verbal skill, personality dominance, value differences, attitude variances, etc. While some of this is inevitable in heterogeneous groups, allowed to simply run their course, splinter groups can be destructive to the group as a whole. Conflict within the group can be helpful and growth producing if the leader is prepared to deal with it openly and fairly. All participants should be encouraged to present their opinions and points of view. An atmosphere of respect can develop between all members when conflict and differences are viewed as natural and healthy and to be expected. The leader can model this behavior be demonstrating respect for all variances and serving as a mediator of conflict and differences.

Power Struggles

Power struggles will occur in the group just as they do in individual relationships. A certain amount of this can be considered natural. Just as in a family, members will jockey for position and a recognizable spot in the pecking order. In the normal course of things this issue is usually quickly resolved. The leader needs to guard against promoting this by equally sharing his/her time and attempting not to show favoritism. In a healthy group, the issue of power is shared and the group remains protean with expertise available as issues emerge. Only when a subgroup remains outside of the mainstream is group growth retarded. This requires direct intervention on the part of the leader if the total group is to be salvaged. Further growth and cohesiveness is impossible if competitive subgroups are allowed to function.

Group Cohesiveness

Cohesiveness in a counseling group refers to the feeling of togetherness experienced by some groups. It is frequently talked about as the "glue" of a group—that difficult to define quality that results from an overall interpersonal attractiveness. In a constructive sense it is related to the chemistry of a group and the overall good, supportive, and respectful attitudes that members have for each other and the group as a whole. Cohesiveness is evidenced when members begin to assign some priority to the group experience, value and equality to other members, a willingness to give as well as to receive, and a certain "we-ness" that can be exclusive of persons not in the group.

While this cohesiveness is a desirable group goal because of its benefits to members in terms of support, what is also possible is for some groups to unconsciously unite and become "too cohesive." This is a difficult process problem for the leader because the underlying motivation is usually anxiety or fear of disclosing, perceived loss of control, and lack of trust in the leader, the group, or the process. Groups like this can become "cousin" groups where what occurs is a lot of rescuing of individual members, denial of problems and conflict, and circular and superficial talk.

Probably the most effective leader intervention is to gently point out the problem and help the group to re-examine their goals and confront their anxieties. Leaders need to guard against becoming personally frustrated when the group refuses to move. All the leader can do is create the conditions for growth. He/she cannot force a group to grow. Taking too much responsibility for the progress of the group is a frequent trap for inexperienced leaders. If all else fails and the group seems committed to staying in one place, the idea of dissolution is a possibility. No guarantee can be given that every collection of individuals will become an effective group.

Resistance in the Group

Most group leaders will encounter resistance in the group at one time or another. Groups will sometimes "agree" at an unconscious level to stand pat or resist moving toward more intense interpersonal levels. This can occur with individuals in the group or among several group members simultaneously. Behaviorally, this is often reflected by group members becoming less verbally involved by returning to relatively superficial issues and then exhausting the subject matter.

Group leaders need to look at their own feelings when a group becomes resistant. Leaders who have unrealistically high expectations for the group can become frustrated with the lack of progress and thereby lose objectivity. A point to remember is that some resistance can be expected in most groups at some time. If leaders are aware of this, they will be less inclined to personalize the resistance and accept too much responsibility for the group.

Remember that resistance typically is related to issues of trust and security. When several individuals are reluctant to take risks in self-disclosure and interpersonal encounter, usually an issue of lack of trust is at the base. Trying new and risky behaviors in the group can put members in touch with their basic feelings of insecurity. "If I disclose my most closely guarded secrets, who will be there to nurture and care for me? Will I still be acceptable to these people if they know what I'm really like? Can I trust these people to care for my personal issues in a gentle and caring way?"

The most effective strategies involve leaders sharing their own immediate observations as to behavior and causation. "The groups seems to be stuck on content issues at this point. I wonder if this means that we're feeling somewhat insecure and a little scared to move toward more honest confrontation—and maybe intimacy?"

Dr. Max Hines (1987) of the University of Wisconsin at Stout recently suggested some success with a very silent and non-contributing member. He might say: "I'm impressed with your ability to quietly internalize and process so much verbal material from the other members of the group and to maintain an unemotional and objective distance."

Whatever the intervention choice is, remember that some resistance is natural and that issues of security and trust are usually the cause. When group members have an opportunity to deal with their individual and collective feelings of doubt and mistrust, the opportunity will exist for a quantum leap in group development. Some of the most powerful opportunities for group progress can grow out of what is initially perceived as resistance.

PROBLEMS ENCOUNTERED
WITH GROUP MEMBERS

Control and Controlling

When the group leader bumps up against various individual member styles and resistances, it can almost invariably be assumed that the issues are related to group members needs for personal control and, by extension, a need to control the situation. Our experience has taught us that members who have a high need for situational control typically feel threatened and anxious about exploring their personal issues too carefully for fear that they will "lose control of self" and be overwhelmed by feelings of insecurity and worthlessness. Fear of the unknown or of ambiguous, unstructured, and confusing situations pose a real threat to these individuals.

Our observation has been that members will call upon their basic personality orientation in attempts to bring order and understanding to these perceived fearful situations in the group. Much of the behavior that might be viewed objectively as rigid and/or resistant seems to occur outside of all conscious awareness of the controlling or controlled member. Within this framework, controlling behavior can be viewed as purposeful, although in many cases extreme and maladaptive, attempt on the part of a member or members to bring reason, stability, and comfort to an unsettling situation.

Naturally, at the deepest intrapsychic levels, needs for control can be viewed as core personality issues that are related to trust in oneself and others. Vague and sometimes highly specific fears need to be treated gently and with much of the reassurance and support that was probably missing in the person's life at an early and impressionable developmental stage. No quick fixes exist for a person's resistance to vulnerability and trust. Empathy and gentle compassion coupled with focus on the behavior tends to lessen the anxiety.

We also have found that a useful procedure is to briefly explain to group members that all normal human beings seek a certain measure of personal control and when monitored and kept within non-neurotic boundaries, the control is useful and is related to a powerful sense of self. The polar opposite or extreme would be "out of control" and the implication of impotence, helplessness, and total dependence. Nobody wants to experience those feelings. Within this general framework of control, we can proceed to a discussion of the various individual members' styles or roles that surface in the group as an attempt to maintain intra-psychic homeostasis. In general, these members' behaviors center around avoidant behaviors, dependent behaviors, aggressive, and/or power behaviors.

Avoidance

Avoiding the encounter with others and self is considered by some group leaders to be among the most difficult member behaviors to impact constructively. The member who uses some form of avoidance is choosing an isolated position in the group and can quickly become a frustration to other group members. Behaviors associated with avoidance can range on a continuum from absence from the group to somewhat more active avoidances such as the pollyanna or naive role. Of course, a member who is habitually *absent* from the group becomes an overt management problem for the leader. Some members will attend a session, sometimes becoming the focus of attention, only to go AWOL for the next three meetings. Naturally, the leader needs to intervene with this behavior and discuss the implications of this "hit and run" behavior for the member and for the group as a whole. Generally, if a member cannot make a concrete commitment to regular attendance, they need to consider exit from the group.

Withdrawal

Distancing behavior in the group begins with the habitually silent member. This extreme form of continual reluctance to participate verbally can set the member up either as a "group project" or as a scapegoat—depending upon the member's overall attractiveness to the group. Either outcome has serious implications for the group. The group might unconsciously join the silent member in offering inappropriate advice and reassurances in order to enlist the member's participation. A person with a low level of attractiveness might become the target of group discontent and even hostility. The group leader needs to heed warning signs that a member is withdrawing by focusing on the behavior and helping the member to risk and develop trust in the process.

A chronically *withdrawn* member might be depressed and the group leader may well suspect depression with any member who is choosing avoidance as a coping mechanism. Social withdrawal is a common symptom of depression and coupled with other observable signs such as crying spells, depressed facial expressions, and lack of animation needs to be checked out by the group leader. Psychological indicators of depression include feelings of worthlessness and guilt, anxiety, and loss of energy. Physical signals associated with depressive states might be an increase in sleep disturbances, changes in appetites, and sexual interest.

The leader must suspect depressive states with any of the avoidance behaviors as they may be early indicators of suicidal intentions. When depression is suspected, the group leader needs to consult with a psychiatrist or the member's family physician as some form of pharmacotherapy may be indicated as an adjunct to psychotherapy—particularly with mild depressions.

Alienation

The *alienated* member may couple his/her withdrawal with active faultfinding and negative assertions in the group. This type behavior, while disconcerting to some members, is actually easier to deal with because the person at least gives some responsiveness to current events. The anger base from which alienated members often come can be linked to early experiences as a way of helping the individual open up and trust.

Naivete

Finally, avoidant behavior is sometimes manifested by *naive* or *pollyanna* type personalities. While they are somewhat related, the naive member may truly lack some essential life problem-solving skills. This is one of the few group member types that can in some instances truly profit from concrete and specific advice from other helping members. Since their experience base is typically limited, other group members can help increase the naive members awareness by sharing their own experiences and ideas. Sometimes group members will share specific verbatim sentences for the naive member to use! When the sentences work, and they often do, and the naive member begins to perceive constructive changes in his or her environment, a change in attitude or perspective often trails along. Naive members typically need a lot of encouragement and reassurance.

Pollyanna

The *pollyanna* has become convinced that the world is Disneyland with a perpetual silver lining. This is an active denial of all things unpleasant—the "rose colored glasses" syndrome. This behavior in group is most often observed in response to another member's problems where the indication is to gloss over and deny pain. The skillful group leader will spend some time instructing the polyanna member, and others in the group, of the benefits of experiencing the fullness of an event. Frequently out of pain, grief, and hurt is when we stretch and grow most.

Dependency

The next major group of resistances center around *dependence* issues. Once again, the seeds of dependent personalities were probably planted early in a person's history. Overly socialized or compliant personalities often label themselves as people-pleasers when they become aware of the motivation for their behavior. In general, this personality type is quite responsive to their environment and "sensitive" to others. They often are perceived as warm and nurturing, as accepting and non-judgmental, and as people who listen well. Nice to be around, if not exciting, they often elevate others at the expense of their own denied wishes and desires. Acutely sensitive to power in relationships they sometimes go to extreme lengths to avoid conflict and the arousal of displeasure in others.

Harmonizer

The *harmonizer* is one example of the dependent type. He or she will tend to gloss over potential growth producing conflict in the group by distracting and changing subjects. Cooperative to a fault the harmonizer will seek to avoid confrontation with his or her own fears by attempting to create an atmosphere free of tension in the group. Closely akin to the harmonizer is the coordinator.

Coordinator

The *coordinator* often takes harmonizing a step further and serves as the unofficial group coordinator. This is a more active defense and frequently involves "doing" things for the group and the members. The coordinator may volunteer for any number of tasks large and small in an attempt to ingratiate the other members.

Group Clown

The *group clown* shares some of these same needs but is also somewhat more exhibitionistic in pleasing others. When handled appropriately, the person with the great sense of humor can provide tension release and opportunities for therapeutic laughter in the group. Laughing, particularly at oneself and our own foibles and mistakes can disfuse some of the deadly seriousness with which we approach our problems. Laughter and humor are signs of a healthy person and are an excellent way to share our humanness with each other.

The flip side is when the clowning is out-of-context or inappropriate. While laughing and depression are incompatible responses, to think that we can laugh our troubles away is to be very naive. Laughter can provide perspective. When the clown uses jokes and silliness at the expense of a true and meaningful encounter, it has the potential to interfere with group progress. The clown needs to be reassured that he or she is O.K. and that they have a secure, stable, and valuable place in the group. The person needs to understand and internally recognize that winning the clown spot each week is not necessary.

Rescuer

Rescuers are probably guilty of projection in the group. When sensing the onset of conflict or discomfort for a particular member the rescuer will often rush in to "save" the person who is perceived to be in the hot seat. Rescues can often be marked as subtle helping so the leader needs to be alert to this phenomenon. A gentle intervention that confronts the behavior respectfully but directly not only helps the rescuer but also the person being rescued. Everyone gets to be an adult and take care of self. Much rescuing behavior happens outside of the rescuer's conscious awareness so the problem is sometimes difficult to manage. Several "reminders" may be needed from the group leader.

Problem Solver

Problem solvers also can pose a unique management situation in the group. People with this orientation are usually quite convinced that they have many helpful suggestions to remedy a person's problem. Persistent advice and problem solving suggestions are most often offered from a "common sense" experiential base, are highly specific, and frequently ignore many of the intra-psychic subleties. This type of helping often comes from persons who have made their way themselves and have an abundance of ego strength. The often cannot understand why another person doesn't "just do it"! They tend to be cognitively oriented and action directed and have a hard time relating to people who experience ambivalence. Subtle interventions typically don't work very well.

Strokes for listening well, attending, and supporting other members will sometimes get the desired behavior as the problem solver gains an appreciation for some of life's complexities.

Poor Me

The *"poor me"* member has become accustomed to staying in self-pity, helplessness, and despair. They seemingly gain a good deal of personal control and power by having a lot of group attention focused on their problems. Members with co-dependent issues and "victim" personalities often fit this picture. Similar in style to naive members, the "poor me" person seems much more invested in maintaining, albeit at unconscious levels, a one-down life position. In relationships they are almost invariably clinging and overly dependent upon the other person for their own feelings of self-worth. They sometimes seem capable of enduring endless abuse.

This member needs enormous reinforcement and affirmation of OKness in order to counter-balance what is probably a lifetime full of diminished self-esteem. Naturally, this is a slow and patient process that hopefully will culminate in increased self-trust.

Compulsive Talker

Compulsive talkers present a somewhat unique problem for the group leader because, unmonitored, their behavior can become overly intrusive in the group. Also because many members feel somewhat impotent in the face of rapid fire verbals, the talker may set himself/herself up to become the group scapegoat—or at least a poorly favored member. We sometimes suspect the talker of having an unconscious fear of death. In many instances, not all, compulsive talkers have a need to affirm their existence by hearing the sound of their own voice. This phenomenon usually has its roots in early developmental experiences so awareness is usually deeply hidden. Talking can be a compensation for feelings of inferiority. "If I can talk and command attention I must be important." This behavior needs to be confronted gently but firmly. Ignoring it can have detrimental effects on the group. Inferiority feelings in the compulsive talker are often linked to self-perceived intellectual deficiencies and sometimes are coupled with perfectionism, particularly in school matters and academic achievement in general. The person is usually well-read and possesses a breath of information.

The final major group of resistances have to do with issues of *aggression* and *power.*

Manipulator

This final category of individual member roles or styles distinguish themselves from the others and are grouped together because they tend to be more *active* resistances in the group. A person in this group could be labeled a *manipulator.* This person will tend to seek control in the group in order to accomplish his/her own internal agenda. Two general types of manipulative personalities are recognizable. The first one is relatively benign but still can have an impact on the group. Type 1, we sometimes refer to as the "Music Man." Such a person frequently is relatively transparent in his/her needs for group control, may use clowning and a highly developed sense of humor, and is most often quite charming and attractive. These people have highly developed social skills, are accustomed to pleasing other people, and have almost a desperate need for approval. Their behavior is often designed to seek leader approval as the group's "favorite son/daughter." This person, with gentle persuasion, will often recognize this behavior and contract to give it up.

Type 2 manipulators are much more difficult to deal with and in some ways are not good candidates for group intervention. Their needs for power, control, and dominance are usually much more repressed and unconscious. This, coupled with a diminished level of social interest and underlying wounds that surface in anger, frequently results in group behavior that is emotionally detached and even hostile. These members often will be suspicious of nurturant and caring behavior in the group and not trust it because no history of that exists in their experiences. They view the world as a place that is unfriendly and to be guarded against so that supportive behaviors in the group tend to be mistrusted.

The double bind this member puts on the group is that when group members become frustrated and begin to match the Type 2 behavior with detachment and/or overt disapproval, the manipulator can then view the groups behavior as further evidence that the world is "out to get him/her" and had better protect self.

Clearly, behavior that is rooted this deeply in a history of deprived significant relationships will not yield to quick or temporary fixes. This person will probably require on-going therapy. The leader needs to be at once gentle but firm. Interestingly, once this type personality is *enlisted* in the therapeutic process, and that is a key variable, they often become excellent group members. An important point is that they view the group leader as a strong and competent person.

Intellectualizers: Super-helpers and Special Interest Pleaders

These intellectual types are similar in their in-group behavior in that they rely heavily upon their cognitive abilities to seize and maintain control in the group. **Helpers** are usually well read in popular psychology and gain a certain amount of group attention by offering their interpretations of others' behaviors and problems. This can be seductive in the group because sometimes they can be very accurate and helpful. Most frequently, however, their interpretations only address part of the problem or are offered too quickly and at the expense of other group members' exploration. Again, they tend to be intellectual solutions based on the assumption that knowledge and information will surely change behavior. Reinforcing helpful suggestions and actively interfering with those that are not helpful seems the most appropriate leader intervention.

The **special interest pleader** is typically locked into a highly focused frame of reference that makes it difficult for him/her to see a large and complex picture. Whatever the special interest, the pleader has typically discovered "the truth" and is so involved in it that he/she will have an almost compulsive need to share experiences and ideas with others so that they too might have "the truth." We have seen this particular orientation surface in group members around religious and spiritual issues, drug and substance use, various kinds of intensive and excludatory "group" experiences, and over exercise and diet regimes. The pleader is typically a recent convert to the cause and is practically obsessive in his/her interest.

In the early stages of the group the leader needs to be accepting of the individual's point of view while also limiting long discourses on any special topics. Interventions need to be fairly direct because those with highly focused special interests often do not perceive and respond to normal social cues that group members might offer.

Attacker

The final difficult member can be labeled an *attacker*. This can often be the most frightening member for the inexperienced group leader because the grab for power is frequently very direct, aggressive, and even hostile. Since this person has probably never felt included, the group pressure to conform to social standards will often elicit responses that are rebellious and challenging. In effect, a resistance to becoming a part of the group. This grows out of a fear of being overwhelmed and incorporated with a loss of individuality and independence.

Attackers almost always stimulate and energize the group. Because of their assertive demands, they help other, more reticent, members of the group get in touch with their own feelings about conflict and self-assertion. Consequently, reframes can accomplish two goals. This first is to reassure the attacker that his place is assured and that boundaries will be respected. The second is to demonstrate to the group that differences in behavioral styles are acceptable and can add to the richness of the group. As an example, "Thank you for pointing that out. We can always count on your honesty and directness in this group."

Once the attacker has attached him or herself to the group therapy process, the leader will want to help investigate the underlying causes of the behavior which results in putting people off or keeping them at a distance.

A final caution with attackers. When the issue under attack has to do with content or depersonalized ideas, it can simply be an annoyance or perhaps an inhibitor to progress. If the attack is directed at a person and is abusive in nature, the group leader needs to take direct action in stopping the behavior. Abusive behavior should not be permitted in groups any more than it should in families or other social collections. For instance, "John, I appreciate your courage in confronting Mike with your feelings. It's clear that you have a lot of investment in this issue. At the same time, you'll need to find more appropriate ways to express your disagreement—your words feel abusive to me and that won't go in here."

Resistance

Kottler (1983) proposed 15 reasons why a group member might be resistant. They bear summarizing here as they can assist the group leader in being objective about perceived resistances.

1. The client doesn't want to be in the group in the first place but is only attending to satisfy the demands of someone else.

2. Resistance is frequently an adjustment reaction to a novel situation. Therapeutic groups are strange places to the uninitiated. Only a fool would take the apparent concern, empathy, and safety at face value until phenomenological confirmations are experienced.

3. Under pressure to conform to group norms, all but the very meek feel the need to flex their individuality. Resistance thus can be an expression of rebellious-ness, and unwillingness to be grouped as a part of the whole.

4. Much client anxiety may be centered on negative expectations of what the group experience might offer.

5. The unusual and flexible leadership style of most group therapists presents a confusing image to clients at first. Authoritarian, democratic, and laissez-faire behaviors might all be in evidence within a single hour. The leader is definitely an authority figure to group members, but a very unconventional authority nevertheless. However warm and caring, the thera-pist's actions still represent "the powers that be" to anyone who doesn't have power. Resistance can therefore be a testing of limits to carve out pecking-order roles. If ever a place existed to challenge authority by resisting compliance to expectations, a therapeutic group is the ideal.

6. People have social fears of groups. This fear of being judged by others and of interacting in groups sparks

a lot of resistance in those who want to speak up but feel they can't perform adequately in front of their peers.

7. A corollary of the social-fear motive is resistance due to a fear of failure. Persons who are used to feeling totally successful in their chosen profession and peer groups feel out of their element in a therapeutic group. They expend every ounce of energy trying to make themselves look good and logically spurn any opportunity that involves the spontaneous or unpredictable, where perfect competence isn't guaranteed on the first trial.

8. The Great Unknown makes people think twice before they leap. Some group members become very slippery to avoid having to take risks. They will work on self-awareness or insight, but when the time comes to apply new knowledge in the real world, they find their courage has left town without them.

9. Resistance can be a sign of someone who enjoys manipulating others. It is, after all, an attention-getting ploy that evokes emotional responses in other members and even in the leader. The resistant client who can stop leader actions dead in their tracks collects laurels of pity from others, and at the same time feels like a poor victim who can't help the situation.

10. Every group member has formulated preferences for how she/he prefers all other participants to be and to act. When they don't cooperate according to the plan, resistance can be used as a way to punish offenders.

11. Resistance also can be an act of jealousy to sabotage forward motion. Every time a group member makes significant life changes, he/she helps other clients to feel more dissatisfied with their inertia. A client then can refuse to cooperate with group proceedings knowing that by resisting he/she no longer has to feel threatened by the rules the productive members are following.

12. The expression of ambivalence is not only evident in sabotaging other clients' progress in the group but is strongly reflected in one's own attitudes toward changing: "I want to be different from what I am, but I don't really want to handle the consequences of this growth—having to be responsible for my life."

13. A group member experimenting with new behaviors experiences a frustration similar to that of an infant trying to practice turning over. Like the infant, who will pout and fight after a desperate effort, the client will resist "handling" when his or her patience is worn thin. What looks so easy for the leader to do is impossible for the client to feel comfortable imitating. Resistance in this case acts as a warning to the therapist to back off until the client's energy supplies are replenished for a counterattack.

14. Resistance also is used as a pacing mechanism to stall for time. In the language of physics, resistance is the drag that slows down the force of movement. When change accelerates too quickly, the human mind will attempt to decelerate progress to more comfortable levels that allow breathing space.

15. Finally, resistance can be a strategy of personality style. Some folks take pleasure in resisting anything because it is intrinsically satisfying for them to participate in conflict. They love the challenge of argument and controversy and will switch sides fluently, depending on which point of view offers the best opportunity for antagonism. Such persons resist because they are strong-willed enough to appreciate the stimulation that comes from locking horns with a powerful adversary. (Kottler, 1983)

SUMMARY

This chapter begins by looking at general characteristics of the group leader and proceeds to methods of assessing the strengths and weaknesses of group members. A Self-

Assessment Scale is presented that allows group members to share their own perceptions of self in the physical, emotional, and intellectual areas of functioning. After a brief summary of pre-group preparations and minimal member expectations, the focus is upon common problems encountered in normal group process. Subgrouping and power struggles are discussed and a sample handout that covers the basic procedural group guidelines is presented.

The concept of group cohesiveness is covered along with a general introduction to resistances in the group. Specific problem group member roles are addressed as they relate to a member's basic personality.

REFERENCES

Cohen, A.M., & Smith, R.C. (1976). *The critical incident in growth groups.* LaJolla, CA: University Associates.

Corey, M.S., & Corey, G. (1987). *Groups: Process and practice (3rd ed.).* Monterey, CA: Brooks/Cole.

Egan, G. (1982). *The skilled helper (2nd ed.).* Monterey, CA: Brooks/Cole.

Hines, M. (1987, March). *Group work with resistant clients.* Paper presented at the annual meeting of the American Association for Counseling and Development, Chicago, IL.

Kottler, J.A. (1983). *Pragmatic group leadership.* Monterey, CA: Brooks/Cole.

Walters, R.H. (1975). *A factor analytic study of the EPIC self-assessment scales.* Unpublished doctoral dissertation, North Texas State University, Denton.

SUGGESTED READING

Kottler, J.A. (1983). *Pragmatic group leadership.* Monterey, CA: Brooks/Cole.

"Because spoken language is the chief medium through which group work occurs, a leader's expertise depends in large measure on how language is employed. It befits the group worker to become a psycholinguist, a semanticist, a student of what is linguistically current as well as of what idioms are peculiar to various ethnic and age groups."

In Part II of his practical and helpful book, Kottler looked at some of the dimensions of group leadership. In addition to exploring the power of language in groups, he addressed the issues of therapeutic modeling and critical incidents and predictable problems. He also devoted a chapter to diagnosis and the functions of labeling.

CHAPTER **8**

TYPICAL ISSUES IN GROUP COUNSELING

In the previous chapter, we discussed many of the specific problems which often develop in the group counseling process. In this chapter, we focus on broad issues which we have found to be typical in working with most groups. How counselors respond to these issues can significantly affect the interaction of the group and thus the group process. Many group counselors remain firmly entrenched in their adherence to the traditional scheduling of once-a-week group sessions. Is their stance on this issue based on an explainable rationale? Is such scheduling for the convenience of the counselor or for the therapeutic enhancement of the group? Another issue with which beginning group counselors must deal is the question of extent and degree of structuring to be utilized. What is the counselor's attitude about structuring? To what extent can structure contribute to the development of interaction in groups. Must the approach to the issue of structure be all or none? An equally perplexing issue for the inexperienced group counselor is how to respond to silences which often occur in counseling groups. Typically periods of silence are viewed as nonproductive. Is it possible that silence is a natural and dynamic part of the interactional process in groups? Although individual member contracts for behavioral change have been used for some time in counseling, whether or not to utilize contracting is still an issue because this procedure has been largely misunderstood. Could contracting for behavioral change contribute in some way to group cohesiveness? These issues are discussed in this chapter.

VARIED TIME

Frank's (1944) summary statements about adolescents and the situation surrounding them seem to be as appropriate today as when written over forty years ago.

> Reports from schools and other sources indicate clearly that restlessness, turbulence and emotional instability are increasing among adolescents everywhere. There are evidences of increasing hostility toward adult authority, of insolence and even of open defiance. (Frank, 1944, p. 34)

> It must be admitted that our procedures in dealing with youth frequently aggravate their difficulties and intensify their deviations and defeats. It sometimes seems as if the schools on the one hand and the family on the other were determined to frustrate adolescents . . . . (Frank, 1944, p. 34)

The fact that this description so aptly fits adolescents in our society today would seem to strongly suggest we still are not meeting their needs.

Gazda (1989) described group counseling as important for all individuals and not just those few who may have adjustment, emotional, or social problems. Everyone has problems. Therefore, group counseling should be for all adolescents not just the "problem cases." Why must we wait until a young person or others have been "labeled" as having a "problem" before group counseling is made available? And then why should help be provided only once a week?

Counseling programs must seek to prevent problems from growing beyond the point where the individual requires special help to deal adequately with them.

Although the unique values of group counseling are generally accepted, a basic question remains involving the effect of the span of time over which group counseling sessions are spread. As in the case of the early history of group counseling, are we to continue our present practice of spacing group counseling sessions one week apart because it has often proved expedient to do so? Perhaps equally effective results could be achieved with other sequencing of sessions.

In striving to extend and intensify the effectiveness of group counseling in an effort to satisfy the counseling needs of all individuals, traditional concepts and scheduling based on counselor convenience must be reexamined. Counselors should determine the effect of varying the amount of time between group counseling sessions in order to further our knowledge of which group activities and procedures best promote the effectiveness of group counseling. Are the most effective results obtained from group counseling sessions meeting the usual once a week? Does the duration or span of time over which group counseling sessions are spread affect the desired results of group counseling? Obviously, five hours in one week, five hours in five weeks, and five hours scattered across a year's time are not equivalents and thus are a factor in outcome.

Although a lack of correlated research in this area exists, several studies, deviating from the traditional one session per week, have reported favorable results. Hobbs (1951); Pine, Gardner, and Tippett (1958); Broedel, Ohlsen, Proff, and Southard (1960); and Gazda (1959) have reported successful results with groups meeting twice a week. Landreth (1966) found groups meeting twice a week and every day to be as effective as groups meeting once a week. Koeppe (1961) investigated the effect of one full day of group counseling and concluded that the sessions were effective. Bach (1966) and Stoller (1968) have reported success with group sessions that last from thirty to forty-eight hours without a major break.

Seemingly, breaking away from the "lock-step" pattern of one session per week has proved beneficial. If ten sessions of group counseling over a two-week period could achieve results similar to that of ten sessions in ten weeks, then an individual or group might be better adjusted and more productive eight weeks sooner. The criterion for selection of the group counseling sequence desired should be based on the needs of group members. Group counseling sessions need not be scheduled on a weekly basis simply because tradition dictates.

STRUCTURING

Probably the chief concern of the beginning group counselor is, How do I start the first session? What should I say? What will we talk about? Should I offer the group a topic to discuss? What group techniques can I use? These are questions counselors often ask themselves again and again as that first group counseling session draws near.

Most experienced group counselors have discovered that the question of how to structure the first session, and succeeding sessions as well, is more of a concern to the counselor than to the members. Such questions also suggest the counselor may be accepting too much responsibility for the group and thus depriving members of the opportunity to struggle with the responsibility of creating a group in which they are willing to invest themselves in the process of exploring what is of primary concern to each member. This is not to suggest however that complete absence of structure must or should exist.

Counselors often avoid what they perceive to be structuring in order to adhere to a particular counseling approach. What is frequently overlooked is the fact that some structuring is evident in all groups. When the counselor explains to the group what group counseling is, he or she is structuring. The topic of discussion in group counseling also is structured to an extent, in that most group counselors are more likely to respond to the feelings they sense in members rather than the expressed verbal content. Likewise, determining when the group will meet, what general topics will be discussed, the importance of keeping confidences, and the setting of limits when necessary are all examples of structuring found in most groups. Appropriate structuring can be facilitative to a group; overstructuring, whereby the counselor becomes the teacher, or adherence to rigid rules can interfere with the therapeutic developmental process inherent in groups. Recognition, therefore, that some degree of structuring exists in all groups results in a shift of focus. The question becomes not whether to structure, but how to select the kind of structuring that will be most appropriate to the group.

One position on structuring is that greater responsibility for self, a goal of most group counseling experiences, can be facilitated by allowing group members to contend with previous questions and to make some decisions for themselves. Another position on structuring is that some groups may not be ready to assume such complete responsibility. Possibly the members may need some assistance in learning how to work together and to conduct productive group discussions if they have had no previous group counseling experience or have not been exposed to small group discussions in other settings such as their classrooms. For example students do not immediately become effective group members simply because they are placed in a counseling group. Some structuring, therefore, may be helpful in the initial session. Structuring does not necessarily imply a "take-over" role for the counselor. Structuring may be helpful in assisting the group to get started in those typically awkward first few minutes of the initial session. In addition, structuring also may help the counselor to approach the experience with more self-confidence, which is a prerequisite to the development of a cohesive group. High anxiety levels on the part of the counselor often contribute directly to the dysfunctioning of a group. This is especially true of groups where the counselor is reluctant to confront and reveal his/her own anxiety to the group. Failure to do so may be perceived by members as the counselor saying to the group, "In here we don't talk about feelings." That is structuring the relationship whether or not the counselor intended to do so.

Structuring For Members

The initial structuring in the first session might go something like the following excerpt from a school counselor's comments during the first few minutes of a new group:

> Well, everyone is here so we can get started. We all know each other, and we all know why we're here. Each one of you is concerned about your progress in school. Your grades aren't what you would like them to be, and you decided to come to this group because you want to work on that problem. There may be other problems or concerns we all share or that you feel the group can help you with. If there are, it is your responsibility to let us know about what you are concerned. It is our responsibility to work together to help each other and ourselves find out some of the reasons for the difficulty, and what we can do.

> We'll be meeting in this room every Tuesday at this time for the next ten weeks. While we're together in this group, you can say anything you want. Whatever is said is just for us and is not to be told to anyone outside the group. I will not talk to your teachers, parents, or the principal or anyone about what goes on here. I'm here to work with you. I don't have a lot of answers to give you, but together perhaps we can work something out that will be helpful to all of us.

At least three alternatives exist at this point in the process of structuring:

1. The counselor may ask, "How do you feel about talking about yourself in this group?"

2. The counselor may ask, "Is there anything else we need to get cleared up or does anyone have a question?" and then move on to the first question; or

3. The counselor could say, "Other groups have found it helpful to go around the circle and have each person tell the group about what they are concerned, and how they think the group can help. Who would like to begin?"

Additional structuring might be helpful to some counselors and some groups in assisting the group to learn how to work together effectively.

Counselor Self-Structuring

The beginning group counselor might find some self-structuring such as the following reminders helpful in his/her efforts to facilitate group interaction.

1. Be patient. Wait for responses to questions. Members need time to think about what they want to say.

2. Help members to interact with each other by clarifying similarities and differences in what members are saying.

3. If a member or several members seem to be confused, ask another member of the group to summarize what he/she thinks the speaker has been saying.

4. Recognize that you, as the counselor, are not the authority. You don't have all the "right" answers. Help members to respond to each other. "Mark, you're talking to Ruth, but you're looking at me. Can you tell her?"

5. Avoid being the answer source. If the counselor is asked for an opinion, refer the question to the whole group by saying, "What do the rest of you think?"

6. Determine who is doing the most talking. If it is the counselor, he/she may be trying too hard to teach everyone something.

7. Try to determine what the central theme of the discussion is and respond to that.

8. Pull things together for the group by verbally linking what one member says with what another member has said if it seems to fit or be related.

9. Listen to the feeling tones behind the words and respond to this inner depth rather than just to the words you hear.

If the counselor attempts to jump the group ahead in order to avoid the initial process of struggling together, the group may never feel safe enough with each other to relate the awkward and confused feelings many members experience. The experience of struggling together provides a degree of equality among members in that each member comes to realize that he/she is not the only one experiencing butterflies in the pit of his/her stomach, a pounding heart that he/she is sure everyone can hear, or the magnetic pull of the floor that has his/her eyes riveted to one spot. Individuals want to look up at the other faces but cannot. Something will not let them. For the counselor to remain completely inactive at this point would seem to provide an absence of structure but may in fact be structuring to such an extent as to be perceived by members as an indication that such feelings are inappropriate. Responding to such feelings however conveys to the group that this is a place where talking about self and feelings is acceptable. Such a move on the part of the counselor also says to the group, "I'm a person who is sensitive to what you feel, and I'm willing to face those feelings openly with you." For most members this kind of structuring is a profound experience: "Hey, she really hears me."

The kind of structuring discussed here allows a great deal of freedom and permissiveness within the group and at the same time provides a framework within which the group can begin to function. If structuring is handled properly, a facilitative relationship will be established which provides the freedom and security necessary for growth-promoting self-exploration.

Structure as a Freeing Agent

Although structuring in group guidance and group counseling is usually thought of as an aid to the group, benefits to the counselor should not be overlooked. Many counselors are hesitant to attempt group work because they may have little specific training in utilizing a group approach. Even those with some training may still be unsure of just how to approach the group or what they should do first. Leader anxiety resulting from unsureness about how to facilitate the group or how members will function is easily detected by most group members. Consequently, they may be reluctant to become involved in the group because "Even the leader feels this whole thing is a bit shaky." When the counselor feels unsure, members usually don't feel safe.

The counselor's own feelings about self and the group have a definite impact on the functioning of the group. What is needed by many counselors is structure which provides a framework within which they can feel more sure of themselves and the group. The addition of structure, therefore, can free the counselor to utilize his/her skills more efficiently while gaining the necessary experience to function more effectively.

Too often groups flounder because the counselor assumes members are knowledgeable about group dynamics and process. In reality, the majority of individuals, especially school age youngsters, may indeed know very little, if anything, about the skills necessary to function as an effective and contributing member of a group. Structuring, especially in the early stages of the group, can help members to learn how to be effective group contributors. As the sessions progress and members become more skillful, less structuring will be needed.

Structure provides direction, concreteness and security, both for the leader and the members, and thus can be a source of maturation and growth in a group situation. Highly structured techniques tend to provide both the group leader and group members maximal amounts of direction and security with the possible consequence of a reduction in personal responsibility. Such structuring techniques typically rely primarily upon structuring by verbal means utilizing a predetermined sequence of questions or instructions. Accompanying pictures or puppets may be utilized in some highly structured approaches.

Moderately structured techniques tend to provide less specific direction and rely upon the group leader and group members to establish some degree of direction related to the initial focus of the structure. Consequently, a higher degree of personal responsibility is required. The vehicle for structuring the focus is usually a combination of some form of media presentation and open-end verbal responses that organize the focus of the group topically, but still allow a wide range of member responses. Structure typically helps group members move from a discussion of what happened there and then to an exploration of self in similar situations here and now.

A limited structure approach allows group members to originate the topic of focus and is assisted by the specific verbal and non-verbal activity of the counselor. Although structuring by counselors is often based on verbal activity, in a school setting non-verbal structuring through the use of carefully selected media materials including pictures, film-strips, films, and transparencies that promote visual stimulation may be at least as helpful, if not more so, than verbal structuring.

Structure can promote group cohesion as members more quickly begin to interact and focus on common problems. A significant benefit is that the frustration of not knowing what is expected can be largely avoided.

Limitations of Structuring

Structuring may initially prevent group members from experiencing the responsibility of determining what content will be important in the group. Also, experientially learning how to cope with the anxiety and frustration of ambiguous situations is precluded. An additional concern is that the introduction of new topics or areas of focus for each meeting, as is recommended when strictly following some structural programs, may break the continuity of the discussions from meeting to meeting or prevent group members from introducing their own immediate concerns. However, our experience has been that group members, regardless of initial structuring, will move quickly to assert their own needs for determining purpose and what is to be discussed. This usually occurs with three to five sessions, and seems largely a result of group members having learned how to function together which in turn promotes a feeling of self confidence and trust in the group. Therefore, it is essential that the group facilitator be sensitive to the group's movement away from the structured focus and remain open as the group explores areas of spontaneous concern.

Kinds of Structuring

The following is a brief discussion of some of the kinds of pre-packaged structured activities available for use with school age children at various levels. No attempt has been made to be all inclusive, but rather the materials discussed are used as illustrations of the types of activities available to counselors. In general, they progress from highly structured to less structured in an attempt to adjust materials to the developmental level of the group members.

Guidance Vistas Audiotapes, for elementary through high school students, are an example of a highly structured technique. Each tape contains six stories. Each story presents a fictionalized problem-solving situation or episode involving children of comparable age and grade level. Included on the tape following each story are questions to be considered by the group and, in some cases, suggestions for role playing. Each story runs from four to seven minutes and the questions read by the storyteller are followed by a signal that the tape recorder should be turned off. The members may then discuss the particular question. Questions are designed to aid children in learning to talk about themselves and their feelings.

The *Magic Circle* program is an example of a highly structured verbal approach for elementary level students that is easily adapted as a moderately structured approach. The popular *DUSO* kits (Level 1 and 2) provide for maximum structure at the elementary level through a unique combination of stories, pictures, and puppets.

Moderately structured techniques also allow the introduction of a topic or "theme" but typically do not deal with it in such great specificity. Such a technique allows the group leader to formulate questions or leads depending upon the needs of the particular group. Specific examples of moderately structured techniques for elementary students are the *Words and Action Series,* and the *Elementary Guidance Transparency Series.* Topics depicted in these pictures and transparencies provide different visual stimuli, one of which is recommended for presentation to the group at the onset of each session. The group leader shows the visual, and then formulates questions such as: "What do you think is happening here?" "How do you suppose that boy feels?" "How would you feel in such a situation?" "What would you do?" The questions should be designed for the individual students and for the specific group with whom the counselor is working and should be formulated to aid students to begin talking about themselves, their feelings and behavior.

For junior high school age youth through adults, somewhat more verbally-oriented structured activities as found in *The Group Leaders Handbook* (Merritt & Walley, 1977) and *RealTalk: Structured Exercises in Friendship and Helping Skills* (Gazda, Childers, & Walters, 1981) can be used. The determining factors as to the complexity of the media and/or activities is more related to the verbal and concept ability of the group members than to simple chronological age. Another factor to be considered in choosing structured activities is the relative interpersonal skill level of potential group members. In general, the fewer group experiences that members have had, the more appropriate will be activities that structure and help in skill development.

Essentially, all group members need skill in giving and receiving feedback in constructive ways, clarifying their feelings and ideas through self-exploration, and opportunities for self-disclosure. In addition to modeling these behaviors, group leaders need to be creative in searching out any number of activities that can enhance these skills in a group.

Using dyads and/or triads to break the group into smaller components often adds a measure of security and gives group members more opportunity to participate. The use of stimulus sentences, open-ended questions, and focused feedback work well and promote group member involvement and commitment. Timed sequences for individual self-disclosure that focus on member strengths and "positive bombardment" as found in the *Handbook of Structured Experiences for Human Relations Training* (Pfeiffer & Jones, 1983) are also examples of structured approaches that promote interaction.

Summary of Structuring

As has been clarified in the special issue of the *Journal for Specialists in Group Work* devoted to the dynamic of structure (Vol. 4, 1979), there is general agreement that structure is a significant dimension in the group counseling process. Although structured techniques can be used to stimulate, to motivate, to teach, and to promote trust, the use of structure should not be abused. The recommendation is that structured approaches be used sequentially beginning with highly structured verbal approaches, followed by moderately structured visual approaches and concluding with an approach involving no externally imposed structured topic thus enabling group members to establish their own speed, direction and personality. When used sequentially, structured approaches become complementary and developmental and are thus compatible with the developmental life cycle of the group.

USING BEHAVIORAL CHANGE CONTRACTS

One of the most common criticisms of traditional low-structure approaches to group counseling is that the group can sometimes get lost in exploration. A member's self-exploration may result in an emotional catharsis followed by relatively unsystematic offers of encouragement and support from fellow members and the leader. A pitfall of this free-flowing, sharing, and caring approach is that the benefits of exploration may be lost for lack of a specific behavioral goal and concrete checkpoints for progress.

Contracting in counselings is not a new concept (Berne, 1966; Corey, 1981; Dustin & George, 1973; & Ezell & Ezell, 1972). This section will focus upon developing a rationale and methodology for the use of individual member behavior change contracts within a traditional counseling group. In addition, some of the advantages and cautions in using this technique will be examined.

Rationale

Contracting for behavior change can be an effective method of introducing increased clarity, definition, and task orientation to verbal material that otherwise might remain vague and abstract. It can involve the member and the group in a specific process of problem identification and solution. Contracting can provide identifiable steps, bilaterally agreed upon, that help the person go beyond mere awareness or recognition to a program for change.

The concept of individual contracting for behavior change within the group is based upon two assumptions. The first is that a reasonable amount of self-exploration has preceded the identification of the specific problem area to be contracted. A potential disadvantage of contracting is that the leader and group members will focus so intently on problem identification and problem solving that more profound areas may be overlooked. This is a particular caution with group members who have highly compliant personalities and are willing to go along with group advice and suggestions.

The second assumption is that the group itself has reached a level of trust so that interdependency within the group is healthy rather than pathological. This is important so that each member is free and autonomous enough to value group input, but at the same time is willing to assume full personal responsibility for the carrying out of the agreed-upon contract.

Within this framework of exploration, trust, and interdependency, contracting for specific change can assist the individual member in bringing historical problem material into the present where it can be worked on in the context of how it is presently affecting behavior.

Procedures

Frequently, group members perceive in themselves a need to make a number of changes in their lives. Constellations of problems can become overwhelming and self-defeating and often contribute to a spiral of depression. An example would be in the sometimes overused term "self-concept." How does one go about improving a self-concept? The answer would seem to lie with a relatively systematic and incremental approach that breaks problems down into behaviors that can be worked on with some assurance of success.

In order to insure that the contracted behavior is specific enough, the following criteria can be applied:

1. The desired behavior must be *valuable.* That is, the outcome should be intrinsically rewarding, and the behavior should be important enough so that the individual will be motivated to stay with the contract. The process of bilaterally negotiating the contract within the group will provide evidence as to the importance of the behavior change to the contracting member. *They must choose - be involved in process*

   Denial, rationalizations, and intellectualizations indicate to the group leader that the member is unready to proceed to the contracting stage—or that the contract is inappropriate.

2. The desired behavior should be *achievable.* Meeting this criterion rewards specificity and avoids goals that are too broad. In effect, the leader is contracting for behaviors over which the member has control. This control has the added benefit of placing the responsibility of choice directly with the group member.

   An example might be a group member who claims he/she "wants to be more assertive." Each group member could be expected to have a reasonable idea of what that means, but it is still a sufficiently broad constellation of behaviors so that progress is difficult to assess. A more manageable and achievable contract might be for the member to initiate verbal interaction three times per group session. This behavior can be monitored directly.

3. The desired behavior should be ***measurable.*** The ability to quantify results removes ambiguity and provides reinforcement as gains are achieved. Even behaviors that might not be observable in the group itself can be tallied by the contracting member and reported back to the group.

Through a process of give-and-take negotiation, the contracting member and the group together decide and agree upon a contract, method of reporting and observing, and a relative timeline for completion.

Berne (1966) discussed what he called amendments to the contract. This is essentially a process of renegotiation that might modify a contract or target an altogether new behavior. It is particularly important to state explicitly this ground rule so that members won't feel overly defeated if they are unable to carry out the conditions of the contract.

In a group setting it is usually satisfactory to use a simple oral contract as opposed to a more formal written document. The group leader might find it helpful to incorporate a brief reporting period at the beginning of each session. The process of negotiating a contract in the group also ensures that several people will be involved in monitoring progress.

Rewards

The incorporation of a desired new behavior in most cases is intrinsically self-rewarding, but many times group members can profit from a more tangible and immediate positive reward for success. An ice cream sundae (particularly if the problem isn't weight reduction) or some similarly pleasurable object or experience frequently can increase the short-term reinforcement. This can be especially effective with group members who experience difficulty in giving themselves permission to have a good time or to do nice things for themselves.

Failure to carry out the contract is usually a punishing consequence in itself since it assumes the continuation of undesirable behavior. Contrived negative punishers are typically not very effective as they can subtly influence the relationship of the group member to the leader and the group.

Advantages of Group Contracting

The contracting process has positive features both for the individual member and for the group as a whole. Since the group is actively assisting in goal achievement, at least an implicit agreement is to work with and support the member. This group commitment not only tends to mobilize group energy but can contribute to the overall development of cohesiveness and shared mission. Also, the group tends to stay involved with the process by providing feedback on the members' progress.

The contractor is the primary beneficiary because he or she is directly involved in choosing the focus behavior. Choosing contributes to a feeling of being in control of oneself. The goal becomes intentional, concrete, and targets very specifically what the focus behavior is.

The process of establishing a contract can facilitate self-exploration as the member and the group attempt to meet the stated criteria. In effect, it adds to the incentive to engage actively in the group process, while at the same time signaling very concretely the member's level of commitment to self and the change process.

Added benefits include the possibility of homework assignments to be completed outside of the group. A brief reporting system also gives the group an ongoing "task" for each session.

Finally, the contracting process can sometimes mean that the member is not totally dependent upon insight before initiating the change process. Intermediate success with measurable behavior change can lay a base for additional risks in the future.

Cautions

A number of traps need to be avoided in the group/contracting process. The group leader is ultimately responsible for recognizing these pitfalls and for taking corrective action when they are observed.

- *Contracting too quickly can subvert the exploration process.* Sometimes the inclination is to target on peripheral behaviors while in pursuit of the goal (contract).

- *Advice-giving can become the predominant mode of relating.* Naive group members particularly, in their genuine attempts to help, can overload the helpee with inappropriate advice and detailed personal stories.

- *Too difficult a contract can be self-defeating.* Compliant members may feel pressure to conform to a contract. Failure to live up to the conditions can add up to another loss for the member and may result in additional guilt and lowered self-esteem. The social (group) consequences of not meeting the goal could cause a member to leave the group. The novelty of a contract tends to wear off with time, and frequently fulfilling the contract isn't as easy as it first seems. The group leader has no real way other than group pressure to hold a member to a contract. This can be a double-edged sword with potential negative implications for total group growth.

- *Occasionally difficulty occurs in defining problems or goals in contract terms.* Often a necessary procedure is to remember the stated criteria and in some cases abandon the contracting process altogether. This requires a value judgement on the part of the leader as to the potential benefits weighed against the time involved in crystallizing a contract.

Summary Regarding Contracts

Contracting for individual member behavior change within the group can have benefits for both the individual and the group as a whole. The contracting process itself provides specificity and goal-directedness if it meets the stated criteria. The target behavior or goal should be valuable, achievable, and measurable.

While the contracting process can be a group process asset, a number of cautions exist of which the group leader needs to be aware while applying this technique. If used in a sensitive and timely way, contracting can help both the individual members and the entire group to grow and profit.

SILENCE

Meaning Of Silence In groups

Although much has been written to help the counselor understand the silent member in group counseling, total group silence is perhaps even more difficult to comprehend. This section is an attempt to help the group counselor anticipate and better understand what is happening when the counseling group experiences periods of silence.

Silence is a significant part of the group counseling process and can be as varied as the feelings experienced and happenings in the group. Each period of silence has a distinctive character. Silence can convey many different messages and seems almost like a contradiction of the word itself because the silences that occur in counseling groups typically "speak loudly" of what is happening. Cohen and Smith (1976) pointed out that each silence has its own "sound" and purpose. Group silence is not silent; it is gestures, unspoken words, unverbalized feelings, facial expressions, and the group atmosphere. As Carroll (1970) stated:

> Silence in a group is not wordless
> Silence in a group is words
> Silence in a group is gesture
> Gesture in a group is not silence
> Silence in a group is not a group
> A group not in silence is not a group. (p. 551)

Silence—Part of the Group Process

Silence in a group is a natural part of the group process. What occurs or is experienced during the silence is not necessarily different from those times when the group is not considered to be silent. Since only one member can be heard at a time, the group membership at any given time is usually silent with but one exception, the speaker. A time of silence then is but a slight departure from the typical setting in that only one more member than usual is silent. When silence is accepted as natural and productive, it becomes a means of growth and not a frustrating villain to be avoided.

That communication exists in silence is often evident in group sessions. Lifton (1968) suggested that at the start of a group session members commonly visit with each other; then, as if by some signal, members become quiet as they shift gears and start up again within the context of the purpose of the group. Lifton suggested that this kind of silence reflects group communication of the need to change behaviors. The unspoken message is, "We're ready to move to a deeper, more personal level." By their silence the group indicates a readiness to work and grants permission for any member to begin.

Silence probably occurs most frequently in initial group counseling sessions and often conveys feelings of awkwardness and apprehension. Although Johnson (1963) suggested silence at this stage of group life is due to the anxiety that members experience and is thus restrictive, Cohen and Smith (1976) stated that silence is a generator of anxiety and thus motivates member involvement. Nevertheless, silence does often happen in beginning stages of the group process and usually conveys a variety of feelings. After an initial group counseling session, one group member wrote in her group log,

> Silence . . . . . on and on and on. I scratched, swung my leg, doodled, and fervently wished that someone would say something, anything, so that I could look up and see the group instead of sneaking furtive glances at them from under down cast eyes. I searched vainly for a question to ask without appearing foolish. No question! What to do?—sneeze, cough loudly, fall out of the chair in

a dead faint? Certainly not! Maybe if I smile crookedly everyone will think that I have all the answers and wish they had them too. No one said anything. There are lots of things I could say, but I'm not about to say anything. NOT A THING! Why don't I ask what I want to know? Can I trust this group? Well, test the water before you plunge headlong into a stump filled lake.

Working Silence

How long a period of silence in the group seems to last, not in actual passing of time but rather how long it feels, is often an indication of the amount of work going on in the group. The point here is not one of what is productive for in terms of the developing group process, a long and frustrating group silence can be productive. However, a working silence is usually experienced as being of short duration. Time seems to be condensed and the silence is hardly noticed as members share through their own thoughts and feelings in the experience of the group. Indeed, the silence is not even experienced as silence. Kemp (1970) pointed out that silent periods become more acceptable and comfortable as members experience a growing sense of adequacy. A non-working silence is felt, is noticed, does drag on, and seems to say, "We are being silent." Such a silence is characterized by darting glances around the group, shifting postures, busy hands or feet, nervous grins, avoidance of eye contact, and a feeling that everyone is waiting for someone to do something. This is especially true when the group is playing the game "there must be something the matter with him" (Laing, 1970, p 5) and works doubly hard at reflecting and probing in order to keep the focus on any other member who happens to say something, whether personal or not. As if by some invisible signal, the members of the group will lapse into a period of silence in which each member seems determined not to be the one to break the silence. The sensitive group facilitator can almost feel the resistance, the pulling back, the holding in that says, "I'm not about to say anything and get put on the spot." At such a time, the group silence certainly communicates.

Silence in a group does not mean "nothing is going on." Quite the contrary, silence by the group may convey support for a member who is having difficulty expressing feelings or ideas. Such a silence is permeated with encouragement which the member seems to feel as much as sense. Support is also evident in the silence of togetherness which follows the sharing of hurt or sadness when the group seems to know words would be inappropriate. Silence can be a time of experiencing deeply one's self when facilitated by an awareness of the support and acceptance of others. Following a fifteen-minute silence in a group, a member remarked, "This has just been the most profound period of deep introspection I have ever experienced. I was able to look closely at some parts of my life I've avoided for ten years." Silence in a group can be a warm blanket.

The silence that occurs in a group after an outburst of anger is certainly not silent. The atmosphere in the group is "charged" and "crackles" with the electrical impulses of emotion. This kind of silence is felt as members experience the weight of the silence. The silence may be alive with the hundreds of unspoken words generated inside each member as they try to understand the reason for the angry outburst. Or the group silence may be reflecting stunned awkwardness which says, "Now what do we do? How do we get going again?"

According to Kemp (1970), silence may be used for thoughtful resolution of conflict, gaining insights, and recognizing ideational relationships. In other situations it expresses hostility, confusion discouragement, or withdrawal. Rosenbaum and Berger (1963) suggested that some silences communicate togetherness and cooperation. Warters (1960) stated that the group may seek relaxation and relief in silence following the exploration of deep feelings and the ventilation of emotions. Cohen and Smith (1976) wrote that silences usually follow an especially meaningful or "peak" experience. In their view members seem to know something meaningful has happened and will sit for long periods of silence feeling quite comfortable and "alive."

Responding To Silence

Just as no single kind of silence exists, no single way for the counselor to respond to silence is apparent. However, the group facilitator may find help by keeping in mind questions suggested by Luchins (1964). Why is the counselor disturbed by the silence? Is the group bothered by the silence? Are the members really not participating because they are silent? What does silence mean to the group? Are nonverbal activities taking place that may be responded to?

Silence can provide the stepping stone to further interaction in the group and yet, the silence often is intra-action. How the counselor responds can determine whether or not group silence is facilitative to the group process or individual introspection. Probably the most helpful thing the counselor can do is to examine his/her own feelings about group silence and try to resolve any anxieties that would interfere with sensitivity to the meaning of group silence. The counselor then can be more facilitative by responding to the meaning rather than the silence.

Silence which conveys acceptance, support, and seems to be encouraging to members working through their own thoughts and feelings is constructive and generally needs no response by the counselor. However, the counselor must be sensitive to those times when silence indicates a nonworking relationship, is not constructive, or has meaning that should be verbalized. At such times, the counselor can be facilitative by sharing with the group personal perceptions of the meaning of the silence or personal feelings or reactions to the silence. The counselor also could facilitate members sharing with a response such as, "It could be helpful to the group is some of you would share what you have been feeling or thinking during this silence," or asking, "Susan, could you share with us what you think has been going on in the silence or what it means? Some counselors might prefer to develop the meaning of the silence through a structured activity. The important thing is that group silence does have meaning and needs to be recognized.

SUMMARY

Some of the significant issues in group counseling have been dealt with in this chapter. A strong recommendation has been presented for the scheduling of some group counseling sessions more frequently than once-a-week. The issue of structuring has been discussed as a potential means for contributing to the development of interaction in groups. In all groups some degree of structuring is present. Silences in group counseling are especially perplexing to inexperienced group facilitators who often feel that something observable must be going on in the group at all times. We have presented silence as a natural and dynamic part of the interactional process in groups. Contracting for behavioral change has been presented as a possible procedure for enhancing group activity, productivity, and cohesiveness.

REFERENCES

Bach, G.R. (1966). The marathon group: Intensive practice of intimate interaction. *Psychological Reports, 18.*

Berne, E. (1966). *Principles of group treatment.* New York: Oxford University Press.

Broedel, J., Ohlsen, M., Proff, F., & Southard D. (1960). The effects of group counseling on gifted under-achieving adolescents. *Journal of Counseling Psychology, 7,* 163-170.

Carroll, M.R. (1970). Silence is the heart's size. *Personnel and Guidance Journal, 48,* 536-551.

Cohen, A.M., & Smith, R.D. (1976). *The critical incident in growth groups: Theory and technique.* La Jolla, CA: University Associates.

Corey, G. (1981). *Theory and practice of group counseling.* Monterey, CA: Brooks/ Cole.

Developing Understanding of Self and Others (DUSO). (1070), Circle Pines, MN: American Guidance Service, Publishers Building.

Dustin, R. & George, R. (1973). *Action counseling for behavior change.* New York: Intext.

Elementary Guidance Transparency Series. Division of Guidance Services, Texas Education Agency, 201 East 11th Street, Austin, Texas.

Ezell, G.T., & Ezell B. (1972). The contract as a counseling technique. *Personnel and Guidance Journal, 51,* 27-32.

Frank, L.K. (1944). Adolescence—a period of transition. *Adolescence.* 43rd Yearbook of the National Society for the Study of Education. Chicago: Univ. of Chicago Press.

Gazda, G.M. (1959). The effects of short-term group counseling on prospective counselors. Unpublished doctoral dissertation, University of Illinois.

Gazda, G.M. (1989). *Group counseling: A developmental approach.* Boston: Allyn and Bacon.

Gazda, G., Childers, W., & Walters, R. (1981). *RealTalk: Structured exercises in friendship and helping skills.* Atlanta: Humanics.

Guidance Vistas Audio Tapes, 2308 Fifth Avenue, Ft Worth, TX.

Hobbs, N. (1951). Group-centered therapy. In C.R. Rogers, *Client-centered therapy.* Boston: Houghton-Mifflin.

Johnson, J.A. (1963). *Group therapy: A practical approach.* New York: McGraw-Hill.

Journal for Specialist in Group Work. (Special Issue: Group Counseling and The Dynamic of Structure), 1979, 4, 4.

Kemp C.G. (1970). *Foundations of group counseling.* New York: McGraw-Hill.

Koeppe, P. (1961). A study of the immediate effect of a one day application of guidance and counseling procedures upon selected ninth grade students. *Dissertion Abstracts.* Ann Arbor, MI: University Microfilms. 22, 1876.

Laing, R.D. (1970). *Knots.* New York: Pantheon Books, 1970.

Landreth, G.L. (1966). Group counseling and varied time effects. Unpublished doctoral dissertation. University of New Mexico.

Lifton, W.M. (1968). Group-centered counseling. In G.M. Gazda (Ed.), *Basic approaches to group psychotherapy and group counseling.* Springfield, IL: Charles C. Thomas.

Luchins, A.S. (1964). *Group therapy: A guide.* New York: Random House.

Magic Circle, Human Development Training Institute, 4455 Twain Avenue, Suite H, San Diego, CA.

Merritt, R.E., & Walley, D.D. (1977). *The group leaders handbook.* Champaign, IL: Research Press.

Pfeiffer, J., & Jones, J. (1983). *Handbook of structured experiences for human relations training.* LaJolla: CA University Associates Press.

Pine, I., Gardner, M., & Tippett, D.L. (1958). Experiences with short-term group psychotherapy. *International Journal of Group Psychotherapy, 8,* 276-284.

Rosenbaum, M., & Berger, M. (1963). *Group therapy and group function.* New York: Basic Books.

Stoller, F.H. (1968). Marathon group therapy. In G.M. Gazda (Ed.), *Innovations to group psychotherapy.* Springfield, IL: Charles C. Thomas.

Warters, J. (1960). *Group guidance: Principles and practices.* New York, NY: McGraw-Hill.

Words and Action Program. New York: Holt, Rinehart, & Winston, 383 Madison Avenue.

SUGGESTED READING

Corey, M.S., & Corey, G. (1987). *Groups: Process and practice (3rd ed.)*. Monterey, CA: Brooks/Cole.

In the third edition of this highly popular group counseling text, the Corey writing team has added significant content that includes specific examples of groups at work, sample leader interventions, a discussion of both effective and ineffective member behaviors and methods of combining research and practice.

The beginning section of the book deals with basic group work issues coupled with an expanded discussion of ethical and professional guidelines for group workers. The major body of the text is organized around the process related to the various stages of group development. The Coreys provide practical suggestions for the group leader to try during the initial, transition, working, and ending stages of the group.

Part three takes a more in depth look at specialized groups for children, adolescents, adults, and the elderly. Beginning group leaders will find this easy to understand book very practical and helpful.

MAINTAINING A GROUP: PROCESS AND DEVELOPMENT

After the group leader has attended to the details involved in getting a group started, attention can be turned to providing constructive leadership for the group. Our position is that no single leadership style automatically insures successful group outcomes. Leaders approach the group with many different personality types and theoretical orientations. Seemingly the leader's ability to integrate his/her leadership skills into a consistent personal style provides the most benefit for the group and its members.

The theoretical orientation of the leader seems to be less important to group outcome than is the nature of the relationship between leader and group members. A number of studies have emphasized the relationship variable and have demonstrated that successful leaders have many characteristics in common regardless of theoretical school of thought (Carkhuff & Berenson, 1977; Lieberman, Yalom, & Miles, 1973b).

Following an investigation of the leadership between leader styles and success of the group, O'Day (1976) reported that leaders of the most successful groups engaged in greater degrees of personal self-disclosure (evidently appropriately so), expressions of self-confidence, demonstrated warmth toward others, and possessed good to excellent manipulative skills. In an intensive analysis of the effects of leaders on encounter group members, Lieberman, Yalom, and Miles (1973a) found that the leader's style, rather than theoretical rationale, was the major contributing cause of casualties in the group. They identified the most ineffective leaders as aggressive, authoritarian, too frequently confrontive, impatient with members' progress, pushing for immediate member self-disclosure, emotional expression, and attitude change. These leaders also were high on self-disclosure and demonstrated little respect for members in that they frequently interrupted and challenged group members.

The relationship of leader effectiveness to self-actualization, relationship skills, and experience is well established. While the "perfect leader" probably doesn't exist, what constitutes effective leadership behavior continues to be researched and defined. We do know that a leader should have a reasonably rich experiential background with a solid exposure to the social sciences. A concrete understanding of human development and an appreciation for the prevailing culture will allow the leader to identify with group members' problems and situations. Finally, the leader needs a keen sense of the dynamics and power of the group and group interactions.

The group leader needs to be in a continuing process of personal actualization and integration that is behaviorally demonstrated through a calm self-confidence and self-acceptance. The leader must be able to communicate to group members high levels of acceptance, empathy, and warmth, and to take calculated risks in disclosing self behaviorally through interpersonal immediacy.

PROBLEMS IN GROUP PROCESS

Even the most skilled of group leaders will encounter problems in group process. Many problems in group development can be anticipated and frequently prevented through careful member selection procedures. In an intake interview potential group members who present highly deviant behavior patterns that might block the healthy development of the group can be eliminated. While heterogeneous balance frequently will compensate for member pathologies, leaders should consider selecting out potential group members who might be maliciously manipulative, very silent and withdrawn verbally monopolistic, insensitive or extremely alienated, and aggressive.

Additionally, we have found that insisting on potential group members being engaged in at least one minimally satisfying and healthy interpersonal relationship outside of and exclusive of the group is a functional necessity. If this is not the case, the person would do better in individual counseling until such time as a constructive relationship is established with the counselor.

We are especially concerned that the group experience be a rewarding and successful venture for the counselor who is not actively involved in group work. Therefore, we encourage beginning group leaders to select, for their first group experience, members who are most likely to ensure a successful group experience.

Group Cohesiveness and Trust

The interpersonal bonding or attraction that takes place in a healthy group is one of the few process variables that has been adequately researched. It has been shown to be a group function that is directly related to positive outcomes.

While too high a level of cohesiveness or "togetherness" can sometimes lead to low levels of group production, research indicates that members of cohesive groups are

1. more productive,

2. more resistant to negative external influences,

3. more open to influence by other group members,

4. able to experience more security,

5. more able to express negative feelings and follow group norms,

6. more willing to attempt to influence others, and

7. able to continue memberships in group longer.

If a high level of interpersonal freedom is a desired atmosphere in the group, seemingly the group leader should give the development of cohesiveness, rapport, and trust a high priority, particularly in the initial stages of group development. Group leader facilitated conditions of personal involvement in the group, a focus upon the expression of feelings, a general affective atmosphere in the group, and interaction among members appear to be the process variables that lead to solidarity and interpersonal trust.

While we feel no such thing as a totally unconditional relationship exists, group leaders are well advised to establish a free and permission giving climate in the early phases of the group. The resultant core of cohesiveness serves as a building block or base of trust that allows increasing behavioral conditionality in later group stages when the primary focus moves from the establishment of an initial feeling of comfort to a more problem-solving orientation.

STAGES OF GROUP DEVELOPMENT

Developmental phases within a group are rarely autonomous and free-standing but tend to overlap with boundaries that frequently are fuzzy. Most writers in the field of group counseling and group psychotherapy have identified stages of group development but they tend to grow from observation and clinical experience, rather than hard data. Because of the number of variables involved and the difficulty in controlling the variations, the number of systematic research studies involving group development is small.

What evidence we do have seems to suggest that groups develop in a cyclical fashion, that is, issues are re-examined in the group but at progressively deeper levels of perspective. Since individual group members have an enormous impact on group development, the portrayal of developmental sequences in any group is highly theoretical. General developmental stages can be thought of as major themes that are complicated by the unpredictability of interpersonal interaction.

Yalom (1985) provided a good overview of prevailing clinical descriptions of group sequences and Cohen and Smith (1976) have attempted to behavioralize ten discreet group stages by exhaustively listing 144 behavioral characteristics of members and groups as they progress through the stages.

The present authors, while bearing in mind the circular nature of group development, generally see groups sequence through two major stages that encompass several minor phases. Also good to remember is that not all members will be at the same stage at the same time, and because each phase represents mastery over individual and group developmental tasks, some members, and some groups, will never progress through the entire sequence.

In general however healthy and cohesive groups tend to follow a similar developmental scheme to the one presented here.

PRECOMMITMENT STAGE

1. Initial Testing of Group Limits

In the beginning stages of a new group, members can be expected to experience a certain amount of expectational anxiety. While some group anxiety can be helpful because it can lead to productivity, high degrees of unspecified anxiety can be counter-productive to the group. The more "group naive" the new members are, the more likely that anxiety will be present because of a general uncertainty of direction and purpose. At deeper levels, group members may be questioning their own ability to handle intensified interpersonal relationships. Initially, most group members will experience some degree of unspecified anxiety that usually relates to an uncertainty about the present and future.

Behaviorally, members will tend to fall back upon social behaviors that have worked well for them in the world in general. They will tend to activate their own prejudices, stereotypes, categorizations, and statuses in an attempt to bring some kind of cognitive order to the group. Some members will become very verbally active and others will be silent and withdrawn. This period of becoming acquainted is characterized by covert testing of the leader, other members, and the group in general.

Confusion, uncertainty, and ambiguity may typify the group in the beginning as members attempt to adjust to a new and strange situation. Irrelevant topics and issues and avoidance of sustained work can be characteristic of the group as members become accustomed to being together.

The major issues in this initial stage involve the resolution of purpose and boundaries.

2. Tentative Self-disclosure and Exploration

In this second phase, members become increasingly sensitive to the power in the group for potential acceptance or rejection, members want to be known and accepted for the person they are but are faced with the prospect of having to risk sharing some part of themselves (usually a feeling, unexpected personal data, or a reaction to a member) in order to ascertain the level of acceptance. Therefore, self-disclosures at this stage are rather tentative and exploratory in nature. In an ambiguous situation, common sense dictates that members look for self-definition and personal status within the group. Leadership struggles are common at this stage as members explore power alliances and attempt to control and influence group direction. Personal attitudes and values, after an initial suspension, begin to emerge and crystalize. While the verbal rate may be high, with some members attempting to keep interaction going smoothly and continuously, the content remains relatively superficial and issue oriented.

A general tendency is present to protect the leader and other group members from criticism and attack coupled with a generalized anxiety related to the prospect of increased intimacy with others. Mini-affiliations tend to occur here in an attempt to form mutual support subgroups. At this point real differences in interpersonal styles become apparent, particularly those who are assertive and independent as opposed to those who project an image of dependency and passivity. Members' typical interpersonal styles will surface in accordance with the ambiguity of the situation and will become a valuable source of information for the leader. Feelings, behaviors, and styles that members have learned in other relationships and situations are the modes used in relating to the group.

Also at this point group members adopt roles that tend to set up a series of expectations by other group members. The chronic rescuer, resident comedian, hostile attacker, to name but a few, have an opportunity to display their behavioral preferences to the group. These roles and labels can be comfortable initially because they give the group definition and expectations while at later stages they obviously can hinder individual growth if group members covertly "force" a member to remain in the formerly defined role.

Through the primary self-disclosures and behavioral expressions associated with this developmental stage, members begin to learn more about each other, the leader, and themselves and using the data available make some initial commitment to a personal level of involvement in the group.

COMMITMENT STAGE

3. Depth Self-exploration and Understanding

As the group progresses through its life, a subtle but discernible movement takes place away from the initial concerns involving purpose and power to an increasing involvement with issues of interpersonal affiliation and intimacy. The issue of closeness will be, in some measure, a major focus for the remainder of the group life.

During this phase, the pattern becomes clear that the group has resolved issues of rules and procedures and is beginning to develop its own unique aura. Standards and norms may become apparent that are unique to the group and may not conform to those outside of the group. An insider/outsider feeling may develop and expressions and behaviors that reinforce "we-ness" are more prevalent.

More focus is on "here and now" transactions in the group and on concerns unique to the group with an increasing disregard for those outside of the group. Even low-status members of the group will be included in intimate exchanges so as to at least preserve the illusion of cohesiveness and solidarity.

Problems of power become more up-front and readable and are dealt with in a more constructive, conscious, immediate manner. The leader typically becomes more confrontive of behavior and serves as the person with a high reality orientation. Informal leaders within the group begin to reemerge without threat to the group.

Group members themselves begin to "check out" or test their perceptions and assumptions about self and others. A higher rate exists of interpersonal risk taking and depth of self-exploration and disclosure not present earlier. Inter-actions between members become more intensive and feeling dominated.

Finally, at this stage, group members begin to demon-strate more helping skills as they become involved with each other as well as self.

4. Commitment to Change and Growth

At this level is an unspoken but more apparent commitment to mutual help and support. The atmosphere of the group takes on a more relaxed and informal tone. Evidence appears of a good deal more interpersonal acceptance and egalitarianism while at the same time a tougher, more demanding orientation to reality becomes apparent. The leader, while not withdrawing, will be able to share more responsibility and facilitation with group members as they begin to exhibit less defensiveness and more helping skills. The leader will notice group members modeling empathic responses and attempting to generate new insights.

5. Working Toward Increased Personal Effectiveness

This is clearly the most productive stage in the life of the group. Most early concerns and developmental tasks have been resolved and mastered. Respect levels are up as group members engage in less "rescuing" behavior. Also apparent is a decrease in aggression and more willingness to compromise on issues concerning the entire group. Group interactions are typified by much more free association of feelings and thoughts and more frequent open, feeling statements and expressions.

More than an illusion of unity appears at this stage as group members become genuinely concerned about the welfare of each other. Missing members become a focal point because of an obvious change in group composition in their absence. The group begins to take on a life of its own that offers the necessary security for individual behavior change.

Group members at this level are approaching a self-therapist existence with increased self-awareness and insight. Self confrontations are frequent as much more reliance upon self-evaluation and independence occurs. Group members now develop a personal autonomy while at the same time the group itself is becoming interdependent.

Fantasies are discussed and shared and group members become more demanding of others and themselves in a quest to discover unconscious motivators for behavior. Interpersonally, members begin to risk new ways of relating to one another and what Rogers (1970) called the basic encounter is in evidence.

6. Preparation to Leave the Group

Clearly the group which progresses through the foregoing stages offers levels of support, behavioral reaffirmation, interdependence, and an intensification of feelings that is frequently missing if not impossible to achieve in the outside society. Equally clear is that the kind of natural high experienced in this setting can create problems of separation at termination.

A certain ambiguity of feelings can be anticipated that approximates the grieving process. Leave taking will produce denial and withdrawal in some and elation in others. Overriding these natural feelings of loss and anticipation should be a general optimism and a sense of completion. The group leader needs to take special care in dealing fully with feelings of anxiety associated with leaving the group.

RESEARCH FINDINGS

Through clinical observations and controlled research studies, most group leaders have attempted to gain some understanding of "normal" group development. While the particular labels might be somewhat different, many researchers and theoreticians agree in general to phases that groups progress through. Martin and Hill (1957) proposed a six phase theory of group development. The developmental process that they described is sectioned out into discrete phases. Each phase is described in terms of the major therapeutic problems and the characteristic behaviors found at each phase level. Additionally, transition stages are described which indicate potential within the group for movement to a new phase. Their *Scale of Group Development* includes the phase and characteristics of the interaction at that particular level.

Phase	Type of Interaction
1	Individual unshared behavior in an imposed structure
2	Reactivation of fixated interpersonal attitudes
3	Exploration of interpersonal potential within the group
4	Awareness of interrelationships, subgroups and power structures
5	Consciousness of group dynamics and process problems
6	The group as an effective, integrative, creative social instrument. (Martin & Hill, 1957)

Bennis and Shepard (1956) saw two major phases and several sub-phases within the normal development of a group. For the group to reach a point where it will function effectively, areas of internal uncertainty and obstacles to communication need to be identified and eliminated. They posited the two major areas of uncertainty as **dependence** (authority relations—those who seek support from persons perceived as being stronger than themselves) and **inter-dependence** (learning to accept dependence in personal relations when it is realistically needed).

They described the dependent member as one who finds comfort in rules of procedure and agendas. This person also may have a high need for intimacy with other group members. The counter-dependent member tends to react to authority with competitiveness, exploitiveness, or withdrawal. Relatively unconflicted, independent group members are seen as catalysts and are usually responsible for major movements in the group from one phase to another. They go on to state that groups will likely encounter difficulty in resolving power and authority problems if it has no catalysts.

If the group is able to progress to the interdependency stage, both sub-groups, over personal and counter personal, join forces to work together. Movement through the dependent and interdependent phases represents a change in emphasis from power to affection and from role dependency to individual personality.

The movement of the group from the initial or **establishment** stage through the **transition** stage was described by Bonney and Foley (1963). After the attempts to define and establish group goals, members enter the transition stage which involves a change from a primarily social setting to one in which the focus will be therapeutic. Members frequently experience resistance and anxiety as they learn that they must discuss their own personal problems if the group is to reach its goal. The authors see the group leader as primarily important in helping reduce the incongruity experienced by members. They recommend that the leader be very active and accepting in the initial stages of the group.

In a later experimental study, the authors (Bonney & Foley, 1966) were unable to demonstrate that several groups of graduate students moved through the hypothesized establishment and transition stages. Group pressures and standards for conformity were cited as possible reasons for non-occurrence.

Forwarding the thesis that group member exposure to levels of personal risk and responsibility congruent with optimal group development can be regulated by group structure was presented as a developmental framework by Bednar and Melnick (1974).

The authors contended that lack of structure in early session not only fails to facilitate early group development but actually may feed client distortions, interpersonal fears, and subjective distress which interfere with group development and contribute to premature client dropouts. They suggested that structured interpersonal exercises can be used early in the life of the group to enhance the learning of new response patterns and behaviors which facilitate both long-term group development and individual member improvement. The essential assumption is that after an appropriate group structure and climate has been established, members will find it easier to express the specific content of their problems and engage themselves more quickly with other members at higher levels of emotional expression and openness.

A common thread that runs through much of the research is the importance of the leader as facilitator in assisting the group to achieve optimal levels. Bonney (1974) stated that the major concern of the group leader should be to assist the group toward mature functioning while allowing the group experience itself to be the primary therapeutic agent. An ancillary finding in the study conducted by Wogan, Getter, Amdur, Nichols, and Okinan (1977) was that greater group member self-disclosure and discussion were primarily related to leadership behaviors rather than cognitive-experiential pre-training. They reported that in the more successful groups, leaders tended to be more active in encouraging discussion of here-and-now, group-related topics.

More recently, Anderson (1984) synthesized the research of several others in the area of interpersonal relationships and proposed what he called the **TACIT model** of group development. He claimed that the development of small groups progress inexorably through sequential themes of Trust, Autonomy, Closeness, Interdependence, and Termination (TACIT). He based his conclusions upon the observed parallels with individual human growth and development and family life cycles which he said seek a balance between autonomy and interdependence.

While hard data are somewhat difficult to find, what seems clear is that groups can progress through relatively recognizable stages given the proper conditions. Equally important is to focus primary attention upon leadership ability, group structure, and composition as the major impactors of group development.

HILL INTERACTION MATRIX

Developed by William F. Hill, the **Hill Interaction Matrix** (HIM) can serve as a particularly valuable tool for the group leader. It is one of the most useful measuring tools for the leader to use in conceptualizing group dynamics and process by examining verbal interaction between members. It also is one way to objectively help determine the extent to which a group is progressing toward meeting it's goals.

Hill's matrix (see Figure 9.1) grew out of the clinical study of hundreds of hours of group observation. Interactions within the groups were intensively examined. A thorough discussion of the developmental process is available in *The Hill Interaction Matrix* (1956). The HIM was developed in a clinical-therapeutic setting and consequently most of the examples are related to mental health. The matrix is generalizable to virtually any group setting, however, as the principles of categorization remain the same.

Within the Matrix the categories are ordered in terms of assumed therapeutic benefit. The rankings are based on the following assumptions:

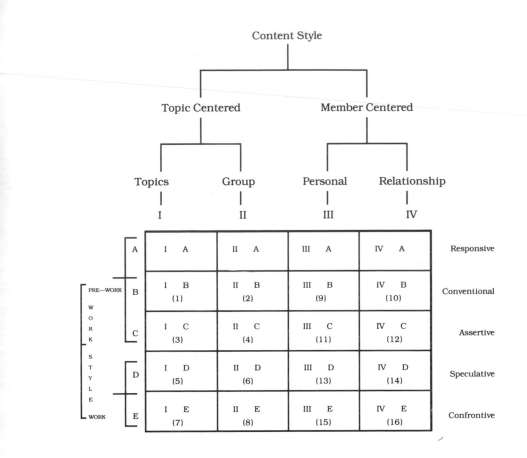

Figure 9.1. The Hill Interaction Matrix.

1. Member centeredness: the desirability of having a focus person in the group much of the time.

2. Interpersonal risk taking: the desirability for group members to give up the need for interpersonal security.

3. Interpersonal feedback: the desirability of all group members acting as both providers and receivers of immediate feedback.

Content Style

The HIM conceptualized verbal interaction in the group along two major dimensions. The first, across the top of the matrix is the **content style.** Content categorizes *what* is being discussed in the group. The second axis has to do with member work styles and is related to the **process** of communication or *how* members relate to each other and the group.

The content dimension is concerned with categorizing the subject matter being discussed. Generally, Hill saw all verbal subject matter as falling into one of the four content categories. Following are some general descriptions of those categories and some points that may help distinguish among them.

Topic. Subjects fitting into this broad and general category include virtually any subject *other than* the group itself, a member of the group, or a relationship *within* the group. General interest material fits here and by definition so would conventional socializing conversation between members of the group. As a further example, most of the content of any discussion group would most probably fit into the topic category.

Group. In this context, verbal interaction is *about* the group exclusively. It may involve an examination of the groups rules and procedures, formation, operation, and goals. The interaction is characterized and limited to the present and immediate group.

Personal. This is almost always a focus person or one who is being discussed. Focus can be by the topic person herself/himself or by other group members directed toward the topic person. The content of the interaction is upon an individual group member, his/her current status, personality characteristics, traits, behaviors, history, or problems.

Relationship. This category is ranked highest of the content dimensions because it involves immediate or "here and now" transactions between present members of the group. It is not *about* relationships, but rather gives evidence of a relationship within the group. It can speak to a relationship between group members or between a member and the group as a whole.

Work Style

The second axis which involves **work style** or process categories concerns itself with the *manner* in which members discuss any of the content possibilities. The critical determiner is how an individual group member initiates or responds to group content. Once again, following are some general descriptors that help distinguish the five process categories:

> **Responsive.** This very basic style dimension indicates an unwillingness on the part of a group member to verbally participate. The member may limit interaction to a brief response to direct questions or encounters. This category is useful only with severely withdrawn members or those who may be highly defensed.

> **Conventional.** Conversation may be about any number of general interest topics, facts or information and is conducted in a socially appropriate manner. A work orientation or context has not been established and the level of interaction could best be termed as descriptive and social rather than problem solving.

> **Assertive.** The present authors' opinion is that this category could more aptly be labeled aggressive in

the context of our current understanding of those terms. This process category is frequently distinguished by a hostile or attacking tone. Statements are *often* argumentative but also may include passive modes of behavior. One of the most valuable clues to watch for in this category is that the tone of the interaction tends to close down discussion rather than enhance it. Speakers tend to be finalistic in their pronouncements, do not appear to be open to another point of view, and exchanges tend to be one-way rather than two way.

Speculative. The tone changes to a discussion of information or problems that is or are task oriented and contains an implicit invitation to further examine two-way, open, and continuing communication. Speculative interaction is characterized by a cooperative desire for understanding of the problem or context.

Confrontive. One of the key words to characterize this category might well be *clarify*. Confrontive statements tend to draw upon what has already been said in an attempt to clarify, evaluate, and resolve issues. Confrontive statements are typically backed up with some form of concrete documentation. The speaker supports his or her opinion. The encounter involved in this style of communication may frequently be as therapeutic for the speaker as it is for the topic or focus person.

We refer to the lower right hand section of the Hill Matrix as the "power-quadrant." The assumption being that the more time a group spends in speculative-personal; speculative-relationship; confrontive-personal; and confrontive-relationship interaction patterns, the greater will be the gain for individuals and the group.

SUMMARY

This chapter offers some suggestions to the group leader regarding selection of new group members. The issue of cohesiveness and the development of a trusting atmosphere is addressed. The study of normal developmental stages in counseling groups is divided into two major phases—the precommitment stage and the commitment stage. Several subphases are listed under each with representative group member behavior for each.

Some of the research and clinical observations available in the literature are discussed regarding normal group development

The *Hill Interaction Matrix* developed by William F. Hill is briefly discussed as a valuable process evaluation instrument available to the group leader. Descriptions of content categories and process work styles are presented.

REFERENCES

Anderson, J. (1984). *Counseling through group process.* New York: Springer.

Bednar, R.L. & Melnick, J. (1974). Risk, responsibility, and structure: A conceptual framework for initiating group counseling and psychotherapy. *Journal of Counseling Psychology, 21,* (1), 31-37.

Bennis, W.G., & Shepard, H.S. (1956). A theory of group development. *Human Relations, 9,* 415 437.

Bonney, W.C. (1974). The maturation of groups. *Small Group Behavior, 5,* (4), 445-461.

Bonney, W.C., & Foley, W.J. (1963). The transition stage in group counseling in terms of congruence theory. *Journal of Counseling Psychology, 10,* 136-138.

Bonney, W.C. & Foley, W.J. (1966). A developmental model for counseling. *Personnel and Guidance Journal, 44,* (6) 576 580.

Carkhuff, R.R., & Berenson, B.G. (1977). *Beyond counseling and therapy* (2nd ed.). New York: Holt, Rinehart, and Winston.

Cohen, A.M. & Smith, R.C. (1976). *The critical incident in growth groups.* LaJolla, CA: University Associates.

Hill, W.F. (1956). *HIM, Hill Interaction Matrix.* Los Angeles: University of Southern California, Youth Studies Center.

Lieberman, M.A., Yalom, I.D., & Miles, M.B. (1973a). *Encounter groups: First facts.* New York: Basic Books.

Lieberman, M.A., Yalom, I.D., & Miles, M.B. (1973b). Encounter: The leader makes the difference. *Psychology Today, 6,* 69ff.

Martin, E.A., & Hill, W.F. (1957). Toward a theory of group development: Six phases of therapy group development. *International Journal of Group Psychotherapy, 7,* 20-30.

O'Day, R. (1976). Individual training styles. *Small Group Behavior, 7,* (2), 147-182.

Rogers, C.R. (1970). *Carl Rogers on encounter groups.* New York: Harper and Row.

Wogan, M., Getter, H., Amdur, M., Nichols, M., & Okinan, G. (1977). Influencing interaction and outcomes in group psychotherapy. *Small Group Behavior, 8,* (1), 25-46.

Yalom, E.D. (1985). *The theory and practice of group psychotherapy (3rd ed.).* New York: Basic Books.

SUGGESTED READING

Luft, J. (1984). *Group processes: An introduction to group dynamics (3rd Ed.).* Palo Alto, CA: Mayfield.

In this much expanded edition of the original book published in 1963 to feature the Johari Window, Luft has added much useful information for the group leader. His general position comes from group dynamics and the laboratory method. He provides a framework for understanding groups—their structure, norms, and roles. for the leader who is able to adapt the concepts to a counseling group setting, this book contains many valuable models and applications.

CHAPTER 10

TERMINATION, EVALUATION, AND FOLLOW-UP

As the group approaches the last session, the facilitator has responsibilities to help members prepare for termination. Steps need to be taken a couple of sessions before the last one. Also the facilitator needs to help members evaluate themselves and their changes if any.

TERMINATION

The ending phase or stage in the group counseling process is as potentially crucial to the growth and development of a group as is the beginning phase. It may seem contradictory to suggest that termination is a significant part of the group development. However, development in human potential terms implies growth, and the ability of the group members to cope with, accept, and effectively explore the ending of significant relationships is a higher order of group development. The dynamics of the process of termination, though, need not be limited to an exploration of the termination of relationship. To do so would restrict growth. According to Yalom (1985), termination is much more than an act signifying the end of the experience; it is an integral part of the group process and can be an important force in promoting change.

Rationale

Perhaps the awareness of the ending of events, happenings, experiences, and relationships in the lives of individuals is what provides the substance for significance and meaning. The very fact that there is a beginning implies that there will be an ending. Human experience consists of a series of beginnings and endings and beginning again. This chapter begins and ends and another follows. The day starts and ends so that another can begin. Semesters begin and end and a new semester commences. Relationships also begin and end and are replaced by new relationships. Termination then is a part of a vital process. It is an ending but that ending can become a beginning.

Allen (1942) also has called attention to termination as an essential part of the life process continuum:

> When the emphasis is placed on the word "ending," it is necessary to keep in mind that this is not a one-sided concept. Actually it describes only half of a life process. The emphasis is not merely on the ending of something already past, but on the new which is being ushered in. The leaving of the old and the beginning of the new constitute the ever-recurring shifting of the scenes in human development. The old is terminated with full regard for the values and satisfactions that have accrued from it. If these values must, however, be measured and felt only in the circumstances in which they were experienced originally, then they cease to be growth-inducing influences and lose their positive meaning. Values from any life experience retain their positive meaning only as the individual is free to use them in the ever-recurring newness of living. This is not forgetting and repressing the old but it is using the old to provide the structure of the new. (p. 102)

When dealt with openly, the impending termination of the group provides members with an opportunity to deal constructively with feelings of loss, to evaluate their own and each others' growth, to identify areas in need of continued work, and to develop plans and direction for continuing without the group. An exploration, then, of how each member can utilize what has been learned becomes equally as significant as learning to effectively cope with the ending of important relationships.

Determining When to Terminate

Closed Groups. Ordinarily the majority of counseling groups in educational settings are closed groups; once begun new members are not added. In such groups the issue of when to terminate is usually not a problem because they typically meet for a predetermined number of sessions. Therefore, termination is a developmental phenomenon with which the whole group must deal. Some closed groups are formed without a fixed ending date and members of the group are allowed to determine early in the group life how many sessions will be needed. Also a closed group may begin with the understanding that they will meet for a determined number of times, usually six to eight sessions, and may at that time decide if additional sessions are needed.

Closed groups often conform to external circumstances such as the ending of the semester or school year which dictate when the group will terminate. Such natural stopping places seem to work well in most instances. The counselor must recognize, however, that predetermined termination may not provide an opportunity for the group to meet the needs of all members and that individuals may be terminating with varying degrees of readiness. The counselor should be open to helping some members join a new group or continue in individual counseling.

Open Groups. An open group accepts new members as individuals terminate; thus maintaining a consistent size by replacing members as they leave. In such groups the question of terminating the group is almost never the issue but rather when an individual member is ready to terminate. This is normally determined by the individual with the help of the counselor and the group. In open groups termination is a reoccurring, extended and comprehensive process. The exiting of members from the group and the assimilation of new members affects not only the dynamics of the group but also the process and level of cohesiveness. Therefore, the establishment of open group is not recommended for inexperienced group counselors.

Additional variables affecting the group counseling process which the counselor must be aware of are readily apparent in the phases described by McGee, Schuman, and Racusen (1972) as typical of open groups:

1. Questions arise about termination during the intake interview. Feelings emerge as other members leave the group.

2. A member verbalizes a desire or intent to leave the group.

3. A discussion ensues about the member's plan to terminate and the potential effect on the member and the rest of the group.

4. Discussion regarding the terminating member will occur during the next several sessions and the decision to terminate will be confirmed.

5. The terminating member attends his/her last group session. Separation occurs.

6. The member's leaving and the resulting implications are discussed periodically during the next few sessions.

7. A new member enters the group.

Resistance to Termination

Reluctance to end a significant experience and to say goodbye to individuals who have become important is a natural reaction and one to be expected. Since individuals may for the first time have experienced this kind of close, intimate, caring relationship, they may face the ending of the group with a sense of loss and resistance. The continuing development of maturity, independence, and responsibility is hindered, though, when resistance is prolonged. A criterion of maturity is the ability to let go when relationships change or end. This willingness to turn loose fosters independence and self responsibility in self and others. Therefore, the counselor must help group members explore feelings related to termination of the group, the resulting ending of meaningful relationships and to engage in the process of turning loose.

The group counselor who anticipates resistance, anxiety, and dependence as probable reactions to termination will be better prepared to respond appropriately. Frequently groups avoid termination by enthusiastically requesting (children plead for) additional sessions beyond the predetermined ending time. The counselor who is unaware of what is prompting the request may get trapped in such situations by his/her own need to be needed. In such situations the counselor should respond to the underlying feelings, rather than the specific requests. Another typical manifestation of reluctance to end is in the planning of reunions. These too should be discouraged because the group will not be able to achieve in a social setting that which has become so significant to them in a therapeutic setting. In our experience of working with almost two hundred groups, we have never known of the members of a group following through on their insistence that "We'll all get together again next semester."

As the date of termination approaches, group members are frequently reluctant to continue the process of working and exploring. Explorations may become less intense and discussions more superficial because members are reluctant to introduce new topics. The unverbalized attitude of the group seems to be a message of "Well, after all we have *only* two more sessions." Our position is that an hour and a half in a counseling group can be profoundly productive; maximized far beyond the limits of time constraints by the intense nature of the therapeutic group. The counselor can help by verbalizing the reluctance sensed, raising the issue of termination, and stating his/her own expectations.

A crucial prerequisite to the effective facilitation of the termination process is the counselor's personal willingness to come to terms with his/her own reactions and feelings about the ending of relationships. The counselor also has shared in the plan and happiness inherent in the development of the group. He/she too has invested in the growth of the organism that has become a cohesive unit. The group leader frequently has felt cared for, liked, needed, and helpful. Such significant feelings are not easily given up. One of the most facilitative things the counselor can do at this point is to share openly with the group his/her feelings of reluctance to end the relationship. Confronting such feelings "opens the door" for group members to begin the process of turning loose and looking ahead to the possibility of new and equally meaningful relationships in their on-going world.

Procedures for Termination

If the group members have not already indicated an awareness of the ending of the group counseling sessions, an important procedure is for the counselor to remind the group of the approaching last session at least two sessions prior to termination. Group members can then make their own decisions as to the investment needed to deal with unfinished business. Introducing the matter of termination too early in the life of the group may result in members focusing their energy on the ending of the group and thus avoiding continuing to work on areas of initial commitment.

Procedures for terminating a group range from allowing the members to decide how they are going to terminate, to the counselor initiating a discussion of feelings associated with the ending of the group, to structured exercises focusing on specific issues related to termination. Ohlsen (1977) recommended the use of termination exercises which focus on growth one or two sessions before termination. He preferred questions such as "Which of your goals have you achieved?" "What do you have left to do?" "Whose help will be required to do it?" "What do each of you think the others have achieved and what they have left to do?"

A slightly different approach is taken by Corey and Corey (1987). During the closing session, they emphasize a focused type of feedback by asking (1) how members have perceived themselves in the group, (2) what the group has meant to them, (3) what conflicts have become more clear, and (4) what, if any, decisions have been made. Other members then give feedback about how they have perceived and how they have felt about that person. Mahler (1969) suggested focusing on the fact of termination with three sessions remaining by initiating a discussion of how members feel about the group coming to an end and how they can utilize later the things learned in the group.

Communication exercises are useful in that they help members review and clarify experiences and changes that have been made and provide encouragement to action. However, a potential problem exists with such exercises in that members too often may give only positive feedback when responding to the above suggested questions, particularly if members have developed a deep, caring relationship. Some balance in what is shared can be structured by having members express additional feelings and reactions by responding to open-end sentences having beginnings such as the following:

My greatest fear for you is ....

My hope for you is ....

I hope that you will seriously consider ....

You block your strengths by ....

Some things I hope you will think about doing for yourself are ....

(Corey & Corey, 1987, p. 211)

In groups where members have been unusually intense and constructively critical in their efforts to better understand themselves and to change, often no need will exist to be concerned about achieving balance in termination feedback. The crucial point seems to be that members utilize the last few sessions to continue the process of implementing what they have learned to do in previous sessions, and that members continue to learn how to transfer these significant learnings to their daily lives outside the group.

Summary About Termination

What is needed by a given group approaching termination will be determined by the uniqueness of the group. No single termination exercise could possibly be appropriate for all groups. Therefore, the group counselor is encouraged to rely on his/her own sensitivity and creativity in determining how to help a group cope with the ending of the group counseling relationship.

EVALUATION

A converse relationship seems to exist between evaluation and years of experience. For the counselor in training, everything done is evaluated and then with increased experience, few, if any, supervisors insist on evaluating the counselor or what takes place in the counselor's groups. Evaluation can contribute to continued growth on the part of the counselor and group members. Therefore, the group facilitator has a continuing responsibility to assess and evaluate the effectiveness of his/her groups.

Leader Self-Evaluation

The first focus of evaluation by the facilitator should be on self. The leader needs to have a genuine concern and openness to learn about self and one's approach to groups. Coleading a group can provide excellent opportunities for feedback from the coleader about projected attitudes, blind spots, missed opportunities, and general facilitative approaches. Also, the opportunity always exists for self critique through audio tapes or video tapes.

Following each group session, the facilitator might find that a helpful procedure is to examine the following questions:

1. How did the group experience me?

2. What feelings did I experience in this session? Did I express those feelings? Did I have some feelings with which I did not feel comfortable?

3. What were my reactions to various group members? Did I feel "turned off" to some members—rejecting? Do all members know I care about them? Do they feel accepted by me?

4. What did I communicate to each member? Did I say what I really wanted to say? Was my message clearly stated?

5. How much time did I spend focused on the content of the discussion rather than on the interaction taking place or feelings and needs subtly expressed.

6. What do I wish I had said or done? What would I do differently next time?

7. Did I dominate? How willing was I for someone else to assume the leadership role?

Member Evaluation of Group and Facilitator

We have found the following open-end sentence/short paragraph beginnings provide an excellent structure for member evaluation feedback. The group facilitator can take a few minutes at the conclusion of the last session or send a response form home to be mailed back. Members are more likely to be honest if they are not required to identify themselves on the form.

> **Instructions:** Write your first reactions to the following sentence beginnings. Please be as open and honest as you possibly can. You may want to view these as short paragraph beginnings. It is not necessary for you to write your name on this page. The sentence beginnings are

1. This group . . . . .

2. This group leader . . . . .

3. I liked best . . . . .

4. I liked least . . . . .

5. I feel . . . . .

For more specific feedback from members about their reactions to the group facilitator, use the rating scale shown in Figure 10.1.

Whether or not questionnaires are administered in the last session or mailed to group members after the group ends, consideration should be given to the length of the questionnaire. Group members may feel overwhelmed with a twenty or thirty item questionnaire requiring lengthy responses to each item. The following is an example of a more specific questionnaire.

1. Of what changes have you become aware in your attitudes, feelings about yourself, and relationships with other people?

2. How did the group experience help these changes to come about?

3. What did the group leader do that was most helpful and least helpful to you?

4. Was the group experience hurtful to you in any way or did it have any negative effect on you?

5. Briefly identify any group exercises you especially liked or disliked?

6. In what ways do you wish you had been different in the group?

7. How are you most different as a result of the group experience?

GROUP COUNSELOR RATING SCALE

Counselor's Name ⎯⎯⎯⎯⎯⎯⎯⎯⎯⎯⎯⎯⎯⎯⎯⎯⎯

INSTRUCTIONS: Rate your group counselor as you see her/him functioning in your group.

RESPECT: Shows a real respect for the group members by attentiveness, warmth, efforts to understand and freedom of personal expression.

5.0	4.5	4.0	3.5	3.0	2.5	2.0	1.5	1.0
very high		high		moderate		low		very low

EMPATHY: Communicates an accurate understanding of the group members' feelings and experiences. The group members know the counselor understands how they feel.

5.0	4.5	4.0	3.5	3.0	2.5	2.0	1.5	1.0
very high		high		moderate		low		very low

GENUINENESS: Realness. Everything he/she does seems to be real. That's the way he/she really is. This person doesn't put up a front.

5.0	4.5	4.0	3.5	3.0	2.5	2.0	1.5	1.0
very high		high		moderate		low		very low

CONCRETENESS: "Tunes in" and responds to specific feelings or experiences of group members. Avoids responding in generalities.

5.0	4.5	4.0	3.5	3.0	2.5	2.0	1.5	1.0
very high		high		moderate		low		very low

SELF-DISCLOSURE: Let's group know about relevant immediate personal feelings. Open, rather than guarded.

5.0	4.5	4.0	3.5	3.0	2.5	2.0	1.5	1.0
very high		high		moderate		low		very low

SPONTANEITY: Can respond without having to "stop and think." Words and actions seem to flow easily.

5.0	4.5	4.0	3.5	3.0	2.5	2.0	1.5	1.0
very high		high		moderate		low		very low

FLEXIBILITY: Adapts to a wide range of conditions without losing his/her composure. Can adapt to meet the needs of the moment.

5.0	4.5	4.0	3.5	3.0	2.5	2.0	1.5	1.0
very high		high		moderate		low		very low

CONFIDENCE: Trusts his/her abilities. Acts with directness and self-assurance.

5.0	4.5	4.0	3.5	3.0	2.5	2.0	1.5	1.0
very high		high		moderate		low		very low

Figure 10.1. Group member evaluation of facilitator.

The experience of writing about the group and self can help members clarify and substantiate for themselves meaningful changes which need to be supported and encouraged.

Member Self-evaluation

Evaluation often seems to be a natural part of the last stages of maturation of the group counseling experience and results from the need members have to feel successful, that something worthwhile has been accomplished. This evaluation process will seldom take the form of members relating specific defined goals but will usually occur in the last few sessions as members share their perception of how they have changed, what the experience has meant to them or changes they perceive in other members. A synthesis of what has gone on before may be described in light of specific group experiences. This is a natural approach to evaluation and should be recognized as such by the group facilitator.

Since groups have a life of their own, members may redefine their goals and expectations as a natural process of changes experienced during the course of the experience. Therefore, in some instances to evaluate the group or changes in members on the basis of initially defined purposes or by contracts established may not be appropriate. Evaluation should always allow for and take into consideration the dynamics of the process of change inherent in counseling groups. In light of such experiences, members may redefine their expectations of self or may set new goals.

If group members are asked to keep a daybook as described in an earlier chapter, this can provide the group facilitator with on-going insight into the member's experiential evaluation of the personal impact of the group. Daybook entries also provide an excellent overview of the on-going process of the group and afford members the opportunity to assess changes in a nonevaluative manner. Thus the daybook is a nonthreatening source of member self evaluation.

FOLLOW-UP SESSIONS

Scheduling a follow-up session two to three months after the group's termination and apprising members of such can provide an impetus for members to continue to work on growth promoting areas of change. For short-term intensive time-limited groups, a follow-up session is essential to afford members the opportunity to deal with unresolved issues and to receive support and encouragement from the group. A major criticism of short-term intensive groups is the failure of the facilitator to provide for such follow-up sessions. According to Gazda (1978), facilitators of short-term groups are responsible for

1. planning a follow-up session,

2. developing a referral source of professionals to whom they can refer group members when continued professional involvement by the facilitator is not possible, and

3. informing group members of other sources of assistance.

The follow-up session can provide an excellent opportunity for group members to identify new goals for themselves and to explore sources for continued growth toward these new goals as well as to work on any unresolved issues. This is typically not a time when major issues are resolved. After being "on their own" for several weeks, members seem to need emotional support and affirmation more than they need answers or advice. Perceptions of changes are shared, gains solidified, and areas of concern for self and others shared.

Evaluation and follow-up are crucial steps in the total group counseling process and should not be viewed as an appendage to be added on to the group experience. A systematic and effective evaluation procedure can greatly enhance the facilitative efforts of the group leader. Follow-up sessions help members to maintain focus on self and to renew commitment to change.

SUMMARY

Termination of a counseling group is much more than just the ending of a group. In this chapter termination has been presented as a dynamic process which is just as vital to the functioning of the group as is any other part. Resistance to termination has been explored and procedures for termination have been discussed.

Evaluation is a necessary and significant factor in the group facilitator's effort to provide effective help to group members. The group facilitator should engage in a process of developing self-awareness and be open to feedback from group members.

Follow-up sessions can be a means of providing an impetus for members to continue to work on growth promoting areas of change. Therefore, group facilitators are encouraged to plan ahead for follow-up sessions.

REFERENCES

Allen, F.H. (1942). *Psychotherapy with children.* New York: W.W. Norton.

Corey, G., & Corey, M.S. (1987). *Groups: Process and practice.* Monterey: Brooks/Cole.

Gazda, G.M. (1978). *Group counseling: A developmental approach.* Boston: Allyn & Bacon.

Mahler, C.A. (1969). *Group counseling in the schools.* Boston: Houghton Mifflin.

McGee, T., Schuman, B., & Racusen, F. (1972). Termination in group psychotherapy. *American Journal of Psychotherapy.* 528-532.

Ohlsen, M.M. (1977). *Group counseling.* New York. Holt, Rinehart and Winston.

Yalom, I.D. (1985). *The theory and practice of group psychotherapy.* New York: Basic Books.

SUGGESTED READING

Yalom, I.D. (1985). *The theory and practice of group psychotherapy (3rd ed.).* New York: Basic Books.

Yalom's classic book is widely considered one of the very best ever published in this field. Dr. Yalom, who is professor of Psychiatry at Stanford University, brings his many years of experience as a writer and practitioner to bear in the 3rd edition of this text. His highly readable style will benefit both the beginning student and the more advanced group leader.

Yalom's consistent brand of eclectic group intervention is in evidence throughout as he addresses therapeutic factors in the group and issues such as interpersonal learning, group cohesiveness, transference and transparency, and the group therapist herself.

Special chapters deal with basic issues such as selection of members, group composition, problem members, and the details of beginning a group. He also discusses characteristics of the advanced group, specialized groups and the training of group leaders.

His integration of clinical experience and pertinent research in the field of group psychotherapy makes this must reading for the serious group leader.

CHAPTER 11

CHILDREN
AND
ADOLESCENTS

Children and adolescents need and want assistance. Group counseling is an excellent means to assist in their development, to learn about themselves and how to prevent negative and increase positive interpersonal relationships, and to explore the here-and-now while considering implications for the future.

GROUP COUNSELING WITH CHILDREN

As an age group, children are probably the least understood and the most difficult to work with for most counselors. Children do not communicate in the customary ways familiar to most adults. They often fail to follow the usual rules of courtesy in groups and are not inclined to be turned on by insight inducing self-exploration as are most adults. They can be blatently disruptive and may even ignore the best facilitation moves the counselor has to offer. While these points are typically true of children's groups, they can also be the most alive, active, sensitively caring and rewarding groups. Greater group faciliation skill may actually be required for working with children's groups because they are developmentally more diverse and more likely to stimulate the subjective values of the facilitator. It may be quite difficult for many group facilitators to refrain from reacting as a typical parent to disruptive behavior in a children's group, something that almost never happens in most adult groups.

Goals and Purposes

In group counseling relationships, children experience the therapeutic releasing qualities of discovering that their peers have problems too, and a diminishing of the barriers of feeling all alone. A feeling of belonging develops and new interpersonal skills are attempted in a "real life" encounter where children learn more effective ways of relating to people through the process of trial and error. The group then is a microcosm of children's everyday world. In this setting children are afforded the opportunity for immediate reactions from peers as well as the opportunity for vicarious learning. Children also develop a sensitivity to others and receive a tremendous boost to their self concept through being helpful to someone else. For abused children who have poor self concepts and a life history of experiencing failure, discovering they can be helpful to someone else may be the most profound therapeutic quality possible. In the counseling group children also discover they are worthy of respect and that their worth is not dependent on what they *do* or what they *produce* but rather on *who* they are.

As in group counseling for adolescents and adults, group counseling for children is basically a psychological and social process in which children learn about themselves and others and the dynamics of interacting in ways which are mutually satisfying and basically encouraging. When children experience difficulty in developing appropriate social relationships, lack self discipline in controlling their own behavior, have poor self-esteem, experience a lack of motivation or in general have difficulty in developing coping behaviors that enable them to make adequate and self-enhancing adjustments, group counseling can be considered a significant intervention process. Emphasis on succeeding coupled with a high incidence of divorce, alcoholic parents, physical abuse, sexual abuse, financially stressed parents, and parents who abuse drugs are all factors that may contribute to stressed children who have difficulty coping or succeeding, especially in classrooms. We believe group counseling experiences should be provided for children before they begin to experience the consistent and cumulative failure that often leads to an unhealthy self-concept.

Special Considerations

Although the basic principles of group counseling apply to working with children in groups, some additional essential considerations are needed regarding the structuring of sessions. A basic rule of thumb is the younger the children, the shorter the attention span and thus the shorter the session. The most effective time frame for preschool and primary grade children seems to be 30 to 45 minute sessions with some groups meeting twice a week.

A second rule of thumb is the younger the children, the greater the degree of physical activity and thus the smaller the group. Groups of five to six children are usually recommended through age nine. Play therapy groups might have only two or three children depending on the needs of the children and the size of the play room or play area.

If the therapeutic group approach is based primarily on verbal discussion, then the third rule of thumb is the younger the children, the less they know about how to function in a group, and thus the more structure is needed. Our own experience has shown that as children learn how to assume responsibility for their behavior in the group, less emphasis is needed on structure.

The same ethical codes of professional conduct required for working with adults apply when working with children. The counselor employed in an agency or private practice must obtain approval from the parent or legal guardian. By law parents are responsible for children and therefore must be informed about the nature of the group counseling procedure and consent secured. Because of the high incidence of divorce in our society, the counselor must ensure that permission is obtained from the adult who has legal custody of the child. In most public schools obtaining parental permission is not an issue because the counseling program is considered to be an extension of the educational program of the school. However, this is not the case in all public schools; so the counselor is well advised to be acquainted with local school policy.

An appropriate procedure in most children's groups is to review basic group rules during the first session. Children need to know what limits are in effect; therefore, reviewing rules for group interaction such as one person talks at a time, remain seated, and listen to others can be a way of helping children to learn how to function effectively as a group. Responsibility can be conveyed to the group by asking the children to share what rules they think are necessary to have a successful group. As will be discussed later, in play therapy groups, limitations on behaviors are best stated at the time they are needed.

Group counseling with children is distinctly different than group counseling with adults. Children are not as capable of verbally expressing themselves as are adults. Their natural means of interaction is play and activity-oriented. Indeed, for children below nine or ten years of age, the natural means of *communication* is play. Therefore, counselors for children's groups must have had supervised training with children so they will know how to effectively utilize this medium to facilitate children's communication with each other and the counselor

Formats

Formats for counseling with children in groups should take into consideration the developmental level of children and should be based on children's natural means of communicating their emotional and social needs. Since children's natural "language" is play, they are much more comfortable acting out their behavior than talking about their problems or concerns. Therefore, exclusive emphasis on the interview or discussion type format of group counseling is not recommended for children below nine years of age.

When children feel uncomfortable trying to conduct themselves appropriately with what is for them an awkward
procedure, the relationship which is so crucial to the group
counseling process is slow to develop. Depending on the age
of the children, the formats for group counseling with
children which are recommended are group play therapy,
activity group therapy, and structured group counseling.

Group Play Therapy

Meaning of Play. Group play therapy is recommended for
children to age nine and takes into consideration the
developmental implications of abstract reasoning and thinking which are not fully developed until approximately age ten
or eleven. Since much of our verbal language is communication based on abstract symbols, children below age nine
experience difficulty using this medium to express feelings
and explore relationships. A difference also exists between
children's production and comprehension of language. The
level of children's understanding typically surpasses the
maturity of their speech. To restrict children to verbal
expression imposes unnecessary limitations on the communication which must take place between children and the
counselor and within the group if the time together is to be a
therapeutic experience. Play is to children what verbalization
is to adults. It is a medium for expressing feelings, exploring
relationships, describing experiences, disclosing wishes, and
achieving self-fulfillment.

Amster (1943, pp. 62-67) has listed six uses of play.

1. Play can be used for diagnostic understanding of the child.

2. Play can be used to establish a working relationship.

3. Play can be used to break through a child's way of playing in
   his daily life and his defenses against anxiety.

4. Play can be used to help a child verbalize certain conscious
   material and associated feelings.

5. Play can be used to help a child act out unconscious material and to relieve the accompanying tension.

6. Play can be used to develop a child's play interests which he can carry over into his daily life and which will strengthen him for his future life.

Play Process. In the natural course of interacting with each other in the playroom, children learn not only about other children but also about themselves. Ginott (1961) suggested the presence of several children in the playroom helps to anchor the experience to the world of reality. In the process of interacting, children help each other assume responsibility in interpersonal relationships. Children then are able to naturally and immediately extend these interactions with peers outside the setting of group play therapy (Barlow, Strother, & Landreth, 1986). Unlike most other approaches to group counseling, in group play therapy no group goals exist and group cohesion is not an essential part of the developing process.

Playroom and Toys. The physical setting for group play therapy can be either a playroom designated for that purpose or a part of a larger room with toys and materials appropriately displayed. A major consideration is a setting that affords privacy and is large enough to afford a certain degree of freedom within the context of limitations on destructiveness. A room that is too small restricts children's expressions and may promote frustration. Likewise a room that is too large may encourage too much activity and inhibits the development of a relationship with the counselor or other children because too little contact and interaction occurs.

Since toys and materials are used by children to communicate their personal world, Landreth (1987) recommended selecting toys and materials that facilitate the following goals:

1. establishment of a positive relationship with a child,

2. expression of a wide range of feelings,

3. exploration of real life experiences,

4. testing of limits,

5. development of a positive image,

6. development of a self-understanding, and

7. opportunity to redirect behaviors unacceptable to others.

He recommended toys that represent the three broad categories of

1. *real-life toys,* such as a doll, bendable doll family, doll house and furniture, nursing bottle, play dishes, small car, airplane, and telephone;

2. *acting-out or aggressive-release toys,* such as handcuffs, dart gun, toy soldiers, pounding bench, rubber knife, and inflatable punching toys; and

3. *toys for creative expression and emotional release,* such as crayons, newsprint, blunt scissors, pipe cleaners, popsicle sticks, Play-Doh, hand puppets, Nerf ball, Gumby, scotch tape, and nontoxic glue or paste.

Activity Group Counseling

Activity group therapy is recommended for children ages nine to thirteen, who are still developmentally play and activity oriented but also to whom the group and team activities are extremely important.

Meaning of Activity. At this age, children generally feel more comfortable in and thus prefer same-sex groups. They are not comfortable talking about their problems and are much more likely to act out their emotional reactions. As Slavson (1945), one of the pioneers of the activity group therapy approach, has stated, "What little children gain through play and acting out, young children in their latency period and early adolescents achieve through manual activity, creative expression, and free play interaction with one another. Older adolescents and adults require verbal expression and insight to gain the same results" (p. 202). Slavson viewed the acting out behavior of children in the therapeutic process as a primary form of communication.

Selection of Members. In activity group counseling, a great deal of attention is paid to member selection and the balancing of groups because there is very little counselor intervention. The activity and the interaction of the group members are viewed as the primary facilitators of change and growth. Ginott (1968) recommended that certain children not be placed in activity group counseling:

1. those with premature and persistent preoccupation with sexual matters,

2. those who have actively engaged in homosexual activities,

3. psychopathic preadolescents,

4. destructive preadolescents whose aggressiveness is deep-rooted in hostility toward self or others,

5. those with long histories of stealing outside the home (those who steal only at home may be seeking affection),

6. those who recently have been involved in a trauma or catastrophe, and

7. those suffering from intense sibling rivalry.

Counselor Role. The role of the counselor is characterized as permissive and nonintervening. "S.R. Slavson has used the term 'neutral' in describing the role of the worker in Activity Group Therapy. He does not use it in the sense that the worker demonstrates fairness in conflict situations between children, which is also true, but rather, as a quality of being available and meaningful to the children in terms of each child's unique need. Each child 'makes' of the worker that which he requires" (Schiffer, 1969, pp. 46-47). Limits on behavior are introjected as suggestions for behavior rather than as attempts to stop behavior. For example, if a child began painting the leg of the easel, the counselor would take newspaper over and place it on the floor and offer the child a smock. This method is viewed as having a compressing effect on the behavior (Schiffer, 1969).

Process. Schiffer (1969) described the therapeutic process in the play group as being set in motion through the purposeful use of permissiveness by the counselor which results in the following phases:

Preparatory Phase

- Introduction to the play group and the children's initial reactions to permissiveness
- Testing the reality of the new experience
- Discovery and relaxation

Therapeutic Phase

- Development of transference on multiple levels—toward the worker and the other children
- Regression
- Aggression
- Abatement of anxiety and guilt
- Catharsis

Reeducational Phase: Integrative, Maturational

- Increased frustration tolerance and capacity for delaying gratifications
- Development of personal skills: expansion of interest areas
- Improved self-image
- Sublimation
- Success in intragroup participation: recognition from the group
- Group controls become more efficient; responsiveness of the individual to the group increases
- Interaction resembles that of normal groups
- Transference becomes diluted; identifications move closer to reality

Termination

- Temporary regression in behavior resulting from separation anxiety
- Acceptance and conclusion (pp. 2-3)

Activity Rooms and Materials. For activity group counseling, a designated activity room is a must. Usually a room of approximately 300 square feet is considered adequate for a group of six children. Schiffer (1969) suggested the following materials for activity group counseling

Objects representing significant persons and animals: dolls, puppets, a large inflatable plastic figure, face masks.

Objects which are identified with significant persons and their activities: adult "dress-up" clothing, crib, carriage, refrigerator, sink, toy size house furniture.

Plastic, multifunctional media: poster paints, finger paints, plasticene clay, self-hardening clay, blocks, water.

Manipulative skill and craft materials: lumber and basic wood working tools, looms for weaving, leather craft, materials for sewing, knitting, crocheting.

Recreational supplies, toys and games: ring toss, a soft rubber ball, a simple boxed game which two or more children can play at one time, dominoes, checkers, pick-up-sticks, Nok Hockey, truck, auto, airplane. (p. 73)

Other standard furnishings are tables, chairs, easel, cabinets, bookshelves, sink, broom, dust pan, mop, pail, newspapers, etc.

Length of Sessions. Sessions of an hour and a half to two hours once a week are generally recommended with the last thirty minutes reserved for refreshment time. The refreshment time is usually the only time when the children come together as a group. The counselor sits with the group but is not the leader. This time usually becomes a time for planning outings and group activities.

Structured Group Counseling

By structured group counseling is meant group counseling experiences which basically rely upon the limited ability of children to verbally discuss topics which have been predetermined by the group counselor and are focused on by presentations through some form of structured media such as puppets, stories, role playing, games, activities, or a highly structured series of questions and discussion stimulus leads.

"Structured groups are developed to meet specific needs of participants by helping them develop specific skills, address certain life transitions, or address specific issues or themes relevant to the lives of those who join the group. The specific topic of the group varies, but there is a focus on providing participating members with new skills, or with helping members address a specific topic relevant to their lives" (Ohlsen, Horne, & Lawe, 1988, p. 316).

Guidelines for Structuring. As has been described in a previous chapter, some degree of structure is evident in all group counseling relationships. Structure should be utilized as a means for achieving goals and not as a means for control. Therefore, the most appropriate structure provides for flexibility. Day and Sparacio (1980) presented the following guidelines for utilizing structure:

1. Structure should be negotiated or requested, not coerced. Clients should be given the opportunity to respond and react to structure as well as to be able to modify it.

2. Structure, particularly restrictions and limitations, should not be applied for punitive reasons or in a punitive manner.

3. The counselor should be aware of his or her rationale for structuring and should explain the reasons at the time of structuring or be prepared to provide rationale in response to the client's request for explanation.

4. The counselor should be guided by the client's readiness for structure and by the context of the relationship and process.

5. Too much or a too-rigid structure can be constraining for both the client and the counselor.

6. Ill-timed, lengthy, or insensitive structuring can result in client frustration or resistance and can interrupt the continuity of the therapeutic process.

7. Unnecessary and purposeless recitation of rules and guidelines can imply that the counselor is more concerned with procedure than with helpfulness. In fact, a compulsive approach to

structuring can be indicative of low levels of counselor self-assurance.

8. The counselor must relate structure to the client's emotional, cognitive, and behavioral predisposition.

9. Structuring can imply that the relationship will continue with this particular client. It may turn out that the counselor will decide not to work with this client, or that the client may not be suitable for this counselor.

10. Structure cannot replace or substitute for therapeutic competence. Structure is not a panacea. It is not the total solution to building a productive therapeutic relationship. Structure is complementary and supplementary to human relations, communications, diagnostic, and intervention skills. (pp. 248-249)

Activity-Interview Group Counseling. Although children lack the verbal facility to express themselves fully and possess inadequate group intervention skills, Gazda (1973) believed appropriate structured and training activities can be utilized to help children learn how to function adequately in groups. In his format, games and activities are followed by discussion of the relevance of experiences or activities to the problem behavior in need of modification. After the first three or four free toy play sessions which are viewed as relationship building experiences, the counselor structures the last half of each 40 to 60-minute session through reading and telling stories and incorporates puppets in the process. Gazda recommended moving from puppets to dolls in structuring situations dealing with problems at hand. The children are asked to use dolls to work out solutions. In many instances, interpersonal problems which develop during the free play part of the session become the focus of the structured problem-solving discussion. Free play activities and games should be selected according to needs of group members and should be varied across sessions in order to accommodate interests of a variety of members. As the children learn how to function more effectively in a group, Gazda suggested moving toward structuring most of a given session.

A word of caution is offered: the completion of a game or planned activity should not supersede a meaningful and appropriate spontaneously generated discussion. Structure should be flexible.

Structured Games and Multimedia. Another approach to structuring is the utilization of simulation games and comprehensive multimedia programs such as the *SRA Focus series* and the *Developing Understanding of Self and Others (DUSO)* kit to structure the entire session. In simulation games, children face reality oriented problems and must work out strategies for surmounting them. Such games teach knowledge and skills and provide for the development of self-awareness. The DUSO program is structured around activities which include open-ended stories, role playing, puppetry activity lessons, and pictures to stimulate group discussion.

Selection of Members. Advocates of simulation games propose that these procedures are appropriate for all ages. Materials such as the *DUSO* program are designed for children in primary and early intermediate grades. Activity-interview counseling is recommended for children ages nine to thirteen.

GROUP COUNSELING FOR ABUSED CHILDREN

Of the many groups of children in our society who are at risk, none is perhaps any more needy or present a wider range of problems than children who have been abused. The U.S. Department of Health, Education and Welfare (1975, p.1) defined child abuse as the "physical or mental injury, sexual abuse, negligent treatment or maltreatment of a child's welfare under circumstances which indicate the child's health or welfare is harmed or threatened." According to some estimates, as many as three million children may be abused each year in the United States. Every state has a child abuse law which requires the reporting child abuse.

Goals and Purposes

Because abusive parents are so inconsistent and unpredictable, children learn to distrust not only their parents but other significant adults in their lives including counselors. In addition they have learned not to trust themselves or their environment. Consequently, abused children have internalized three significant messages. "Don't talk. Don't trust. Don't feel." To work with abused children is very difficult and requires great patience on the part of the counselor. Abused children may be aggressive, extremely withdrawn, isolated, and/or exhibit academic problems or socially maladaptive behavior. The first major goal with such children is the building of a relationship in which they will feel safe enough to risk trusting a new adult in their lives.

As in the case of other special population children, abused children need to be helped to discover that they are not alone in their experiences and feelings. Such children need opportunities to act out these intrusive experiences and in the process they experience a feeling of being in control. In addition, abused children need opportunities to express the full range of mixed and confusing feelings felt toward the perpetrator.

Selection of Members

Caution must be exercised in placing abused children in group counseling experiences. The feelings associated with abuse are so potentially intense, especially in cases of sexual abuse, that individual counseling may be required initially or in conjunction with group counseling. In cases of recent traumatic sexual abuse, individual counseling would be recommended. Same sex groups are recommended for children of all ages in cases of sexual abuse. This does not seem to be a necessary prerequisite for other forms of abuse.

Intervention Strategies

Group play therapy is the most preferred format for children below ten years of age because it affords children who are unable to verbalize an opportunity to express their feelings. For older children, the structured group counseling format could use focused discussion topics and simulated games to help children share and explore what they have experienced and their feelings and reactions.

GROUP COUNSELING FOR
CHILDREN OF DIVORCE

The incidence of divorce touches at least fifty percent of the children in the United States and leaves many of them feeling bewildered, confused, hurt, angry, rejected, or abandoned. Since children are egocentric, many feel guilty, believing that something they did caused the divorce. Some children experience serious problems in development as a result of the trauma of divorce. Younger children experience their world in a very concrete manner, and therefore, many fear that if parents can "abandon" each other, they too can be abandoned. This fear may result in a developing distrust of any adult who seems to care.

Goals and Purposes

Children of divorce need opportunities to express their feelings and reactions in a safe and constructive environment which breaks down the barriers of isolation and provides experiential communication with which they feel comfortable. Hammond (1981) suggested the following goals for group counseling with children of divorce:

1. To help children talk about and come to understand their feelings about their parents' divorce.

2. To help children understand that they are not alone in their feelings and experiences.

3. To give children an opportunity to learn new coping skills and to share successful coping strategies with others in the group.

4. To help children gain a more realistic view of the divorce situation and move toward acceptance of themselves and their family.

Selection of Members

Eleven and twelve year old children would seem to be best suited for the structured group counseling format because of their abstract reasoning ability and their ability to generalize from the group experience to daily life. Group play therapy would provide younger children with constructive physical outlets for their anger and the opportunity through play to develop a feeling of control at a crucial time when their world seems to be out of control. Both formats would help children to discover they are not alone.

Intervention Strategies

The *Children's Divorce Group* described by Wilkinson and Bleck (1977) consists of eight 45-minute sessions for upper-grade elementary school students. The sessions are structured around introductions, agreeing on rules for the group, activities focused on feelings, drawing the family, problem-solving techniques, integrating role playing, and puppets.

Hammond (1981) described a six session format utilizing get acquainted exercises, films, role playing, brainstorming, bibliotherapy, assertiveness training, games, strength bombardment exercises, and group discussion.

GROUP COUNSELING WITH ADOLESCENTS

Adolescence is generally regarded as a period of great change. For many adolescents, this stage of development is characterized by conflict, questioning of values, a bewildering array of choices, confusing physiological changes, and an overwhelming need for approval by peers. Added to these stressors is an increased pressure to be responsible for one's own actions. During this stage of development many adolescents feel they are alone in their mire of self-doubt. They seek approval from others, especially peers, and at the same time struggle with the issue of independence-dependence in relationships involving significant others. For most adolescents, this is a time of enormous peer pressure. Values and traditions are questioned in light of peer group reaction and standards. The need for peer approval and acceptance may often be stronger than their own issues of self-respect. Adolescents often look to their peer group for self-identity. Therefore, this is an opportune time to utilize group counseling to deal with feelings of isolation and the overwhelming number of choices facing adolescents.

A couple of cautions about working with adolescent groups would seem to be in order at this point. As with all counseling groups, a facilitator has the ethical responsibility to clarify group functions and actions. A counselor who haphazardly brings together groups for no clear purpose cannot expect trust and respect to develop within the group. The prospective members must know why the group has been established. Since adolescents are often sent to counseling under duress and are made to feel that whatever happened is their fault, counselors need to be very careful that they are not perceived as defender of authority figures.

Purpose and Goals

Since adolescents have such a strong need for peer identification and approval, group counseling is especially appropriate because it provides a supportive atmosphere in which they feel safe enough to risk sharing their concerns. Through the interaction process in the group, they discover other adolescents have similar problems, and that they are not alone. Within the group counseling structure, many adolescents experience for the first time that they can give as well as receive help. To receive help from another person or a group is a positive experience, but indeed a much more powerful experience is for adolescents to discover they can be helpful to another person. Out of such experiences comes a respect for self as adolescents experience a sense of usefulness and an acceptance of themselves as contributing persons in the lives of other members. Adolescents also learn they are unique and special and that they are genuinely accepted by a group of peers whom they have come to admire and respect. These therapeutic factors contribute to the development of a cohesive, growth promoting group. Adolescent's perceptions of the therapeutic factors in group counseling provide helpful insight into the importance of such a group experience. The factors selected by adolescents as most helpful, according to Corder, Whiteside, and Haizlip (1981, p. 348) are as follows:

Learning to express my feelings.

Learning that I must take ultimate responsibility for the way I live my life.

Other members honestly telling me what they think of me.

Being in the group was, in a sense, like being in a big family, only this time, a more-accepting and understanding family.

Belonging to a group of people who understand and accept me.

The group giving me an opportunity to learn to approach others.

Seeing I was just as well off as others.

Helping others and being important in their lives.

These therapeutic factors could easily be translated into general goals for adolescent group members. As with any group, however, the adolescent group members must decide for themselves what specific goals are appropriate. Ohlsen, Horne, and Lawe (1988) have taken a unique approach to stating the general goals for adolescent counseling groups by identifying adolescent's needs as follows:

1. Search for identity by defining meaningful goals for various facets of life.

2. Increase understanding of their interests, abilities, and aptitudes.

3. Improving skills for identifying opportunities and for evaluating them in terms of their own interests, abilities, and aptitudes.

4. Increasing interpersonal skills and self-confidence to recognize and solve their problems.

5. Improving interpersonal skills and self-confidence to recognize when decisions are required, how to make them, and how to implement them.

6. Increasing sensitivity to others' needs and improving skills for helping others satisfy their needs.

7. Improving communication skills for conveying their real feelings directly to relevant persons, and with considerations for their feelings.

8. Independence to examine what they believe, to make their own decisions, to take reasonable risks, to make mistakes, and to learn from their mistakes.

9. Improving interpersonal skills to deal with authority figures in a mature manner; for example, employers, police, government officials as well as parents and teachers.

10. Meaningful participation in developing and maintaining limits on their own behavior.

11. Growing knowledge and skills for coping with their physical and emotional changes associated with maturation.

12. Improving skills to learn and live new roles. (pp. 275-276)

Intervention Strategies

Topics addressed in adolescent groups should be directly related to changes occurring in their lives. For example, junior high students are generally concerned with socialization issues, while high school students are more concerned with self. Other common topics or themes which arise in adolescent counseling groups are alcohol and drug abuse, relationships with parents, conflicts at school, making one's own decisions, feeling rejected and unloved, learning to repress feelings appropriately, and relating to the opposite sex.

Although to specify a topic is sometimes advisable for certain sessions or to develop a group theme, spontaneously generated problems or concerns of members not related to the topic should be encouraged. Such spontaneous discussions are often the most productive and usually touch areas of concern or feelings of other group members.

Adolescents are not as developmentally capable of coping with uncertainty as are most adults. Therefore, some structuring of sessions will help group members to feel more secure and thus more willing to risk sharing in keeping with the direction provided by the structure. Apparent disinterest by some adolescents in the group may mask their fear of being unable to express appropriately and comfortably their feelings and needs. **Role playing,** one of the most easily utilized intervention strategies, is especially effective with adolescents because they are allowed to be someone else and thus are not as likely to be self conscious.

Role playing can be a means of gaining practical experience in expression of feelings. This informal here-and-now reality dramatization allows adolescents an opportunity to take on various roles and in the process to develop insight into how another person thinks, feels, and experiences. It is a learning through experiencing activity and thus can have a significant impact on experience prone teenagers. Role playing also affords teenagers the opportunity to practice human-relations skills and is highly recommended for practicing communication with parents, teachers, peers, and employers. Role playing fosters creative problem-solving, helps members express themselves more spontaneously, improves communication, increases involvement in the group inter-action, increases feelings of empathy for others, and facilitates the development of new insights into self.

Other techniques or intervention strategies which have been found to be helpful in working with adolescents are **human potential lab exercises** for teaching adolescents how to give positive feedback, assertiveness training, decision making training, and socialization skill building exercises. These techniques are described in *Group Techniques* by Corey, Corey, Callahan, and Russell, (1982), *Self-Awareness Through Group Dynamics* by Reichert (1970), *Human Relations Development* by Gazda, Asbury, Balzer, Childers, and Walters (1984), and *Handbook of Structured Experiences for Human Relations Training* by Pfeiffer and Jones (1983).

Problem Focused Groups

Topic or theme oriented groups fit naturally into the developmental concerns of adolescents and have been shown to be quite effective with those adolescents typically labeled as difficult or hard to reach. These are the adolescents who do not feel they fit in and thus do not identify with or feel they are a part of the school setting. They lack motivation in the direction desired by most adults in schools but nevertheless are motivated in the direction of what seems to them to be important in their lives. We believe all adolescents are motivated. *The counselor's task, therefore, becomes one of developing the kind of setting and atmosphere which builds upon this motivation rather than trying to develop motivation.* Peer identification among "hard to reach" adolescents is one of the most powerful sources of motivation they experience and can be utilized in the group counseling setting to help such adolescents to examine and change their attitudes, goals, and self-defeating behaviors. Beginning group counselors are often amazed at the constructive suggestions and creative problem-solving ideas generated by adolescents who have been labeled as problem students by other adults. This inherent group move or push toward positive, constructive behavior has been noted in a wide variety of special high risk groups focusing on topics such as school truancy, classroom management problems, repeated discipline violations, drug abuse, and run-aways. In a caring supportive environment such as develops in a counseling group, adolescents can move toward accepting greater self-responsibility and in turn encourage other members to do the same.

Example of Problem Focused Group. One of the most exciting topic or theme oriented groups we have organized was structured around teen-age chronic traffic violators. The project is described here as an example of how such groups can be organized.

1. Identified Group: Teen-Age Chronic Traffic Violators.

2. Rationale: Teen-age drivers are experimenting with new found freedom, are notorious for taking unnecessary risks, and use automobiles as an avenue and extension for expressing their feelings. They lack the maturity which comes with experience in making decisions in a wide variety of situations and often respond impulsively when driving, using the automobile as an expression of their frustrations. Traffic fines seem to have little or no significant or lasting impact on the recurrence of traffic violations by teen-agers. A group of teen-agers who are all traffic violators can provide the opportunity for peers to share their feelings, gain insight into their behavior and learn to delay gratification or feelings by bringing them to the group for sharing rather than acting out with an automobile. An assumption is that many chronic teen-age traffic violators have poor self-concepts. A supportive peer group can be a powerful instrument in helping teen-agers develop more positive attitudes and feelings about self.

3. Group Membership: This group was composed of high school students who had committed more than five major traffic violations in the past year. Expiration of a safety sticker, exceeding the speed limit by no more than five miles per hour, etc., were not considered major traffic violations. The program was explained to court officials and they agreed to give these teen-agers a choice. They could choose to pay the fines or go to group counseling for an undetermined length of time with no guarantee at the end of that time that the fines would not have to be paid. The judge would consider the recommendation of the peer group. Screening was conducted in individual sessions where the nature and purpose of the group was explained, choices were clearly stated, and questions answered. Five boys and three girls were selected.

4. Organization of the Group: The group was an open-end group and met for an hour and a half once a week after school hours. Group members understood that a member could not exit the group experience and request a hearing with the judge until the group decided they were ready to terminate the group experience. Group members were free to leave the group at any time but with the understanding that they had not completed their part of the contract and therefore would have to pay the outstanding fines. More than two absences would result in removal from the group.

Written consent was obtained from parents for permission to participate in the group. General basic ground rules were discussed and the point was stressed that members must maintain the confidential nature of other members' disclosures.

5. Topics for Discussion: In the first session, members were invited to share their reason for being in the group and considerable unsolicited discussion occurred of details surrounding traffic tickets received. This was viewed as a natural stage in the group's movement toward getting acquainted and establishing trust. An explanation was made to the group that this was their group and they could each get out of the group what they felt was important for them. They were encouraged to say what they thought and felt. The point was emphasized that all topics were appropriate for discussion, not just traffic violations. After the first session, very little discussion of traffic violations or driving habits occurred other than an occasional updating by members of the most recent location of radar units. Recurring themes throughout the sessions involved feeling unloved by parents, feeling no one cared about them, dating relationships, and feeling restricted by too many rules. The group's facilitator never made any attempt to "set the members straight" about their driving habits.

6. Structure of Sessions: A continual task for the facilitator was the necessity of working hard to help members to speak for themselves in concrete terms, to own their behavior, and to focus on the here and now. Role playing was frequently utilized in sessions to assist members in expressing themselves more effectively and to provide opportunities to test reality and practice new behaviors. Some topics such as, "When do you get angry and how do you express your anger?" were introduced into the group, but overall this was a lively group with spontaneously generated topics and concerns which were quite appropriate for the group to explore. An interesting point to note was that members rather quickly began to assume responsibility in the group. This was first observed by members squashing attempts to side track the group.

7. Results. What became apparent early was that the group experienced rather quickly a move from a level of being an opportune way to hopefully avoid paying a traffic ticket to an experience in which members were invested. One example was David who graduated from high school, took a job in a town thirty miles away, worked until the very last minute he could on group day, then jumped into his car and drove as fast as the law permits so he wouldn't be late for group. Encouragement that it was o.k. for him to be late for group was to no avail. He was a leader in the group and found the experience to be tremendously rewarding. Another group member tried to bribe members to allow him to terminate the group early so he could earn more money, and they refused.

A one, two, and three year follow-up of the three groups that completed this program for teen-age chronic traffic violators found that the average number of traffic citations per member per year was reduced from five to less than one per member. Several members received no traffic citations during the three years following the group experience.

SUMMARY

Children need help in learning about themselves, others, and the process of interacting, and the group setting affords all the dynamics necessary for engaging in this significant process. What better way to learn the dimensions of self-control necessary in social interactions than in a play therapy group or activity group setting. These modalities for working with children allow them to utilize their natural means for self expression and in the process easily keep the focus of exploration in the here-and-now because spontaneous and structured play can only occur in the present.

Because of the developmental issue of peer pressure, perhaps no other age group needs group counseling more than adolescents. Socialization issues and self-awareness are key areas of focus and exploration by adolescents, and unlike children's groups, are dealt with primarily through verbal interaction. Insight and self-discovery are exciting adventures for adolescents, especially those adolescents who have poor self-concepts, unsatisfying social relationships and poor impulse control. The group affords an excellent opportunity for adolescents to learn appropriate ways to express feelings, to accept responsibility for self, to discover they are not alone, to experience acceptance, and to discover they can give as well as receive help.

For many adolescents, this is a time of isolation and introversion, and a struggle for independence and a need for dependence. How confusing! There are pressures to conform on the one hand and admonishments on the other to be different and accompanying this bewildering confusion is an overpowering need for approval. The setting is ripe for stress and the inner process of struggle often bubbles over or just simply explodes. Counselors must be sensitive to this process and should be actively involved in providing group counseling experiences for adolescents that will match the inner dynamics of their struggles with an equally dynamic process of therapeutic interaction.

REFERENCES

Amster, F. (1943). Differential uses of play in treatment of young children. *American Journal of Orthopsychiatry, 13*, 62-68.

Barlow, K., Strother, J., & Landreth, G. (1986). Sibling group play therapy. An effective alternative with a mute child. *The School Counselor, 33*, 44-50.

Corder, B., Whiteside, L., & Haizlip, T. (1981). A study of the curative factors in group psychotherapy with adolescents. *International Journal of Group Psychotherapy, 31*, 345-354.

Corey, G., Corey, M.S., Callahan, P.J., & Russell, J.M. (1982). *Group techniques.* Monterey, CA: Brooks/Cole.

Day, R., & Sparacio, R. (1980). Structuring the counseling process. *Personnel and Guidance Journal, 59*, 246-249.

Gazda, G. (1973). Group procedures with children: A developmental approach. In M. Ohlsen (Ed.), *Counseling children in groups.* New York: Holt, Rinehart, Winston.

Gazda, G., Asbury, F., Balzer, F, Childers, C., & Walters, R. (1984). *Human relations development.* Boston: Allyn & Bacon.

Ginott, II. (1961). *Group psychotherapy with children.* New York: McGraw-Hill.

Ginott, H. (1968). Innovations in group psychotherapy with preadolescents. In G. Gazda (Ed.), *Innovations to group psychotherapy.* Springfield, IL: Charles C. Thomas.

Hammond, J. (1981). *Group counseling for children of divorce.* Ann Arbor, MI: Cranbrook.

Landreth, G. (1987). Facilitative use of child's play in elementary school counseling. *Elementary School Guidance and Counseling Journal, 21*, 253-261.

Ohlsen, M., Horne, A., & Lawe, C. (1988). *Group counseling.* New York: Holt, Rinehart & Winston.

Pfeiffer, W., & Jones, J. (1983). *Handbook of structured experiences for human behavior training.* La Jolla, CA: University Associates.

Reichert, R. (1970). *Self-awareness through group dynamics.* Dayton, OH: Pflaum.

Schiffer, M. (1969). *The therapeutic play group.* New York: Grune & Stratton.

Slavson, S. (1945). Differential methods of group therapy in relation to age levels. *Nervous child, 4,* 196-210.

U.S. Department of Health, Education, and Welfare. (1975). *Child abuse and neglect: A report on the status of research.* Washington, D.C.: U.S. Government Printing Office.

Wilkinson, G., & Bleck, E. (1977). Children's divorce groups. *Elementary School Guidance and Counseling, 11,* 204-213.

CHAPTER 12

ADULTS AND ELDERLY

In this chapter we will consider some of the special groups that concern themselves primarily with adult membership. While our sampling in this section is certainly by no means exhaustive, our goal is to present a representation of some of the more commonly encountered groups for mature individuals. We'll begin with family groups, groups for couples, women, the elderly, and conclude with a framework for differentiating among the many kinds of "self-help" groups that are proliferating in our culture. In a later chapter, we will examine and highlight a few of these special interest groups.

FAMILIES

Some consider families to be among the purest kinds of groups in that they occur naturally in our culture. Group counseling for families typically centers around a problem member or identified patient. A "different" family member frequently provides the impetus to enter some kind of therapy program. Family group counseling can occur with one family or with several families together. The larger the group, the more structured activities are usually necessary.

Intra-family issues that normally emerge are those that might be expected in most groups. The major difference is that families are usually living together under the same roof so the potential for conflict is multiplied. Families are concerned with issues of communication, cooperation, trust, competition, and support. Additionally, developmental issues that involve guidance and leadership, independence, risking and growing, and problem solving typically will emerge in group sessions.

Goals and Purposes

Two major focuses in family groups are involved with resolving issues that cause stress and conflict among members thus resulting in what is commonly referred to as the "dysfunctional family," and secondly, an educative function that is both remedial and preventative in nature in that it is designed to equip the family with the necessary skills to manage problems of living on their own.

Selection of Members

Most family practitioners prefer to work with an entire family when significant dysfunction exists. This gives the group leader an opportunity to observe and intervene with the interaction patterns that have developed uniquely with that family. Also, family roles become apparent and provide a rich source for intervention as they impact upon intra-family relationships and the manner in which conflict is dealt with and problems are solved.

Time frames for severely disabled family units may be open-ended. Meeting once per week is usually satisfactory but the duration is less predictable. Families that are more highly motivated and have resolved some of the more basic issues can often profit from a time limited structure of from 10 to 12 sessions where the focus is upon improving living skills.

Intervention Strategies

With most families the therapeutic function of the group needs to be attended to initially. This involves enlisting the various members in the process, developing trust in each other and in the therapist, and examining the way that family members interrelate. In many, it will involve focus upon the presenting problem (or person) with behavioral methods of reducing conflict and eliminating abusive relationships.

As members become involved in the group and family positions are reaffirmed or redesigned, *role-reversal techniques* can be effective in helping family members appreciate the point of view of another. Focus should be upon *listening skills*. *Compromise* and *cooperative tasks* help provide the family with needed awareness and skills. Bonney and Gillis (1986) have proposed a model that includes *adventure activities* and *physical activity* that challenge families in groups.

Finally, creative *homework* assignments that involve the family can help keep the therapy a focus between sessions.

RELATIONSHIP GROUPS FOR COUPLES

The preponderance of couples who seek group counseling for their relationship are in what could be considered traditional marriages that include a man and wife. Some seek pre-marital counsel and others are living together. We believe couple counseling in groups is appropriate for any two people who are in or are in the process of defining themselves in a committed relationship. Most couples will seek counseling because their relationship is in disrepair or at the least, is not approaching the expectations they may have initially had. In some cases couples are looking to strengthen, enrich, or renew their relationships.

Goals and Purposes

The very fact that a couple seeks professional intervention in their relationship is normally a very positive sign that they are motivated to explore the possibility of enhancing their time together as a couple. Even in cases where the relationship may have deteriorated to the point of ambivalence on the part of one or another of the partners, the act of committing to a group is encouraging and represents a reaffirmation of energy devoted to making it better. Corey and Corey (1987) listed several themes that regularly emerge in their work with couples in a weekend retreat format. They include

how to remain separate individuals while benefiting from an intimate relationship,

the myths about marriage and how they lead to unrealistic expectations,

sex roles as they affect a marriage,

alternatives to traditional marriages,

open versus closed marriages,

the importance of commitment in a relationship,

how to reinvent a relationship,

sex and loving in intimate relationships,

the sources of conflict in a marriage,

how to detect communication pitfalls and learn to express one's thoughts and feelings directly, and

how to deal with stress. (p.322)

Selection of Members

Depending upon the format, counseling groups for couples can range from the traditional 8 to 10 persons to several dozen or more in a structured weekend or retreat format. Obviously, with larger numbers the big group would be broken down for small group interaction. In the weekend configuration a good deal of general information can be given to the large group. Small groups can be used to personalize the material, discuss specific issues as they relate to couples, and practice skills that have been modeled in the large group. Fixed duration groups seem to be the most prevalent format due, at least in part, to the more structured and educational nature of the material presented.

Intervention Strategies

One of the primary advantages of the group in working with couples is that it seems to have a socializing impact. According to George and Dustin (1988):

> Within a group setting, spouses appear to be more likely to accept responsibility for talking openly about their own concerns, rather than simply criticizing their mates. They also seem to make greater progress in learning to listen to their spouse, to communicate, to make requests, and to share warmly private feelings. In addition, marriage counseling clients within a group learn to recognize the early signs of conflict, to help each other reveal early what is annoying, and to cooperate with each other in resolving conflicts. (p.144)

Clearly, sensitizing the couple to their unique methods of communication will be a primary focus in the early stages of the group. Focused **bibliotherapy** and **informational lecturettes** centered on common problems and processes within a relationship are an efficient method of broadening a couple's appreciation for the complexities of making a relationship work.

Contracting with couples to give up or modify relationship defeating behaviors from the catastrophic (suicide, insanity, divorce) to the subtle (hobbies, work, recreations) will redirect energy into the relationship and provide a basis for moving from existing *together* to a more enhanced and sharing partnership.

Most couples get stuck in power struggles that occur when their initial illusions of how the relationship was supposed to be gradually give way to the reality of daily living. Discovering that the illusion was created by their own internalized projections can help a couple to move beyond the power struggle to a re-romanticized and working relationship.

GROUPS FOR WOMEN

One of the legacies of the women's movement has been a clearer understanding and appreciation for the special and unique needs of women in our culture. As women continue the struggle to define themselves and their many roles a concurrent emergence of single-issue or special focus groups is evident. Coping with the process of change in a society that puts a high premium on perfectionistic performance has contributed to a need for groups to deal with women's stress, career decisions, the superwoman myth, anger and conflict, relationship dependency, as well as weight control, eating disorders, and recovery from various chemical dependencies. In short, as women have won fuller membership in the social scheme of things, they are consequently faced with all of the attending stresses and anxieties plus a few that are unique to them.

As women attempt to balance traditional roles of wife, mother, and family manager with demanding professional lives, the expectation can be an increase in job dissatisfaction, troubled relationships, and even illnesses.

Goals and Purposes

The relative absence of constructive role models for women provides a strong rationale for support groups that allow members to share some of their universal concerns and anxieties as they attempt to find balance in their priorities. Frequently a healthful procedure is for women to learn that others share their fears and that no one is perfect. The development of a social support system and the establishment of the belief that women are in *control of their own lives* are important learnings that can grow out of the group.

A common problem that women share with many overly responsible and achieving people is that they have very little idea of how to take good care of themselves. They often have become accustomed to and defined themselves as helpers of others (husband, family, colleagues, etc.) frequently at their own expense. This particular personality often suffers from a lack of assertiveness so that they only attend to their own needs when all of their responsibilities and obligations to others have been retired! To behave in even a remotely self-caring manner causes guilt.

A group can be a very reinforcing place for women to learn to be "healthily-selfish" and take better care of themselves. As they begin to see that they can be *better quality* partners, caretakers, and co-workers if they also tend to their own needs for reassurance, praise, support, and quality alone-time, they also can provide a stable support system for each other in the group.

Selection of Members

Issue specific groups will naturally provide for a certain homogeneity of membership. Chronological age and life position will impact on the focus of energy, as women with young children will be concerned with different issues than will those approaching the "empty-nest" stage of life. While much can be gained from the experience of others, probably more benefit both to individuals and to group development will occur if a great disparity in age and life concerns is not existing in members selected.

The more generic "growth" group that may deal with global issues lends itself to an open-ended duration. The more issue-specific groups often profit from a time limited format.

Intervention Strategies

The more issue-specific the group, typically the more structured the format will be. Since members share common concerns, the focus can be more defined which also lends itself to an informational and educative function. ***Informational handouts, bibliotherapy, leader lecturettes, brainstorming,*** and ***behavioral rehearsal*** are examples of techniques that can enhance individual learning in the group.

Requesting members to identify their personal goals and agendas helps focus the group and the individual members.

The use of **daily logs** to record behaviors tends to help group members obtain personal base-line data on their activities as well as providing an opportunity to become more fully aware of feelings associated with those behaviors.

Corey and Corey (1987) in their work with residential workshops have a list of rather broad internal struggles that continue to appear in their participants. They include the following:

> The struggle between the desire to know oneself and the fear of discovering only emptiness inside.
>
> The struggle between the desire to know oneself and the fear of finding that one is like one's parents.
>
> The struggle between the desire to be self-sufficient and the desire to lean on others.
>
> The struggle between the desire to drop one's hard exterior shell and the desire to protect oneself.
>
> The struggle between the desire to respect oneself and the desire to feel sorry for oneself.
>
> The struggle between the desire to get revenge and the desire to forgive. (p.335)

These themes or struggles are general enough so that many women would be able to identify with several of them. As such, they can serve as a springboard to more specific and personalized issues.

OLDER ADULTS

The greying of America is a frequently mentioned cultural phenomenon whose time is upon us. The over 60 age group is the fastest growing segment of the American population. The projections for the future, with more effective health care, increased awareness of healthier life-styles, and the maturation of the baby boom generation is for an even larger group of elderly. This substantial part of the population will require psychological intervention at a rate greater than ever before.

Naturally, not all people over 60 are alike just as all 21 year old adults are not. Some people well into their 80s continue to lead vital and dynamic lives while some who are much younger have begun to experience some of the losses that occur naturally with age. The point is that aging is not so much a matter of chronology as it is with physical and emotional well-being.

Most of the group intervention systems that we will discuss are designed to minimize loss, maintain available levels of functioning, and enhance the lives of those individuals.

Goals and Purposes

Developmentally, older adults must cope with change and loss. Some of the most severe changes and losses occur at times when an individual is seemingly less well equipped to deal with the loss of a spouse and friends, changes in living arrangements, decreased opportunities for social interaction, and the possible loss of physical functioning through illness and disabilities.

For many older persons the aging process is accompanied by a lessening of environmental supports. Particularly for minority elderly, Blacks, Hispanics, Native Americans and Asian Americans, the problems of aging are exacerbated by poverty, sub-standard housing, and inadequate services. Cultural prejudices against the elderly have resulted in stereotypes and beliefs that are now referred to as ageism. All of these factors combined potentially add to feelings of isolation, loneliness, dependency, and despair.

Group counseling can be the treatment of choice as it offers many benefits that individual therapy cannot. Socialization and involvement factors alone can help diminish feelings of helplessness and isolation. Reasonable goals for older persons would include improved relationships with others, increases in self-esteem and confidence, and a renewed sense of purpose. When working with the elderly one often gains a sense that a "Hawthorne-type" effect might influence the process. That is, the very fact that they are being "treated" in the group (paid attention to) may account for some increase in interest and functioning.

In general, group leaders should consider keeping goals rather specific and concrete. They should be immediate and short-term rather than global and poorly defined.

Selection of Members

Pre-group orientation sessions and, if possible, individual interviews, can help in constructing a group with a reasonable chance for success. As with other populations, some initial enthusiasm might wane as realities become apparent. Potential group members should have a good understanding of why the group is being organized, what will be expected of them, and what they might reasonably hope to gain from the group.

Minimal criteria for inclusion in the group might include

- wants to be a member of the group,

- is able to physically get to the group with or without assistance,

- is relatively free of severe hearing impairment,

- has a reasonable level of personal cleanliness,

- is relatively alert and able to express feelings and ideas, and

- has a willingness to communicate.

Careful attention should be paid to the time when group meetings are held so as to not interfere with other important activities.

Intervention Strategies

The most commonly used group interventions with institutionalized elderly include the following:

1. **Reality Oriented Groups.** The focus of the group is on the present. Repetition of current concerns and facts seek to stimulate recent thoughts and memory. The orientation and structure of the group are in the "here and now," with the goal of helping members spend more time in the present. Dates, time, weather, food, activities, and current events are subject matter for the groups.

2. **Remotivation Groups.** The use of selected topics for the group members to discuss that are appealing helps stimulate group involvement. Goals of the group are to assist older people in becoming reinvolved with ideas, feelings, and other people. Music and art are materials that help stimulate the sensory abilities and add to the interest of the groups. Leaders encourage members to become increasingly verbally involved in the group.

3. **Resocialization Groups.** Members of these groups might be more severely withdrawn and suffering from memory impairment. The group is relatively unstructured and members are encouraged to talk about the positive experiences in their past. Group members are supported for learning about other group members— their names, interests, hobbies, etc.

4. **Reminiscing Groups.** Developed by Ebersole (1976) around the concept of life review, this type of group provides an opportunity for older persons to look at the past events of their lives in an attempt to come to some personal resolution. It differs from resocialization in that the reflections are not limited to positive experiences but may include significant life events that were negative. A warm, supportive atmosphere of trust is developed and confrontation is discouraged. This kind of group is more therapeutic in nature because the content can create intense personal reactions. Leaders need to have experience with these kinds of groups or be under supervision.

Generally groups for the elderly need to be brief and time-limited in duration. Ten to twelve weeks is usual. Two or perhaps three sessions per week is useful particularly with reality and remotivation groups. Group leaders will find themselves intervening more frequently with direct, slow, and concrete sentences. An advisable procedure is to pay attention to more complete closure at the end of each session so that unfinished business will be kept to a minimum.

SELF-HELP AND SUPPORT GROUPS

Support groups, mutual-aid groups, leaderless groups, and specific-interest groups are all labels at one time or another attached to a rapidly growing type of group in our society. (The estimate is that during the past decade one-half million groups have developed with 15 million members.)

Support groups are getting more attention in the literature as the need for them increases. As Rosenberg (1984) pointed out, support groups can be defined by the homogeneity of the problem, members who share a common stress as opposed to an illness, members who are willing to publicly state the stress that qualifies them for membership, and members who speak a common language.

Support groups are usually facilitated by professional leaders. While the goals of support groups differ from traditional therapy groups and self-help groups, many leadership functions tend to be similar. Leaders model appropriate behaviors, link members together, interpret the dynamics of the group, and serve as the primary manager of the group. Goals of the support group include increasing a members coping abilities, increased interpersonal insight, and providing members with structured feedback. Clearly, as the label support-group implies, a major component of the group will be to focus upon the supportive nature of the cohesive group (Rosenberg, 1984).

Self-help group leadership is different from support groups in that leaders are typically persons who have "been there." That is, they may be in recovery and are in a position to offer their help to others. Group leaders may have had some formal or informal training in group process and often a professional leader will serve as a consultant to the group. Leaders may be para-professionals or peer leaders. A unique feature of self-help groups is that each member is potentially a future leader.

Types of self-help groups tend to fall into one of four categories.

1. **Physical and/or Emotional Problems.** Examples would include cancer, AIDS, ALS, Parkinsons, depression, phobia, and PMS groups.

2. **Addictive Disorders.** Chemical dependency, relationship addictions, and sexual compulsivity.

3. **Crisis Intervention or Transition Groups.** Groups for grief, step-parenting, divorce, rape trauma, and post-traumatic stress disorders.

4. **Environmental Support Groups.** These groups are organized for family members and others in a position to be impacted by a disease or disorder. Examples include Al-Anon and Alateen, ADD parent groups, Parents of Teens, Co-dependent groups, and groups for male partners as they adjust to sexual assault trauma.

Many local newspapers attest to the burgeoning phenomenon. Extensive lists of local groups and meeting times and places are published weekly. In addition, the National Self-Help Clearing House, 33 W. 42nd St., New York, NY, 10036 is organized to provide information about the availability of self-help groups in many metropolitan areas.

With this framework for differentiating among the many kinds of groups available, we will proceed to highlight in Chapter 13 a few of the special interest groups.

REFERENCES

Bonney, W., & Gillis, H. (1986). Group counseling with couples or families: Adding adventure activities. *Journal for Specialists in Group Work.* *11*(4), 213-219.

Corey, M.S., & Corey, G. (1987). *Groups: Process and practice (3rd ed.).* Monterey, CA: Brooks/Cole.

Ebersole, P. (1976). Problems of group reminiscing with the institutionalized aged. *Journal of Gerontological Nursing, 2,* (6), 23-27.

George, R., & Dustin, D. (1988). *Group counseling: Theory and Practice.* Englewood Cliffs, NJ: Prentice Hall.

Rosenberg, P.P. (1984). Support groups: A special therapeutic entity. *Small Group Behavior, 15,* (2), 173-186.

CHAPTER 13

INDIVIDUALS WITH CHRONIC DISEASES, EMOTIONAL DIFFICULTIES, OR ADDICTIVE BEHAVIORS

INTRODUCTION

A s we move further into discussions of special populations or issue specific groups, it may need to be reiterated that the processes and techniques that we elaborate upon in other sections of this book are *generally* applicable to all groups regardless of their focus or particular group composition. At the same time, some groups deserve special attention because of their unique needs and specific problems. As we have observed in previous chapters, children and adolescents will have different developmental concerns than will groups of adults and elderly persons. Additionally, as we point out in this chapter, issue specific groups such as those organized around chemical dependency, issues of abuse, depression, chronic illnesses, eating disorders and other addictions or co-addictions often require special knowledge and perhaps even intervention and management skills on the part of the group leader.

This chapter is in no way to be considered inclusive. Even to list the sundry types of groups designed for special emotional problems would be an exhaustive enterprise. One of the major group trends during the past decade has been the evolution of treatment groups for all kinds of functional and organic disorders. It is hoped that those we present here will serve as representative illustrations of some of the groups currently available. From this general framework we will proceed to a discussion of some of the more common and emerging special populations and topics.

CHRONIC DISEASES

Cancer Patients

Since cancer is such a potentially fear and stress producing diagnosis, groups for cancer patients are singled out as an example of interventions with chronic diseases. Complicating this diagnosis is that more than 100 different types of cancer exist from the relatively benign and treatable to those that resist treatment and whose course is volatile and rapid.

In as much as all kinds of cancer are presently second only to heart disease as a leading cause of death in the U.S., at least in the foreseeable future, a continuing need will be present to assist patients in dealing with their lives during the course of the disease. Some patients will live for many years with a cancer diagnosis because of continuing medical treatment advances. Approximately 6 out of 10, however, have a prognosis that is potentially life threatening and, as such, qualifies as a chronic disease.

Goals and Purposes. Many researchers have attempted to identify what might be termed a "cancer personality." Is there a personality profile that lends itself to the eventual development of cancer? Most studies have failed to demonstrate that any particular personality type predisposes a person to the development of cancer, but there remains an interest in this area.

The researchers who have developed the most compre hensive model of personality that contributes to the development of cancer are Simonton and Simonton (1975). They postulated that in addition to experiencing a significant loss of a love object some 6 to 18 months prior to the onset of cancer, the cancer personality demonstrates a tendency to hold onto resentments, an inability to forgive, has poor self-esteem and self-pity, and a poor ability to develop and sustain long-term relationships. While they fail to present hard evidence, their speculations are related to immune system dysfunction in the development of cancer. Their hypotheses are even more interesting with the more recent AIDS epidemic.

Most clinicians who work with the chronically ill verify the stage or phase model that victims progress through as they learn to cope with their disease. Most recognizable are the grieving stages first proposed by Kubler-Ross. These predictable stages include (1) denial, (2) anger, (3) bargaining, (4) depression, and lastly (5) acceptance.

In addition to helping the cancer patient deal with the grieving process, Richert and Koffman (1982) through their examination of the literature, identified several other issues with which cancer patients must deal. They include the following:

> *Loss of Identity:* Feelings of depersonalization as if, in effect, they *become* the diagnosis of cancer. Dazed shock, numbness, and apathy often result in an inhibition of action.

> *Loss of Control:* Many patients feel powerless over the course of the disease so that they must deliver

their personal power to the bewildering health care system. Also, because of the nature of some treatment, often a real loss of control occurs over one's bodily functions.

Loss of Social Support: Because of the demands of the disease treatment, many patients find their social support systems shrinking just at the time when they need more. Feelings of abandonment and loss are almost inevitable.

Loss of Time: Facing death and coming to grips with one's own mortality suddenly becomes more immediate and real. Living with what can be termed permanent uncertainty regarding the future places a much greater need to deal with plans and also an emphasis on living fully in the present.

Selection of Members. The suggested number is seven to ten cancer patients in a counseling group that is either fixed duration or more open-ended. Weekly meetings seem most plausible in as much as there may be heavy treatment demands on the patients.

Intervention Strategies. Telch and Telch (1986) conducted a study comparing a structured counseling skills acquisition group with a more traditional supportive counseling group. The skills group were taught *relaxation and stress management, communication and assertion, problem solving, feelings management,* and *pleasant activity* planning. The findings lent strong support for the skills training approach as an enhancement of patients' psychological and psychosocial adjustment to their illness. They reported more satisfaction related to work, social activities, communication, and coping with medical problems.

Achterberg and Lawlis (1980) in an extension of the Simonton's research studied cancer patients who had significantly outlived predicted life expectancies. They concluded that a patient's emotional experience can impact bodily functions with regard to onset, course, and treatment of the disease. They presented a composite personality profile for the successful cancer patient characterized as follows: (1) refusal to give up, (2) flexibility, (3) no physical decompensation when under stress, (4) rejection of the invalid role, (5) nonconformity, (6) aggressiveness, (7) assertiveness, (8) high ego-strength, (9) self-reliance, (10) creativeness, (11) past history of success, (12) a limited belief that "powerful others" were in charge of their well-being, and (13) insightfulness (p.122).

Typically, cancer patients need to adjust to their illness, as well as attendant family and sexual problems. Additionally, they may have to cope with the adverse reactions to various chemical and radiation therapies.

Group intervention with chronically ill patients would suggest a *combination of structured informational content coupled with a supportive and encouraging group atmosphere.*

AIDS and Counseling Groups

In the relatively few years since Acquired Immune Deficiency Syndrome was initially recognized, it has spread in such a fashion that it now touches virtually every corner of our culture. Since it is presently incurable, and the HIV virus so insidious, it will continue to be a major health problem into the foreseeable future. While researchers are at work on many fronts in an attempt to discover methods to control and prevent the disease, its prevention and eradication will require enormous resources before a solution is found.

Our intention in including a section on AIDS is to help sensitize readers to the present and continuing need for mental health professionals to provide support services for victims of AIDS and their families and friends. Secondly, our opinion is that counselors have a responsibility to be as well informed as possible about the mechanical aspects of the infection, how it is transmitted, and what segments of the population are most at risk, so that they can be educators of correct information and dispellers of misinformation and rumor.

The Surgeon General of the United States has issued a very comprehensive and authoritative brochure that is quite readable. AIDS information is readily available to the counselor through printed material and workshops. Since information and statistical data are accumulating almost daily, these materials are not presented here.

At the present time some prevailing *myths* are associated with AIDS.

Myth 1. *AIDS is a disease that really only affects large metropolitan areas such as San Francisco and New York City.* While these two cities have been the major areas of reported cases of HIV infections, the rest of the country is rapidly catching up. In as much as AIDS is a disease that is spread from person to person, it has become potentially a universal problem that will impact all segments of society.

Myth 2. *AIDS is a disease that is limited to male homosexuals and intravenous drug users.* While homosexual intercourse and reused and contaminated needles are major conveyers of the infection, the HIV virus has infiltrated all segments of the population and any sexually active person who has multiple partners is at risk of contracting the disease. Presently in the U.S. the ratio of male to female cases is roughly ten to one. However in parts of Africa and the Caribbean area, heterosexual transmission is predominant with closer to one to one male/female ratios.

Myth 3. *Since I'm in a monogamous sexual relationship with a partner whose sexual history I trust, I won't be personally impacted by AIDS.* The best method of personal protection from the virus remains knowing one's partner and practicing responsible sex. Nevertheless, we will all be impacted by the spread of AIDS because of it's enormous economic and social dimensions. To prevent and/or cure AIDS will require large sums of money for research and dissemination of accurate information. Likely all stratas of society will feel the impact of AIDS economically and in lost productivity.

Taboos and Stigmas. AIDS is frequently coupled with the words crisis and epidemic. In truth, with some justification, it has been compared to the Bubonic Plague epidemic. Never before have health care providers and mental health workers been confronted with treating a disease and patients that are potentially lethal. It raises serious questions within all support workers. AIDS has a way of activating both courageous and compassionate acts and some of the most mean-spirited and destructive behaviors in our culture. Not long ago a colleague shared a story with us of an AIDS patient in the final stages of the disease. As he lay in his hospital bed fighting for his life he was confronted by members of his own family—accused of a deviant lifestyle and excoriated for the shame he had visited upon his family. He died that very night. We'd like to think that this was an isolated example but the evidence suggests otherwise. In ignorance and shame, families are rejecting their own, leaving them to suffer and die in their own isolation.

Many AIDS sufferers in the U.S. are burdened with the double stigma of a sexual lifestyle that runs contrary to the mainstream along with a frightening terminal disease. Some homophobics have seized upon the AIDS phenomenon as an opportunity to strengthen their anti-gay positions from both social and religious points of view. Mental health workers will, of necessity, be in the forefront in creating supportive intervention systems to assist AIDS victims as they attempt to reconcile their disease and make order of their lives.

Counselors will find a need to inspect their own biases and value systems. Current and accurate information regarding the virus is imperative. Counselors will need to keep up to date with advances in knowledge. Additionally, we will need to assess our own values and honestly look at beliefs that may interfere with and inhibit our ability to assist AIDS patients and their families in an objective and constructive way.

Specifically, chronic and terminal diseases will cause the helper to get in touch with his or her own feelings regarding mortality. Standing by in a supportive manner while we watch young people die before their time will arouse serious questions regarding the purpose of life. Personal feelings of frustration and fear will surface as helpers deal with hopelessness, suffering, and despair.

Helpers will need to grapple with their own needs to "fix-things" in the face of unsolvable injustice. The moral outrage and hostility may be focused on the helper as patients struggle to make sense of the disease. How we respond to anger and despair in others will impact on our ability to support and encourage.

Finally, we'll need to examine ethical questions related to protecting our clients while at the same time protecting potential sexual partners from infection. How can this best be done and what are the helpers' responsibilities?

Issues. Models are beginning to emerge as helpers direct groups of AIDS victims in community agencies and other socially supportive settings. Our synthesis of the literature and reports from our students in groups that we have supervised suggest that AIDS support groups will deal with the following issues as patients experience the journey.

> *Despair.* Newly diagnosed persons will exhibit the greatest need for the group as they begin to deal with initial support from feelings of isolation and helplessness. For the first time they may come fully in contact with their own vulnerability. The group, in being accepting and non-critical, can provide validation for the new member's feelings and behaviors.

> *Denial.* Some helpers will find this stage most difficult to work with. As the AIDS patient begins to experience a loss of social contact and support systems, some will become angry and hostile, sometimes displacing these feelings onto the group leader. They may irrationally strike out against the very persons who want most to support them as they

prepare to confront their own fears. Accepting this behavior without sanctioning it will provide the atmosphere for the person to marshall new defenses while at the same time giving full expression to the grief associated with the loss of health and self-image.

Ownership. Feelings of depression will most likely surface at this stage with the acceptance of an almost complete loss of the former self. Group members will want to reflect upon their past life and begin to create a new identity that includes the illness. Basic social management questions can be addressed such as who should be told about the illness, what needs to be told, how to go about telling them, and consideration of appropriate timing.

Another concern has to do with what lifestyle changes will be necessary so that the AIDS patient can care for himself and, finally, what preparations will be necessary for the inevitable multiple hospitalizations.

Moving Through and Forward. Paradoxically, in this final stage of acceptance there is a reclaimed power as the person accepts personal responsibility for future treatments and life choices. Decisions regarding how to deal with family and friends help increase feelings of self-worth and identity. The member also can serve as a model for newer members of the group.

Research. The struggle to control AIDS is progressing primarily along three avenues of research. The field of *pharmacology* is exploring new anti-viral drugs. Secondly, the search is continuing for even newer information on how the immune system can eventually neutralize HIV. Most informed sources believe that ultimately, the only feasible way to control AIDS in the future will be through the development of an effective vaccine. Lastly, researchers are looking into the human immune system since most AIDS patients eventually die from opportunistic infections other than HIV itself. Advances have been made and health care providers are able to fend off and control these extraneous diseases with more confidence, thereby at least prolonging life. Though AIDS is an extremely complex problem, the AIDS problem is solvable—therein lies the hope for the future (Thomas, 1988). Until then we remind ourselves that AIDS is a venereal disease that is transmitted from man to man, man to woman, women to unborn children, and woman to woman.

EMOTIONAL DIFFICULTIES

Depression

The use of groups for the treatment of depression is becoming more prevalent because of its apparent increase in incidence, either as a symptom or a syndrome. While no single unifying theory of depression exists commonly accepted professional guidelines do exist for diagnosis and treatment. Generally, depressions are grouped in two primary categories. The first being *situational depressions* that also may be called justified or reactive in that the depression can normally be directly linked to psychosocial stressors that may precipitate and maintain the depression. The second group may be termed *somatic* or *autonomous depressions* that may have a more neurotic etiology, higher rates of recurrence and are longer term in duration. Another way to view this is whether a depression is the *primary disorder (somatic)* or is the result of some external cause including physical disease *(secondary).*

Major depressions also can be differentiated according to unipolar and bipolar subtypes. *Bipolar depressions* are those that display episodes of cyclic behavior—mania and depression. Manic-depressive episodes typically require both psychopharmacological treatment and psychotherapy. *Unipolar depressions* are those characterized only by depression.

Goals and Purposes. Group leaders need to have a reasonably good understanding of the various symptoms associated with the various kinds of depression in order to select the most appropriate treatment course. The DSM III-R offers the most helpful diagnostic tool when evaluating depressions. Criteria for major depression include the following:

Mood Disturbance—Feeling sad, blue, and even hopeless with a loss of interest in activities that were previously pleasurable. A noticeable change in activity patterns and decreased ability to concentrate. Additionally, at least four of the following symptoms will be present every day for at least two weeks.

Weight Gain or Loss—Poor appetite or increased appetite, sometimes with a craving for carbohydrates.

Sleep Disturbances—Patterns differ from insomnia, staying up and not being able to sleep to hypersomnia which involves sleeping much more than normal and feeling tired all the time.

Movement Disturbances—Characterized by excessively slow and deliberate movements or by increased agitation and hyperactivity. This may vary according to the time of day.

Decreased Interest in Sexual Activities

Loss of Energy and Fatigue

Feelings of Worthlessness and Excessive Guilt—Feeling inappropriately overly responsible for even minor events that may not be particularly bad.

Reduced Ability to Think or Concentrate—Even though more time may be spent with certain tasks, a fall off occurs in productivity. Students may experience a decline in their grades.

Suicidal Ideation or Attempts—Preoccupation with thoughts of death is a very common symptom of depression. References to suicide should always be taken very seriously and evaluated for lethality.

An intriguing theory developed by Martin Seligman (1975) has some broad implications for group treatment of depression. "Learned Helplessness" may provide a model of what happens when people perceive themselves to be out of control of their environment in the sense that circumstances exist over which their behavior will make little difference. In effect, the theory states that uncontrollable events may cause an *expectancy* that stressors cannot be controlled thus resulting in feelings of hopelessness and resignation.

Group programs that teach members about depression, offer support and encouragement, and provide skills to help members begin to exert control over themselves and their world seem to offer the most benefits.

Selection of Members. Group members who have been evaluated as depressed, either primarily or secondarily, and whose depression is mild to moderate will experience the best chances to profit from group intervention. The usual organization for open-ended groups is a weekly meeting with 12 or less members so that each person will have opportunities to become verbally involved in the process. Closed groups with fixed duration have also reported successes in treating depression from a psychoeducational treatment mode (Haberman, Lewinsohn, & Tilson, 1988). These groups typically meet from 8 to 12 weeks with treatment based on a social learning model of depression. About 80% of participants report positive results in coping with unipolar depressions

Intervention Strategies. Groups that combine *structured, educational information* with a *supportive group environment* seem to offer most benefits for mildly to moderately depressed clients. Additional member characteristics that seem to be related to the prediction of improvement in groups are (1) an expectation of improvement, (2) good reading ability, (3) young age, (4) perceptions of family as supportive, and (5) perceptions of self-control (Haberman, Lewinsohn, & Tilson, 1988).

Groups that are high in support and low in criticism will offer the best chances for success. Depressed individuals frequently are "Type A" personalities with high needs for achievement and perfectionism. Criticism often widens the gap between performance and self-expectation.

Coping skills that include assertiveness and self caring while helping the individual to experience the feeling of being in control of self are important to include in the treatment package. *Depression management lecturettes* coupled with a group experience that validates the feelings of the person and helps to provide new coping strategies while treating the concerns of members in a serious and respectful manner offer the most hope to members.

ADDICTIVE BEHAVIORS

Chemical Dependency

Although treatment formats for substance abuse vary as do definitions of substance abuse, the format most commonly recommended by authorities in the field is group work. The effectiveness of Alcoholics Anonymous self-help groups has greatly influenced this emphasis.

Individuals with a long history of substance abuse are particularly difficult to work with because they have strong defenses against change and minimal abilities for carrying out commitments. Consequently the group facilitator must have an especially strong commitment to the group and the group process.

Lcite's (1983) summary of findings related to substance abuse persons presents a picture of a person who has difficulty handling frustrations, anxiety, depression; someone who wants immediate gratification of desires; someone who is lonely and unsuccessful in family and other relationships; someone with low self-esteem; someone who is impulsive and has little regard, for health and safety; and someone who resents authority and scorns rules.

Brill (1981) identified four types of chemically dependent individuals. First type are individuals who are socialized in the drug culture. They have learned behaviors suitable for the drug subculture primarily for reasons of group identification. Involvement in the drug culture may be traced to sociological instead of psychological causes. Second type are individuals who are inadequately socialized into society's values. This type of chemically dependent person has had few opportunities to learn from adequate models, which normally occurs early in life. These persons generally have some capacity for current learning. Third type are individuals who are unsocialized in conventional values. They have been severely neglected and deprived as children and have consequently internalized few social values. They are often destructive to themselves and to others and project their difficulties onto the external environment. Fourth type are individuals who are presocialized. They realize they are in trouble with their chemical dependency but have not yet succumbed to the drug culture. They have achieved some socialization in cultural values but not enough to withstand drug temptations.

Goals and Purposes. Typically the goals of groups for substance abusers are to help members identify and modify personal coping behaviors, learn new communication and interpersonal relationship skills, recognize and build personal strengths, take responsibility for personal decisions and behavior, and integrate values, lifestyles and life goals with behavior choice and decision making. A purpose of the group is to bring into the open the problems, resentments, and frustrations that the members have not been able to put into words.

Vanicelli, Canning, and Griefen (1984) list the objectives for group members as (1) to share and to identify with others who are going through problems of chemical abuse, (2) to understand the group member's own attitudes and defenses in others, and (3) to learn to communicate needs and feelings more directly. Shields (1985-86) reported that substance abuse members of mutual aid groups showed increased evidence of coping skills, fewer instances of acting out, less isolation from peers, and increased decision-making capabilities to choose abstinence. Contracting was described as a major variable in the progress. Other studies have shown that members increase their self-awareness, self-respect, and self-esteem.

According to Brill (1981), the four goals of group work with drug abusers are (1) to develop adaptive behaviors and attitudes competitive with drug abuse to ameliorate skill deficits, (2) identification and practice of verbal and non-verbal components of assertiveness, (3) learning appropriate and effective expression of personal needs, and (4) to produce changes designed to promote self-sufficiency and positive self-appraisals without drug dependency.

The strong therapeutic attachments that develop in the group facilitate the development of attitudes of commitment and hopefulness which are prerequisites to the changes described above. Peer group support is a powerful force assisting individuals with the maintenance of these changed behaviors.

Selection of Members. Self help and support groups for substance abusers usually consist of six to ten members meeting one and one-half hours once a week although some groups may meet twice a week. Groups are open-ended. Membership is limited to individuals in recovery.

Intervention Strategies. Denial is a major inhibitor of change for most substance abusers. Few will readily admit they have a problem. In the group, through the process of observing, interacting with other members, and being confronted, they gradually begin to accept the fact that they too are substance abusers.

George and Dustin (1988) reported that individuals who are chemically dependent tend to have a great deal of unexpressed anger which has typically been repressed except when drinking or using chemical substances. The group setting offers a safe opportunity for members to express their anger and to discover they can do so and still be in control. George and Dustin recommended that because the chemically dependent person's life has been out of control, major emphasis should be placed on providing structure in the group so members will realize that at least one area of their life is under control.

Techniques and intervention strategies that have been found to be helpful with substance abusers are ***confrontation,*** various ***cognitive techniques, role playing,*** and

behavior rehearsal to help members gain confidence in handling interpersonal situations.

Eating Disorders

The three classifications of individuals who have eating disorders are anorexics, bulimics, and compulsive overeaters. Individuals diagnosed as ***anorexic*** have an intense fear of becoming obese and this fear does not diminish as weight loss progresses. They have suffered severe weight loss, experience extreme disturbance of body image, and are preoccupied with a goal of being thin. Such individuals may "feel fat" even when emaciated (DSM-III-R, 1987).

Individuals diagnosed as ***bulimic*** experience recurrent episodes of binge eating often followed by attempts to purge themselves by self-induced vomiting or the use of cathartics or diuretics. They experience frequent fluctuations in weight due to alternating binges and fasts and have an intense desire to be thin. They fear not being able to stop eating voluntarily and are aware that their eating pattern is abnormal. They are often depressed following eating binges (DSM-III-R, 1987).

Compulsive overeaters are individuals who experience great difficulty in controlling the amount of eating they do.

Goals and Purposes. The symptoms of denial, preoccupation with self, lack of coping skills, and anger which anorexics and bulimics exhibit make them excellent candidates for group work. Individuals who have eating disorders also frequently experience social isolation. The group minimizes social isolation and provides needed peer support. The group format provides a setting where individuals can learn how to reach out to peers instead of food and for many authorities, this is the preferred mode of treatment.

The characteristics of bulimics listed by Schwartz, Barrett, and Saba (1985) seem just as appropriate for anorexics and can easily be translated into issues for work in the group. These characteristics include

(a) a feeling of being unable to control the direction of their lives or of all important relationships; (b) an inability to know what they really want or who they really are, including a sense of constant mental turmoil and confusion at having to wear a mask of happiness for the sake of others; (c) an obsession with the way they look, a strong fear of getting fat, and a state of chronic depression over their eating patterns; (d) an overriding feeling of obligation toward or protectiveness for certain other family members; and (e) an orientation toward poor extremes of faking, affect, and behavior. (p. 285)

Generally, the goals in eating disorder groups are to deal with issues of authority control, perceived helplessness, fear of rejection, denial, anger, social isolation, and to return to and maintain healthy eating patterns.

Selection of Members. Self-help and support groups for individuals with eating disorders usually consist of six to ten members meeting one and one-half hours once or twice a week. Another pattern suggested by Brisman and Siegal (1985) is a weekend format with a follow-up several days later and bimonthly support group meetings. Groups are typically open-ended and often are led by a male and female co-facilitator team.

According to Hall (1985) those individuals suffering from anorexia nervosa who are most likely to benefit from a group approach are

1. those who are not severely ill, but are gaining weight or are relatively stable;

2. those who are highly motivated;

3. those who have benefited psychologically from other treatments;

4. those who are not totally isolated or withdrawn;

5. those in whom denial or intellectualization is not predominant and who show some capacity for psychological-mindedness, ability to reveal feelings, and sensitivity to others;

6. those for whom another treatment approach (e.g., family therapy) is not indicated or where a combination of other treatment with group therapy is practical; and

7. those who are liked by the group leader and have the potential to be liked by other group members. (p. 220)

Intervention Strategies. Since individuals who have eating disorders often feel their lives are out of control, a helpful procedure is to provide some **structure** so members will feel security in some part of their lives. Food journals are often assigned in the first session to help members become aware of their dysfunctional eating patterns. Group sessions typically include the utilization of *relaxation techniques, guided imagery, assertiveness training, social skills training,* and *cognitive behavioral skills.* Educational instruction may be utilized along with *modeling, self-monitoring,* and *goal setting.*

Adult Children of Alcoholics (ACOA)

The estimate is that at least one in every eight Americans have at least one alcoholic parent (Cermak, 1985). The psychosocial consequences for adults who have grown up in such a home include "denial of perceptions, needs, and experiences (including parental alcoholism); frozen or re-pressed feelings, difficulties in trusting others; compulsive behavior (e.g., "workaholism"); high needs for control; and an inflated, inappropriate sense of personal responsibility" (Downing & Walker, 1987, p. 440). No wonder Adult Children of Alcoholics (ACOAs) have great difficulty expressing their feelings when it is recognized that as children they developed survival roles based on don't trust, don't talk, and don't feel (Black, 1981).

Children who grow up in homes with alcoholic parents often develop coping styles such as the superhero, the scapegoat, the lost child, and the mascot (Wegscheider, 1981). These adaptive coping styles may be quite effective survival roles for children but are at best maladaptive when these individuals reach adulthood and try to establish effective relationships with other adults.

Goals and Purposes. Since Adult Children of Alcoholics have poor interpersonal relationships, low self-esteem, and high incidence of chemical dependency (Wegscheider-Cruse, 1985), intervention plans are likely to be effective if they include experiential interpersonal interactions such as those possible in self-help and support groups. Through such interactions the isolation of individuation is broken down and members are confronted with the reality that they are not alone. This can be a profound experience for individuals who have lived their life hiding, denying, controlling, and feeling responsible.

Appropriate objectives for ACOA psychoeducational groups include "assistance in lessening the severity of current concerns, creating an informed and favorable attitude toward mental health services (so that they may seek appropriate help sooner in the future, and preventing the onset of certain concerns entirely" (Downing & Walker, 1987, p. 441).

Selection of Members. Groups may be either heterogeneous or homogeneous consisting only of ACOA and usually are open-ended consisting of 8 to 10 or more members meeting for one to two hours once or twice a week. Corazzini, Williams, and Harris (1987) proposed that heterogeneous, open-ended groups are especially effective. Downing and Walker (1987) recommended excluding from the group individuals who are in immediate or intense crisis, abusers of mood-altering chemicals, individuals whose life circumstances differ significantly from other group members, and individuals the group leaders believe may deter the group's functioning.

Intervention Strategies. Because Adult Children of Alcoholics have peer interpersonal skills and a long history of unrewarding interpersonal relationships, the first few sessions should be highly *structured* and designed to facilitate nonthreatening contact and sharing between group members. Focus on *exploration of feelings* should be gradually addressed since most Adult Children of Alcoholics have either denied their feelings, especially feelings of anger and self worth, or doubted them.

Downing and Walker (1987) described a psychoeducational group structured to provide a safe place to talk while *focusing* on confronting denial and helping participants recognize and begin to recover lost or distorted feelings. Their group also has an educational focus based on the use of *films, discussions,* and *handouts.* The group meets for eight sessions structured around "Week 1—building universality and decreasing denial; Weeks 2 and 3—confronting denial and learning about alcoholism and co-dependency; Weeks 4-8—recognizing and recovering feelings" (p. 441).

Al-Anon groups are a popular example of support groups. College-based support groups also have become quite popular and in many instances have been established with federal grant support.

REFERENCES

Achterberg, J., & Lawlis, F.G. (1980). *Bridges of the body-mind.* Champaign, IL: Institute for Personality and Ability Testing.

American Psychiatric Association. (1987). *Diagnostic and Statistical Manual of Mental Disorders, DSM-III, (3rd ed.)* Washington, D.C.

Black, C. (1981). *It will never happen to me.* Denver: M.A.C. Printing.

Brill, L. (1981). *The clinical treatment of substance abusers.* New York: Free Press.

Brisman, J., & Siegel, M. (1985). The bulimia workshop: A unique integration of group treatment approaches. *International Journal of Group Psychotherapy, 35,* 585-601.

Cermak, T. (1985). *A primer on adult children of alcoholics.* Pompano Beach, FL: Health Communications.

Corazzini, J., Williams, K., & Harris, S. (1987). Group therapy for adult children of alcoholics: Case studies. *Journal for Specialists in Group Work, 12,* 156-161.

Diagnostic and Statistical Manual of Mental Disorders III-Revised (1987). Washington, D.C.: American Psychiatric Association.

Downing, N., & Walker, M. (1987). A psychoeducational group for adult children of alcoholics. *Journal of Counseling and Development, 65,* 440-442.

George, R., & Dustin, D. (1988). *Group counseling: Theory and practice.* Englewood Cliffs, NJ: Prentice Hall.

Haberman, H., Lewinsohn, P.M., & Tilson, M. (1988). Group treatment of depression: Individual predictors of outcome. *Journal of Consulting and Clinical Psychology, 56,* (3), 393-398.

Hall, A. (1985). Group psychotherapy for anorexia nervosa. In D. Garner & P. Garfindel (Eds.), *Handbook of psychotherapy for anorexia nervosa and bulimia* (pp. 213-239). New York: Guilford Press.

Leite, E. (1983). Understanding and ministering to the drug abuser. Unpublished dissertation, Southwestern Baptist Theological Seminary.

Rickert, M.L., & Koffman, A. (1982). The use of groups with cancer patients. In Seligman, M. (Ed.), *Group psychotherapy and counseling with special populations.* Baltimore: University Park Press.

Schwartz, R., Barrett, M., & Saba, G. (1985). Family therapy for bulimia. In D. Garner & P. Garfindel (Eds.), *Handbook of psychotherapy for anorexia nervosa and bulimia* (pp. 280-307). New York: Guilford Press.

Seligman, M.E.P. (1975). *Helplessness: On depression, development, and death.* San Francisco, CA: Freeman.

Shields, S. (1985-86). Busted and branded: Group work with substance abusing adolescents in schools. *Social Work Journal, 8,* 61-81.

Simonton, O.C., & Simonton, S.S. (1975). Belief systems and management of the emotional aspects of malignancy. *Journal of Transpersonal Psychology, 7,* 29-47.

Telch, C.F., & Telch, M.J. (1986). Group coping skills instruction and supportive group therapy for cancer patients: A comparison of strategies. *Journal of Consulting and Clinical Psychology, 54,* 802-808.

Thomas, L. (1988). AIDS: An unknown distance still to go. *Scientific American,* October, p. 152.

Vanicelli, M., Canning, D., & Griefen, M. (1984). Group therapy with alcoholics: A group case study. *The International Journal of Group Psychotherapy, 34*(1), 127-147.

Wegscheider, S. (1981). *Another chance: Hope and health for the alcoholic family.* Palo Alto, CA: Science and Behavior Books.

Wegscheider-Cruse, S. (1985). *Choice-making.* Pompano Beach, FL: Health Communications.

APPENDIX

Ethical Guidelines
for
Group Counselors

Ethical Guidelines for Group Counselors

Preamble

One characteristic of any professional group is the possession of a body of knowledge, skills, and voluntarily self-professed standards for ethical practice.* A Code of Ethics consists of those standards that have been formally and publicly acknowledged by the members of a profession to serve as the guidelines for professional conduct, discharge of duties, and the resolution of moral dilemmas. By this document, the Association for Specialists in Group Work (ASGW) has identified the standards of conduct appropriate for ethical behavior among its members.

ASGW recognizes the basic commitment of its members to the Ethical Standards of its parent organization, the American Association for Counseling and Development (AACD) and nothing in this document shall be construed to supplant that code. These standards are intended to complement AACD standards in the area of group work by clarifying the nature of ethical responsibility of the counselor in the group setting and by stimulating a greater concern for competent group leadership.

The group counselor is expected to be a professional agent and to take the processes of ethical responsibility seriously. ASGW views "ethical process" as being integral to group work and views group counselors as "ethical agents." Group counselors, by their very nature in being responsible and responsive to their group members, necessarily embrace a certain potential for ethical vulnerability. It is incumbent upon group counselors to give considerable attention to the intent and context of their actions because the attempts of counselors to influence human behavior through group work always have ethical implications.

The following ethical guidelines have been developed to encourage ethical behavior of group counselors. These

---

*These guidelines, approved June 1, 1989, by the Association for Specialists in Group Work (ASGW), Executive Committee, have been reprinted by permission of the American Association for Counseling and Development (AACD), 5999 Stevenson Avenue, Alexandria, VA 22304.

guidelines are written for students and practitioners, and are meant to stimulate reflection, self-examination, and discussion of issues and practices. They address the group counselor's responsibility for providing information about group work to clients and the group counselor's responsibility for providing group counseling services to clients. A final section discusses the group counselor's responsibility for safeguarding ethical practice and procedures for reporting unethical behavior. Group counselors are expected to make known these standards to group members.

Ethical Guidelines

1. **Orientation and Providing Information:** Group counselors adequately prepare prospective or new group members by providing as much information about the existing or proposed group as necessary. Minimally, information related to each of the following areas should be provided.

   (a) Entrance procedures, time parameters of the group experience, group participation expectations, methods of payment (where appropriate), and termination procedures are explained by the group counselor as appropriate to the level of maturity of group members and the nature and purpose(s) of the group.

   (b) Group counselors have available for distribution a professional disclosure statement that includes information on the group counselor's qualifications and group services that can be provided, particularly as related to the nature and purpose(s) of the specific group.

   (c) Group counselors communicate the role expectations, rights, and responsibilities of group members and group counselor(s).

   (d) The group goals are stated as concisely as possible by the group counselor, including "whose" goal it is (the group counselor's, the institution's, the parent's, the law's, society's, etc.) and the role of group members in influencing or determining the group's goal(s).

(e) Group counselors explore with group members the risks of potential life changes that may occur because of the group experience and help members explore their readiness to face these possibilities.

(f) Group members are informed by the group counselor of unusual or experimental procedures that might be expected in their group experience.

(g) Group counselors explain, as realistically as possible, what services can and cannot be provided within the particular group structure offered.

(h) Group counselors emphasize the need to promote full psychological functioning and presence among group members. They inquire from prospective group members whether they are using any kind of drug or medication that may affect functioning in the group. They do not permit any use of alcohol and/or illegal drugs during group sessions and they discourage the use of alcohol and/or drugs (legal or illegal) prior to group meetings which may affect the physical or emotional presence of the member or other group members.

(i) Group counselors inquire from prospective group members whether they have ever been a client in counseling or psychotherapy. If a prospective group member is already in a counseling relationship with another professional person, the group counselor advises the prospective group member to notify the other professional of their participation in the group.

(j) Group counselors clearly inform group members about the policies pertaining to the group counselor's willingness to consult with them between group sessions.

(k) In establishing fees for group counseling services, group counselors consider the financial status and the locality of prospective group members. Group members are not charged fees for group sessions where the group counselor is not present and the policy of charging for sessions missed by a group member is clearly communicated. Fees for participating as a group member are contracted between group counselor and group member for a specified period of time. Group counselors do not increase fees for group counseling services until the existing contracted fee structure has expired. In the event that the established fee structure is inappropriate for a prospective member, group counselor assist in finding comparable services of acceptable cost.

2. **Screening of Members:** The group counselor screens prospective group members (when appropriate to their theoretical orientation). Insofar as possible, the counselor selects group members whose needs and goals are compatible with the goals of the group, who will not impede the group process, and whose well-being will not be jeopardized by the group experience. An orientation to the group (i.e., ASGW Ethical Guideline #1), is included during the screening process.

Screening may be accomplished in one or more ways, such as the following:

(a) Individual interview,

(b) Group interview of prospective group members,

(c) Interview as part of a team staffing, and

(d) Completion of a written questionnaire by prospective group members.

3. **Confidentiality:** Group counselors protect members by defining clearly what confidentiality means, why it is important, and the difficulties involved in enforcement.

(a) Group counselors take steps to protect members by defining confidentiality and the limits of confidentiality (i.e., when a group member's condition indicates that there is clear and imminent danger to the member, others, or physical property, the group counselor takes reasonable personal action and/or informs responsible authorities).

(b) Group counselors stress the importance of confidentiality and set a norm of confidentiality regarding all group participants' disclosures. The importance of maintaining confidentiality is emphasized before the group begins and at various times in the group. The fact that confidentiality cannot be guaranteed is clearly stated.

(c) Members are made aware of the difficulties involved in enforcing and ensuring confidentiality in a group setting. The counselor provides examples of how confidentiality can non-maliciously be broken to increase members' awareness, and helps to lessen the likelihood that this breach of confidence will occur. Group counselors inform group members about the potential consequences of intentionally breaching confidentiality.

(d) Group counselors can only ensure confidentiality on their part and not on the part of the members.

(e) Group counselors video or audio tape a group session only with the prior consent and the members' knowledge of how the tape will be used.

(f) When working with minors, the group counselor specifies the limits of confidentiality.

(g) Participants in a mandatory group are made aware of any reporting procedures required of the group counselor.

(h) Group counselors store or dispose of group members records (written, audio, video, etc.) in ways that maintain confidentiality.

(i) Instructors of group counseling courses maintain the anonymity of group members whenever discussing group counseling cases.

4. **Voluntary/Involuntary Participation:** Group counselors inform members whether participation is voluntary or involuntary.

   (a) Group counselors take steps to ensure informed consent procedures in both voluntary and involuntary groups.

   (b) When working with minors in a group, counselors are expected to follow the procedures specified by the institution in which they are practicing.

   (c) With involuntary groups, every attempt is made to enlist the cooperation of the members and their continuance in the group on a voluntary basis.

   (d) Group counselors do not certify that group treatment has been received by members who merely attend sessions, but did not meet the defined group expectations. Group members are informed about the consequences for failing to participate in a group.

5. **Leaving a Group:** Provisions are made to assist a group member to terminate in an effective way.

   (a) Procedures to be followed for a group member who chooses to exit a group prematurely are discussed by the counselor with all group members either before the group begins, during a pre-screening interview, or during the initial group session.

   (b) In the case of legally mandated group counseling, group counselors inform members of the possible consequences for premature self-termination.

   (c) Ideally, both the group counselor and the member can work cooperatively to determine the degree to which a group experience is productive or counter-productive for that individual.

   (d) Members ultimately have a right to discontinue membership in the group, at a designated time, if the predetermined trial period proves to be unsatisfactory.

(e) Members have the right to exit a group, but it is important that they be made aware of the importance of informing the counselor and the group members prior to deciding to leave. The counselor discusses the possible risks of leaving the group prematurely with a member who is considering this option.

(f) Before leaving a group, the group counselor encourages members (if appropriate) to discuss their reasons for wanting to discontinue membership in the group. Counselors intervene if other members use undue pressure to force a member to remain in the group.

6. **Coercion and Pressure:** Group counselors protect member rights against physical threats, intimidation, coercion, and undue peer pressure insofar as is reasonably possible.

(a) It is essential to differentiate between "therapeutic pressure" that is part of any group and "undue pressure," which is not therapeutic.

(b) The purpose of a group is to help participants find their own answer, not to pressure them into doing what the group thinks is appropriate.

(c) Counselors exert care not to coerce participants to change in directions which they clearly state they do not choose.

(d) Counselors have a responsibility to intervene when others use undue pressure or attempt to persuade members against their will.

(e) Counselors intervene when any member attempts to act out aggression in a physical way that might harm another member or themselves.

(f) Counselors intervene when a member is verbally abusive or inappropriately confrontive to another member.

7. **Imposing Counselor Values:** Group counselors develop an awareness of their own values and needs and the potential impact they have on the interventions likely to be made.

   (a) Although group counselors take care to avoid imposing their values on members, it is appropriate that they expose their own beliefs, decisions, needs, and values, when concealing them would create problems for the members.

   (b) There are values implicit in any group, and these are made clear to potential members before they join the group. (Examples of certain values include: expressing feelings, being direct and honest, sharing personal material with others, learning how to trust, improving interpersonal communication, and deciding for oneself.)

   (c) Personal and professional needs of group counselors are not met at the members' expense.

   (d) Group counselors avoid using the group for their own therapy.

   (e) Group counselors are aware of their own values and assumptions and how these apply in a multicultural context.

   (f) Group counselors take steps to increase their awareness of ways that their personal reactions to members might inhibit the group process and they monitor their countertransference. Through an awareness of the impact of stereotyping and discrimination (i.e., biases based on age, disability, ethnicity, gender, race, religion, or sexual preference), group counselors guard the individual rights and personal dignity of all group members.

8. **Equitable Treatment:** Group counselors make every reasonable effort to treat each member individually and equally.

   (a) Group counselors recognize and respect differences (e.g., cultural, racial, religious, lifestyle, age, disability, gender) among group members.

(b) Group counselors maintain an awareness of their behavior toward individual group members and are alert to the potential detrimental effects of favoritism or partiality toward any particular group member to the exclusion or detriment of any other member(s). It is likely that group counselors will favor some members over others, yet all group members deserve to be treated equally.

(c) Group counselors ensure equitable use of group time for each member by inviting silent members to become involved, acknowledging nonverbal attempts to communicate, and discouraging rambling and monopolizing of time by members.

(d) If a large group is planned, counselors consider enlisting another qualified professional to serve as a co-leader for the group sessions.

9. **Dual Relationships:** Group counselors avoid dual relationships with group members that might impair their objectivity and professional judgment, as well as those which are likely to compromise a group member's ability to participate fully in the group.

(a) Group counselors do not misuse their professional role and power as group leader to advance personal or social contacts with members throughout the duration of the group.

(b) Group counselors do not use their professional relationship with group members to further their own interest either during the group or after the termination of the group.

(c) Sexual intimacies between group counselors and members are unethical.

(d) Group counselors do not barter (exchange) professional services with group members for services.

(e) Group counselors do not admit their own family members, relatives, employees, or personal friends as members to their groups.

(f) Group counselors discuss with group members the potential detrimental effects of group members engaging in intimate inter-member relationships outside of the group.

(g) Students who participate in a group as a partial course requirement for a group course are not evaluated for an academic grade based upon their degree of participation as a member in a group. Instructors of group counseling courses take steps to minimize the possible negative impact on students when they participate in a group course by separating course grades from participation in the group and by allowing students to decide what issues to explore and when to stop.

(h) It is inappropriate to solicit members from a class (or institutional affiliation) for one's private counseling or therapeutic groups.

10. **Use of Techniques:** Group counselors do not attempt any technique unless trained in its use or under supervision by a counselor familiar with the intervention.

(a) Group counselors are able to articulate a theoretical orientation that guides their practice, and they are able to provide a rationale for their interventions.

(b) Depending upon the type of an intervention, group counselors have training commensurate with the potential impact of a technique.

(c) Group counselors are aware of the necessity to modify their techniques to fit the unique needs of various cultural and ethnic groups.

(d) Group counselors assist members in translating in-group learnings to daily life.

11. **Goal Development:** Group counselors make every effort to assist members in developing their personal goals.

   (a) Group counselors use their skills to assist members in making their goals specific so that others present in the group will understand the nature of the goals.

   (b) Throughout the course of a group, group counselors assist members in assessing the degree to which personal goals are being met, and assist in revising any goals when it is appropriate.

   (c) Group counselors help members clarify the degree to which the goals can be met within the context of a particular group.

12. **Consultation:** Group counselors develop and explain policies about between-session consultation to group members.

   (a) Group counselors take care to make certain that members do not use between-session consultation to avoid dealing with issues pertaining to the group that would be dealt with best in the group.

   (b) Group counselors urge members to bring the issues discussed during between-session consultations into the group if they pertain to the group.

   (c) Group counselors seek out consultation and/or supervision regarding ethical concerns or when encountering difficulties which interfere with their effective functioning as group leaders.

   (d) Group counselors seek appropriate professional assistance for their own personal problems or conflicts that are likely to impair their professional judgment and work performance.

   (e) Group counselors discuss their group cases only for professional consultation and educational purposes.

   (f) Group counselors inform members about policies regarding whether consultations will be held confidential.

13. **Termination from the Group:** Depending upon the purpose of participation in the group, counselors promote termination of members from the group in the most efficient period of time.

   (a) Group counselors maintain a constant awareness of the progress made by each group member and periodically invite the group members to explore and reevaluate their experiences in the group. It is the responsibility of group counselors to help promote the independence of members from the group in a timely manner.

14. **Evaluation and Follow-up:** Group counselors make every attempt to engage in ongoing assessment and to design follow-up procedures for their groups.

   (a) Group counselors recognize the importance of ongoing assessment of a group, and they assist members in evaluating their own progress.

   (b) Group counselors conduct evaluation of the total group experience at the final meeting (or before termination), as well as ongoing evaluation.

   (c) Group counselors monitor their own behavior and become aware of what they are modeling in the group.

   (d) Follow-up procedures might take the form of personal contact, telephone contact, or written contact.

   (e) Follow-up meetings might be with individuals, or groups, or both to determine the degree to which: (i) members have reached their goals, (ii) the group had a positive or negative effect on the participants, (iii) members could profit from some type of referral, and (iv) as information for possible modification of future groups. If there is no follow-up meeting, provisions are made available for individual follow-up meetings to any member who needs or requests such a contact.

15. **Referrals:** If the needs of a particular member cannot be met within the type of group being offered, the group

counselor suggests other appropriate professional referrals.

(a) Group counselors are knowledgeable of local community resources for assisting group members regarding professional referrals.

(b) Group counselors help members seek further professional assistance, if needed.

16. **Professional Development:** Group counselors recognize
that professional growth is a continuous, ongoing,
developmental process throughout their career.

(a) Group counselors maintain and upgrade their knowledge and skill competencies through educational
activities, clinical experiences, and participation in
professional development activities.

(b) Group counselors keep abreast of research findings
and new developments as applied to groups.

Safeguarding Ethical Practice and Procedures
for Reporting Unethical Behavior

The preceding remarks have been advanced as guidelines
which are generally representative of ethical and professional
group practice. They have not been proposed as rigidly
defined prescriptions. However, practitioners who are thought
to be grossly unresponsive to the ethical concerns addressed
in this document may be subject to a review of their
practices by the AACD Ethics Committee and ASGW peers.

For consultation and/or questions regarding these ASGW
Ethical Guidelines or group ethical dilemmas, you may
contact the Chairperson of the ASGW Ethics Committee. The
name, address, and telephone number of the current ASGW
Ethics Committee Chairperson may be acquired by tele-
phoning the AACD office in Alexandria, Virginia at
(703) 823-9800.

If group counselor's behavior is suspected as being unethical, the following procedures are to be followed:

1. Collect more information and investigate further to confirm the unethical practice as determined by the ASGW Ethical Guidelines.

2. Confront the individual with the apparent violation of ethical guidelines for the purposes of protecting the safety of any clients and to help the group counselor correct any inappropriate behaviors. If satisfactory resolution is not reached through this contact then:

3. A complaint should be made in writing, including the specific facts and dates of the alleged violation and all relevant supporting data. The complaint should be included in an envelope marked "CONFIDENTIAL" to ensure confidentiality for both the accuser(s) and the alleged violator(s) and forwarded to all of the following sources:

   (a) The name and address of the Chairperson of the state Counselor Licensure Board for the respective state, if in existence.

   (b) The Ethics Committee
   c/o The President
   American Association for
       Counseling and Development
   5999 Stevenson Avenue
   Alexandria, Virginia   22304

   (c) The name and address of all private credentialing agencies in which the alleged violator maintains credentials or holds professional membership.

INDEX

INDEX

A

Abused children, group counseling
  intervention strategies 270
  purposes 269-70
  selection of members 270
Achterberg, J. 300, 317
Ackerman, N.W. 9, 18
Activities
  pre-group 136-43
Activity group counseling
  activity room 266
  counselor role 264-5
  length of sessions 266
  materials 266
  meaning of activity 263-4
  process 265
  selection of members 264
Activity group therapy 27
Activity-interview group counseling
  268-9
ADD parent groups 295
Adler, A. 26, 35, 61
Adolescents 272-280
Adolescents, group counseling
  272-80
  intervention strategies 275-6
  purposes 273-5
Adult children of alcoholics (ACOA)
  group counseling
  intervention strategies 315-6
  purposes 314-5
  selection of members 315
Adults, group counseling 283-95
Advantage of co-leadership 52-3
Advantages
  group contract 209
Advantages of group counseling
  developing interpersonal
    awareness 6
  discovering others 4-5
  learning to help 7-9
  observe a model of helping 8
  pressure for growth 9
  reality testing 7
  redefining self 5-6
  self discovery 3
  supportive environment 9-10

AGPA (American Group Psycho-
  therapy Association) 104
AIDS and counseling groups 301-6
  denial 304-5
  despair 304
  issues 304-5
  moving through and forward
    305
  myths 302-3
  ownership 305
  research 305-6
  stigmas 303-4
  taboos 303-4
Al-Anon groups 295, 316
Alateen groups 295
Alienation 179
Allen, F.H. 242, 255
Allen, R. D. 27, 36
Altruism 30
Amdur, M. 232, 240
American Association for Coun-
  seling and Development (AACD)
  22, 92
American Psychiatric Association
  (APA) 22, 312, 317
Amster, F. 261, 281
Anderson, J. 233, 239
Approaches
  theoretical 32-5
Arkansas Rehabilitation Research
  and Training Center 62
Asbury, F. 276, 281
Assertive
  work style 236
Association for Counselor Educa-
  tion and Supervision (ACES) 96
Association for Specialists in
  Group Work (ASGW) 22, 36, 87,
  104, 107, 108, 144
  ethical guidelines 106-7, *Figure*
    108-11
  professional standards 92,
    Figure 93-5
Assumptions
  basic in helping 64
Attacker 186
Attitudes 167
Authoritarian leader 57

Hobbs, N. 11, 18, 39, 56, 195, 218
Hope
    instillation of 30
Horne, A.M. 1, 6, 11, 18, 49, 56, 267, 274, 281
Human potential lab exercises 276
Human Potential Movement 35

I

Immediacy 64, 69, 85-6, *Figure* 70
Information
    imparting 30
Instructional aids 139
Intellective skill bundles 167
Interaction
    phase 230
    type 230
Interdependence 231
Interpersonal
    See skills
    skills development 60-77
Interpersonal skills 166
Intervention strategies
    abused children 270
Intervention strategies
    adolescents, group counseling 275-6
    children of divorce 272
Intervention strategies
    cancer patients, group counseling 300-1
Intervention strategies
    ACOA, group counseling 315-6
    chemical dependency 311-2
    depression, group counseling 308-9
    eating disorders, group counseling 314
    elderly, group counseling 292-4
    family, group counseling 285-7
Intervention techniques 163-90
Issues 193-216
    behavioral change contract 205-11
    related to AIDS and group counseling 304-5
    silence 211-5
    structuring 196-205
    varied time 194-6

J

Johnson, J.A. 23, 36, 212, 218
Jones, J. 11, 19, 205, 218, 276, 281,
Journal for Specialist in Group Work 205, 218

K

Kemp, C.G. 213, 214, 218
Koeppe, P. 195, 218
Koffman, A. 299, 317
Kohlberg, L. 64
Kottler, J. 59, 60, 92, 112, 187, 189, 191
Krumboltz, J.D. 3, 18
Kubler, Ross, E. 299

L

Laboratory reality testing 7
Laboratory group 88-9
Laing, R.D. 213, 218
Laissez-faire leader 58
Landau, H. 152, 160
Landreth, G. 87, 92, 112, 195, 218, 262, 281
Lawe, C.F. 1, 6, 11, 18, 267, 274, 281
Lawlis, F.G. 300, 317
Leader
    authoritarian 57
    characteristics 163-5
    democratic 58
    laissez-faire 58
    self-evaluation 248-9
Leadership
    group stability 151
Leadership styles 117
Leadership training 87-92
Learning
    group 119-21, 151-3
    interpersonal 31
    self 118-9
Lecky, P. 4, 18, 287, 289
Lee, J.L. 218
Leite, E. 309, 317
Lewin, K. 27, 57, 107, 112

R

W

Walker, M. 314, 315, 317
Walley, D.D. 204, 218
Walters, R. 204, 217, 276, 281
Walters, R.H. 170, 191
Warner, R.W. 11, 18, 115, 133
Warters, J. 5, 9, 214, 218
Weaknesses
    group members 165-7
Wedding, D. 56
Wegscheider-Cruse, S. 314, 318
Weir, J. 126
Whipple, G.M. 36
White, R. 57, 107, 112, 113
Whiteside, L. 273, 281
Whole person 67-8, *Figure* 67
Wilkinson, G. 272, 282
Williams, K. 315, 317
Withdrawal 178-9
Wogan, M. 232, 240
Wolf, A. 11, 19

Women, group counseling 288-90
    intervention strategies 289-90
    purposes 288-9
    selection of members 289
Words and Action Program 204, 218
Words and Action series 204
Work
    style 236-7
Wrenn, C.G. 27, 36

Y

Yalom, E.D. 225, 240
Yalom, I.D. 7, 19, 30, 36, 104, 113, 116, 117, 133, 158, 160, 222, 239, 242, 255

Z

Zander, A. 112, 113, 150, 160

ROBERT C. BERG

Dr. Robert C. Berg is Professor of Counselor Education at the University of North Texas. He has been a counselor in public schools, at the junior college level and in private practice. He holds an Ed.D. from Northern Illinois University and has been a counselor educator for over twenty years. In the state of Texas he holds credentials as a licensed professional counselor and as a licensed psychologist.

Berg's major fields of interest include the training and supervision of group leaders, interpersonal skills development, relationship therapy, and sports psychology. He has lectured, presented workshops and served as a consultant on these topics throughout the United States to various professional and private organizations that include American Airlines, the Federal Aviation Administration, the Internal Revenue Service, the New Orleans Saints Football Club, Braniff Airways, the Chicago Board of Education, and the Dallas Cowboys.

Berg is a past member of the Ethics Committee and the Generic Standards Committee and is a charter member of The Association for Specialists in Group Work. The Association for Counseling and Development and The American Psychological Association are also among his professional affiliations.

Dr. Berg has authored or co-authored over 30 articles in professional journals in addition to several books. Other books include *Group Counseling: A Sourcebook of Theory and Practice* with James A. Johnson and *Counseling the Elderly* with Garry Landreth.

GARRY LANDRETH

Dr. Garry L. Landreth is a Regents Professor in the Counselor Education Department at the University of North Texas and Director of the Center for Play Therapy. He has been a teacher and counselor in public schools, has worked extensively with children in therapy relationships and has conducted workshops focusing on relationships with children for parents, teachers, and counselors throughout the United States. Garry was also invited to conduct workshops in group counseling and play therapy for counselors and psychologists in China.

His more than sixty publications include the text *Play Therapy: Dynamics of the Process of Counseling With Children* and three texts published by Accelerated Development Incorporated, *Group Counseling: Fundamental Concepts and Procedures* (1st and 2nd editions) and *Child Centered Play Therapy: The Art of the Relationship* (in press). Garry is a licensed professional counselor and licensed psychologist in the state of Texas.

Garry received the 1985 Meadows Honor Professor Award, the 1986 President's Outstanding Teacher Award, the 1987 Toulouse Scholar Award, the 1987 Regents Distinguished Professor Award, and the 1988 American Association for Counseling and Development Humanitarian and Caring Person Award.